译言英美 文化教程

Translating America and Britain:
A Cultural Textbook

主　编　张　姝　王贵华

副主编　高　长　夏延华　王稀婧

编　者　乔　平　李孝婷　何宗慧　谭竹修

　　　　王小雨　何　丹　裴舒晨　樊文娟

　　　　丁恒尧　刘　湘　邱　阳

重庆大学出版社

图书在版编目(CIP)数据

译言英美文化教程 / 张姝,王贵华主编. — 重庆:
重庆大学出版社,2025.2. — ISBN 978-7-5689-5100-5

Ⅰ.H315.9

中国国家版本馆CIP数据核字第2025LS6235号

译言英美文化教程

张 姝 王贵华 主编

责任编辑:牟 妮 版式设计:欧阳荣庆
责任校对:谢 芳 责任印制:赵 晟

*

重庆大学出版社出版发行
出版人:陈晓阳
社址:重庆市沙坪坝区大学城西路21号
邮编:401331
电话:(023)88617190 88617185(中小学)
传真:(023)88617186 88617166
网址:http://www.cqup.com.cn
邮箱:fxk@cqup.com.cn(营销中心)
全国新华书店经销
重庆市国丰印务有限责任公司印刷

*

开本:889mm×1194mm 1/16 印张:14.5 字数:381千
2025年2月第1版 2025年2月第1次印刷
ISBN 978-7-5689-5100-5 定价:60.00元

前言 PREFACE

英语不仅是一种语言，是一种文化的载体，一座沟通的桥梁，更是一扇打开国际视野的窗口。《译言英美文化教程》的诞生，源于国家级一流本科混合式课程——"译言英美"慕课的教学实践与学术探索。本教材旨在引领学习者穿梭于英美文化的丰富脉络之中，提升翻译技能，深化跨文化交流，培养具有全球胜任力的新时代青年。

"译言英美"是由西华师范大学建设的慕课，获批四川省省级线上线下混合式本科课程，与国家级一流本科课程（线上线下混合式）。课程启动以来，它以其独特的研建理念和创新教学模式，吸引了国内众多高校学子的目光，成为连接语言学生与英美文化的课程纽带。教材的编写遵循了《中国教育现代化 2035》的战略部署，响应了教育部混合式教学的倡导，深刻融合了现代信息技术，推动了传统课堂教学的革新；同时，促进了优质教育资源的开放共享，加强了教师教技融合水平的提升，并致力于培养学生的自主学习能力，全面符合新时代教育教学改革的要求。

《译言英美文化教程》精心编织了英美文化的七大领域：从地理人文的壮阔画卷，到节日文化的缤纷色彩；从人生典礼的情感纽带，到酒水饮食的生活情趣；从音乐电影的艺术魅力，到英美文学的思想深度；再到体育运动的激情活力。每个单元都是一次文化的探索之旅，每篇文本都是一扇窥探世界的窗口。通过各个单元英译汉关键翻译原则的学习和训练，本教程致力于提升学生的语言技能，拓宽他们的知识视野，激发他们的文化思考。

使用本教材时，我们建议师生采用线上线下混合式教学模式，充分利用在线资源和课堂互动，激发学生的学习兴趣和参与程度。同时，鼓励学习者在比较、对照、思辨、吸收、升华的基础上汲取外来文化精华，追求中华文化创新性发展，树立文化自信。

我们期待《译言英美文化教程》能够助力学习英美文化、提升翻译技能，为培养具有国际视野和文化自信的新时代人才贡献力量。愿每一位读者都能在译言英美课程与教程引导下，博采英美文明，厚植家国情怀，提升翻译素养，增进文化交流。

2024年11月

CONTENTS

Unit 1
GEOGRAPHY

I The Mississippi River

↳ 1. Cultural Background

The Mississippi River is the longest and most important river in the United States and the chief river of the second largest **drainage**[1] **system**[2] on the North American continent, second only to the Hudson Bay drainage system. The river drains the **basin**[3] of the Middle Western United States between the Appalachians and the **Rocky Mountains**①. As a matter of fact, all the rivers west of the **Appalachian Mountains**② and east of the Rocky Mountains flow toward each other and finally empty into the Mississippi. The river together with its numerous **tributaries**[4] forms an enormous water-course network, with a drainage area of 3.2 million square kilometers.

The Mississippi River is so important that it is involved in every side of the American life. **Native Americans**③ have lived along the Mississippi River and its tributaries for thousands of years. The arrival of Europeans in the 16th century changed the native way of life as first explorers, then settlers, **ventured**[5] into the basin in increasing numbers. In the early days, the Mississippi was the most important means of transportation for people and **commercial**[6] goods, and now it is still one of the major inland carriers of **freight**[7].

The Mississippi River Basin is one of the largest areas of flatland in the world, which takes up about half of the **continental**[8] United States and covers a distance of some 2,000 km in width. The northeastern part of the Mississippi River Basin is called **the Midwest**[9], or the Middle West. It lies in the general area of the **Great Lakes**④. From east to west, the

◇◇◇◇◇◇

① Rocky Mountains 落基山脉，是北美洲科迪勒拉山系东部山脉的主体，因其多岩石的地貌特征而得名。落基山脉纵贯加拿大和美国西部，北连阿拉斯加的布鲁克斯岭，南接墨西哥境内的东马德雷山脉。全长 4 800 千米。海拔一般为 2 000~3 000 米，最高峰埃尔伯特山的海拔为 4 399 米。

② Appalachian Mountains 阿巴拉契亚山脉，是北美洲东部众多山脉的统称，又称阿巴拉契亚高地、阿巴拉契亚山系。山脉北端起源于加拿大的纽芬兰和拉布拉多地区，主体位于美国境内，绵亘于北美洲东部，向南至美国亚拉巴马州中部止，呈东北—西南走向。全长近 3 200 千米，宽 130~560 千米。

③ Native Americans 美洲原住民

④ Great Lakes 五大湖，是北美洲中部彼此相连的五个大湖的总称，即苏必利尔湖、密歇根湖、休伦湖、伊利湖及安大略湖，构成世界上最大的淡水水域。密歇根湖完全位于美国境内，其他四个湖均位于美国和加拿大的边境线上，为两国共有；五大湖通过圣劳伦斯航道与大西洋相连，构成具有重要经济价值的水道。

states in the Midwest are **Ohio**, **Michigan**, **Indiana**, **Illinois**, **Wisconsin**, **Missouri**, **Iowa and Minnesota**⑤ . This region has great **mineral**[10] resources, rich soil, a good climate for agriculture, **fertile**[11] plains, low **rolling**[12] hills and no high mountains.

The large area between the Appalachians and the Rockies is called the **Great Plains**⑥ . It covers, from north to south, six states: **North and South Dakotas**, **Nebraska**, **Kansas**, **Oklahoma and Texas**⑦ . The land in this region is very flat and open. Except for a few **separated**[13] sections, there are no trees or forests in this whole region. The soil here is generally fertile, but the dry climate limits farming to a few important **crops**[14]. Wheat and corn are the main crops in the plain states. But in the west sections, **cattle raising**[15] is more important.

Words and Expressions:

1 drainage /ˈdreɪnɪdʒ/ *n.* 排水；放水

2 drainage system 水系；排水系统

3 basin /ˈbeɪsn/ *n.* 流域；盆地；内湾

4 tributary /ˈtrɪbjəteri/ *n.*（流入大河或湖泊的）支流

5 venture /ˈventʃər/ *v.* 敢于去（危险或令人不快的地方）；冒险

6 commercial /kəˈmɜːrʃl/ *adj.* 贸易的，商业的；以获利为目的的

7 freight /freɪt/ *n.* 海运、空运或陆运的货物；货运

8 continental /ˌkɑːntɪˈnentl/ *adj.* 北美大陆的；大洲的，大陆的

9 the Midwest （美国）中西部，中西部地区

10 mineral /ˈmɪnərəl/ *adj.* 矿物的 *n.* 矿物

11 fertile /ˈfɜːrtl/ *adj.* 肥沃的，富饶的

12 rolling /ˈrəʊlɪŋ/ *adj.* 起伏的；连绵的

13 separated /ˈsepəreɪtɪd/ *adj.* 相距遥远的；分开的，分居的

14 crop /krɑːp/ *n.* 作物；庄稼

15 cattle raising 养牛业，牧牛业

◇◇◇◇◇◇◇

⑤ Ohio, Michigan, Indiana, Illinois, Wisconsin, Missouri, Iowa and Minnesota 均为美国州名，依次是俄亥俄州、密歇根州、印第安纳州、伊利诺伊州、威斯康星州、密苏里州、爱荷华州和明尼苏达州。

⑥ Great Plains 大平原，即北美洲落基山脉以东的大平原地区，从加拿大的马更些河谷延伸至美国得克萨斯州南部。

⑦ North and South Dakotas, Nebraska, Kansas, Oklahoma and Texas 均为美国州名，依次是北达科他州、南达科他州、内布拉斯加州、堪萨斯州、俄克拉荷马州和德克萨斯州。

2. Translation Examples Explained

When translating a text, the very first step lies in the translator's accurate comprehension of its original meaning. This section will explore how to achieve an accurate comprehension during the translation process by translating a short passage about the Mississippi River. Here is the passage, with the two underlined sample sentences being the focus.

> *The Mississippi is the largest and the most important river in the United States.* ①*The name of the river comes from the Indian language meaning "Father of Waters", or "Great River".* ②*Rising in Lake Itasca in Northwestern Minnesota, the Mississippi flows southward for more than 3,700 kilometers and finally empties into the Gulf of Mexico. Its waters are gathered from two-thirds of the United States, together with its chief branch—the Missouri River. If measured from the source of the Missouri, the whole river is 6,021 kilometers long. The Mississippi is among the world's great continental rivers, like the Nile in Africa, the Amazon in South America, and the Yangtze in China.*
>
> ① The name of the river comes from the <u>Indian language</u> meaning "<u>Father of Waters</u>", or "Great River".

The first sentence informs about the origin of the river's name. But the translation might be hindered by the two items "Indian language" and "Father of Waters", because either of them has more than one meaning. Firstly, "Indian language" might be literally translated as "印度语", the language spoken in the country India. However, the topic of this text is about a river in the USA, which has nothing to do with a South Asian country. To achieve an accurate understanding, we need to work out other solutions. Actually, this phrase also refers to a group of languages spoken by the original inhabitants of America and their modern descendants. So, the word "Indian" here refers to "American Indian" or "native Americans".

To correctly understand the word "waters" in this sentence, the above-mentioned tip is also adopted. A little search on the geographical background information tells that a number of major rivers like the Missouri River (密苏里河), the Arkansas River (阿肯色河) and the Ohio River (俄亥俄河) flow into the Mississippi River. And tens of smaller rivers flow into those. So, the Mississippi River is a huge river system, acting like a father dominating numerous rivers. Thus, the word "waters" in the text refers to "rivers". Besides information search, there is another way to define the term "Father of Waters". In this passage, the contextual connection between this sentence and the fourth sentence is obvious, which informs us that the Mississippi is a gathering of numerous branches. This definitely provides readers the context to understand the word "waters". The word "waters" here refers to "branches" or "rivers". So, with background information research and the context inferring strategy, this sentence can be accordingly translated as: 这条河的名字源自印第安语，意为"众河之父"或"伟大之河"。

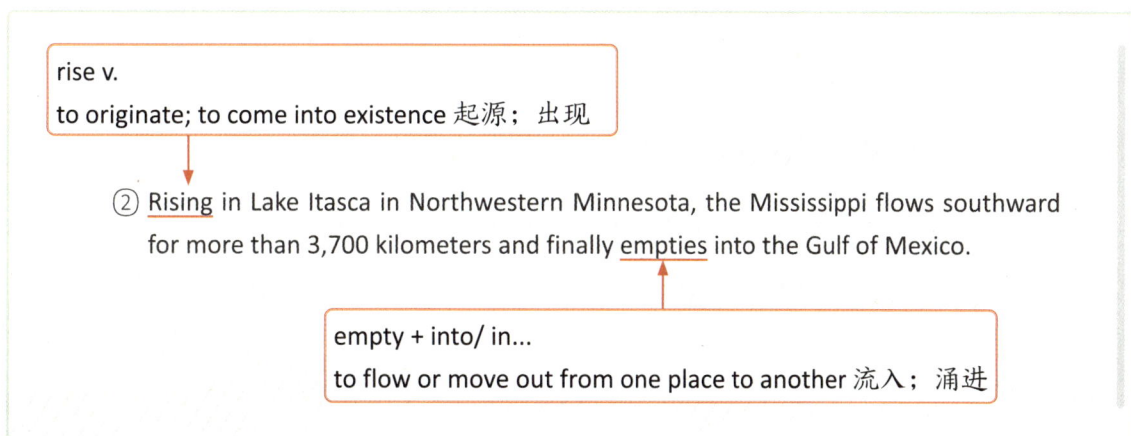

---

rise v.
to originate; to come into existence 起源；出现

② Rising in Lake Itasca in Northwestern Minnesota, the Mississippi flows southward for more than 3,700 kilometers and finally empties into the Gulf of Mexico.

empty + into/ in...
to flow or move out from one place to another 流入；涌进

The second sample sentence reveals the whole course of the Mississippi. Two words are not that easy to be understood. The first one is "Rising", which is the present participle of the verb "rise". Its meanings the readers are familiar with are three types: "起来" as in the sentence "She rises from the chair", "升起" as in "The sun has just risen", and "增加" as in "Land prices had risen." But none of them perfectly match the meaning of the given sentence. By looking up the dictionary for more possibilities, we can find another explanation "to originate; to come into existence". Then as in the sample, "rising in Lake Itasca" means that the Mississippi River has its source in that lake.

The other puzzling word in this sentence is "empties". The word "empty" usually means "空的", an adjective which apparently doesn't fit the grammatical structure here. As a verb, "empty" can indicate "to make empty of contents", just like the word "empty" in the example "He emptied the ashtrays." However, being lifeless, the Mississippi River cannot actually move anything from the inside to the outside. Then it is reasonable to infer that the word "empty" here is an intransitive verb with the corresponding explanation of "to become empty" in dictionary, just like the verb in the example: "The streets soon emptied when the rain started." Moreover, "empty into" is often used as a regular collocation describing the water or something "flow or move out from one place to another".

In addition to the help of dictionary, there is another way to define the verb "empty" here. After reading through the whole sentence, it's easy to infer from the context that the Mississippi, with Lake Itasca as its source, must have a mouth or an exit in a bigger river or a sea. Reading between lines will help readers to know that the Gulf of Mexico is its very mouth. Based on the context, the word "empty" should be understood as the action of a river flowing to somewhere and translated as "流入". So the second example sentence should be translated as: "密西西比河发源于明尼苏达州西北部的依塔斯卡湖，往南流经 3700 多公里，最后流入墨西哥湾。"

3. Parallel Texts

Here are the original and the translated texts for comparison. Each sentence in the original, in fact, needs to be understood accurately before a faithful translation.

The Mississippi River

The Mississippi is the largest and the most important river in the United States. The name of the river comes from the Indian language meaning "Father of Waters", or "Great River". Rising in Lake Itasca in Northwestern Minnesota, the Mississippi flows southward for more than 3,700 kilometers and finally empties into the Gulf of Mexico. Its waters are gathered from two-thirds of the United States, together with its chief branch – the Missouri River. If measured from the source of the Missouri, the whole river is 6,021 kilometers long. The Mississippi is among the world's great continental rivers, like the Nile in Africa, the Amazon in South America, and the Yangtze in China.

密西西比河

密西西比河是美国最大和最重要的河流。这条河的名字源自印第安语，意为"众河之父"或"伟大之河"。密西西比河发源于明尼苏达州西北部的依塔斯卡湖，往南流经 3 700 多公里，最后流入墨西哥湾。河水由美国三分之二地区的河流与其主要支流密苏里河汇集而来。如果从密苏里河的发源地算起，整条河长约 6 021 公里。正如非洲的尼罗河、南美洲的亚马逊河和中国的长江一样，密西西比河是世界上最大的大陆河道之一。

4. Translation Skills Summarized

Accurate comprehension is the primary step in English-Chinese (E-C) translation. The elements to be concerned include: the correct understanding of linguistic elements like word meanings, idiomatic collocations (惯用表达) and sentence structures; a good command of background information such as social settings, historical allusions (典故), technical terms, writing styles, and contrasts between languages; and a careful analysis of the logic relationship between lines by inferring from the context.

Comprehension

Background Information

social settings
historical allusions
technical terms
writing styles
contrasts between languages
...

Lingustic Elememts

word meanings
idiomatic collocations
grammatical structures

Logic Between Lines

the logic relationship between lines
by inferring from the context

5. Cultural Expressions

The Mississippi, with its numerous tributaries, flows through 10 states in the United States, and its drainage basin stretches out 31 states. As the most important inland waterway, it has a drainage area of approximately 3.22 million square kilometers. The huge Mississippi River watershed has been introduced with many lively nicknames like the "Father of Waters", the "Great River", the "Body of a Nation", the "Old Man River" and "The Mighty Mississippi".

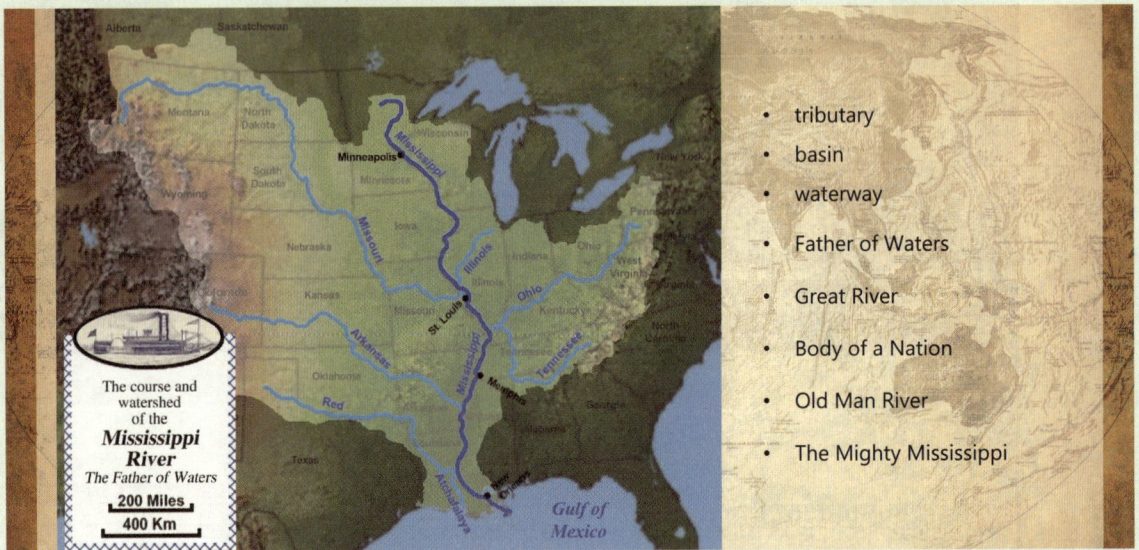

- tributary
- basin
- waterway
- Father of Waters
- Great River
- Body of a Nation
- Old Man River
- The Mighty Mississippi

When you cast a keen eye on the geographical features on the map of America, you may discover that it is the Mississippi that forms the traditional dividing line in this country between "west" and "east". From the Appalachian Mountains in the East to the Rocky

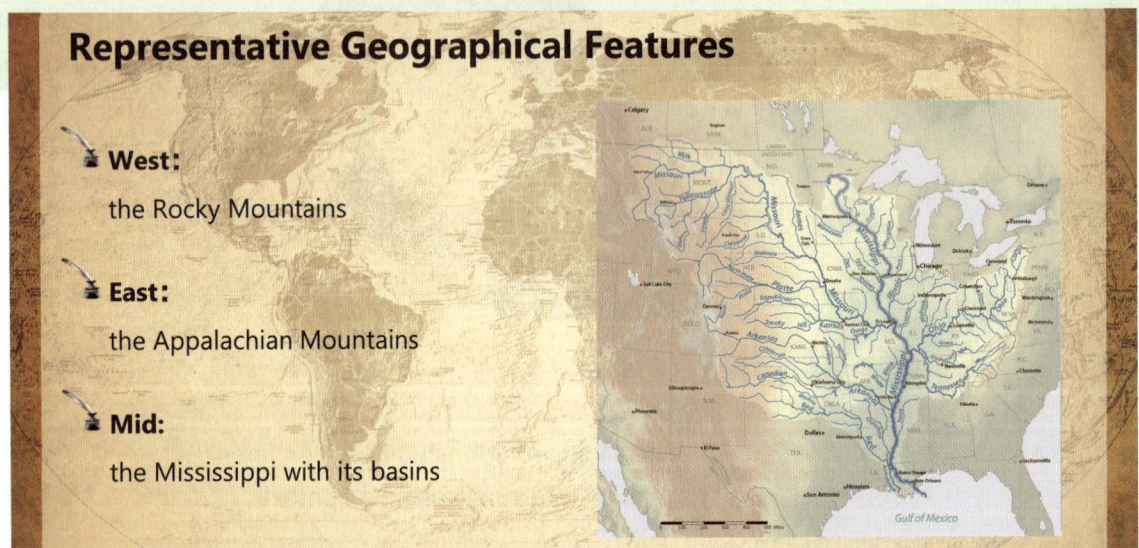

Representative Geographical Features

West:
the Rocky Mountains

East:
the Appalachian Mountains

Mid:
the Mississippi with its basins

Mountains in the West, the center of the country is drained by the Mississippi and its basins. The Mississippi watershed flows right through the heart of America and drains over three fifths of the American landscape. To some extent, the Mississippi has made America what it is today.

North America

Alaska 阿拉斯加
Canada 加拿大
Pacific Ocean 太平洋
Atlantic Ocean 大西洋
the continental US 美国本土
Hawaii 夏威夷
Mexico 墨西哥

This is a country consisting of 50 states with an independent district of Columbia where the capital Washington D. C. is located. Forty-eight states which border on one another constitute the mainland America, also known as the continental United States. The other two states are Alaska and Hawaii. Alaska, the largest state, is separated from the mainland and borders on northwestern Canada. Hawaii, an island group, lies in the central Pacific, southwest of North America. The continental United States stretches 4,500 kilometers from the Atlantic Ocean on the east to the Pacific Ocean on the west. It borders Canada on the north and neighbors Mexico in the south.

⌐ 6. Questions for Discussion

1) What are other nicknames for the Mississippi River? What characteristics of the river do these nicknames contain?

2) In E-C translation, what elements should be considered in order to achieve an accurate comprehension of the original text?

Yellowstone National Park

↳ 1. Cultural Background

The Yellowstone National Park is the first US national park, established in 1872, and one of the largest. Native Americans have lived in the Yellowstone region for at least 11,000 years. The park is located at the headwaters of the Yellowstone River, from which it takes its historical name. Near the end of the 18th century, French **trappers**[1] named the river "Roche Jaune", which is probably a translation of the **Hidatsa**[2] name. Later, American trappers **rendered**[3] the French name into English as "Yellow Stone". The region was bypassed during the **Lewis and Clark Expedition**① in the early 19th century. Aside from visits by mountain men during the early-to-mid-19th century, organized exploration did not begin until the late 1860s. The US Army was commissioned to oversee the park just after its establishment. In 1917, **administration**[4] of the park was transferred to the **National Park Service**[5].

Yellowstone National Park covers about 9,066 square kilometers in north-west **Wyoming** and parts of **Montana** and **Idaho**②, **comprising**[6] lakes, canyons, rivers and mountain ranges. The vast forests and grasslands also include unique species of plants. Yellowstone Lake is one of the largest high-**altitude**[7] lakes in North America and is centered over the Yellowstone Caldera, the largest supervolcano on the continent. The caldera is considered an active **volcano**[8]. It has erupted with **tremendous**[9] force several times in the last two million years. Half of the world's geothermal features are in Yellowstone, fueled by this ongoing volcanism. Lava flows and rocks from volcanic **eruptions**[10] cover most of the land area of Yellowstone.

Yellowstone is known for its wildlife and hundreds of species of **mammals**[11], birds, fish and **reptiles**[12] have been documented, including several that are either endangered or threatened. Yellowstone Park is the largest and most famous **megafauna's**[13] location in the Continental United States. **Grizzly bears**[14], wolves, free-ranging herds of **bison**[15] and

◇◇◇◇◇◇◇◇

① Lewis and Clark Expedition 刘易斯与克拉克远征，是美国国内首次横越大陆西抵太平洋沿岸的往返考察活动。

② Wyoming, Montana and Idaho 均为美国州名，依次是怀俄明州、蒙大拿州和爱达荷州。

elk[16] live in the park. The Yellowstone Park bison herd is the oldest and largest public bison herd in the United States. Forest fires occur in the park each year. In the large forest fires of 1988, nearly one third of the park was burnt.

Yellowstone has numerous **recreational**[17] opportunities, including hiking, camping, boating, fishing and sightseeing. The nearby town of Jackson Hole, Wyoming offers fine lodging and a range of year-round outdoor activities. Paved roads provide close access to the major **geothermal**[18] areas as well as some of the lakes and waterfalls. During the winter, visitors often access the park by way of guided tours that use either snow coaches or snowmobiles.

1 trapper /ˈtræpər/ n. 设陷阱捕兽者

2 Hidatsa /hiˈdɑːtsɑː/ n. 希多特萨人（居住在美国密苏里河岸的印第安人）

3 render /ˈrendər/ v.（用不同的语言）表达；翻译；把……译成

4 administration /ədˌmɪnɪˈstreɪʃn/ n. 管理；管理部门，行政部门

5 National Park Service （美国）国家公园管理局

6 comprise /kəmˈpraɪz/ v. 包括；包含；由……组成

7 altitude /ˈæltɪtuːd/ v. 海拔；高度

8 volcano /vɑːlˈkeɪnəʊ/ n. 火山

9 tremendous /trəˈmendəs/ adj. 巨大的；极大的

10 eruption /ɪˈrʌpʃn/ n. 喷发；爆发

11 mammal /ˈmæml/ n. 哺乳动物

12 reptile /ˈreptaɪl/ n. 爬行动物

13 megafauna /ˈmɛɡəˌfɔnə/ n. 巨型动物群

14 grizzly bear n. 灰熊，银尖熊（生活在北美和俄罗斯等的大型棕熊）

15 bison /ˈbaɪsn/ n. 野牛（分北美野牛和欧洲野牛两类）

16 elk /elk/ n. 驼鹿 (亦作 moose)；美洲赤鹿 (亦作 wapiti)

17 recreational /ˌrekriˈeɪʃənl/ adj. 娱乐的；消遣的

18 geothermal /ˌdʒiːəʊˈθɜːrml/ adj. 地热的

2. Translation Examples Explained

Once the original text is accurately comprehended, what comes next as a vital thing is to express it properly in the target language. This section is to discuss how to handle expression in translation by translating a short passage about the Yellowstone National Park. Below is the passage with four underlined sample sentences serving as the focus of discussion.

The Yellowstone National Park is the oldest and the best-known park of the United States. Yellowstone has lots of unusual geologic phenomena. Hundreds of miles of clear streams flow from the park's mountains and plateaus. The Grand Canyon of the Yellowstone is a colorful gorge 30.6 kilometers long. It is a remarkable display of the work of weathering and other erosive forces. ①The brilliant walls of red, pink, yellow, buff, lavender and white are its crowning glory. ②Rugged ridges, sinuous rivers, white cascades and emerald green waters enhance its spectacular character.

③The plant covering of the park varies from microscopic algae in hot spring runoffs to forest trees. The Yellowstone is 90% forested. In season, wild flowers splash the landscape with color. ④Dainty, rare and less conspicuous plants bloom in secretive woodland environments. The park fauna typifies the native animals of the Rocky Mountain region. The bird list includes 237 species as permanent residents and seasonal migrants. Waterfowl are especially abundant on the lakes and streams. The park waters are stocked with a variety of fishes, and the native black-spotted trout is eagerly sought by fishermen.

> Literal meaning: 光辉的，灿烂的

① The **brilliant** walls of red, pink, yellow, buff, lavender and white are its crowning glory.
那由红色、粉红色、黄色、暗黄色、淡紫色和白色组成的**光辉的峭壁**是它最美的地方。

> 光彩夺目的峭壁

The first example sentence brings out the charm of Yellowstone Canyon. The word "brilliant" literally means "光辉的、灿烂的", which is used here to describe walls. However, the expression "光辉的峭壁" does not sound idiomatic and is not a good lexical collocation in Chinese. The phrase "光辉的" means honor and glory and Chinese people often say "光辉的时代" or "光辉的事业". But people hardly ever say "光辉的峭壁". Instead, "光彩夺目的峭壁" is an idiomatic and fluent expression in Chinese. So, this sentence can be translated as "那由红色、粉红色、黄色、暗黄色、淡紫色和白色组成的光彩夺目的峭壁，正是它最美之处".

② Rugged ridges, sinuous rivers, white cascades and emerald green waters enhance its spectacular character.

起伏的山脉、蜿蜒的河流、白色的瀑布和翠绿的海水使其更加壮观。

| 绵延起伏 | 蜿蜒曲折 | 银珠飞溅 | 碧波粼粼 | 蔚为壮观 |

Four-character idioms

In the second sentence, the word "Rugged" "sinuous" "white" "emerald green" and "spectacular" can be initially translated as "起伏" "蜿蜒" "白色" "翠绿" and "壮观" with their Chinese equivalents given by dictionaries. But there is room for improvement in expression. What if the former translation is replaced by "绵延起伏" "蜿蜒曲折" "银珠飞溅" "碧波粼粼" and "蔚为壮观"? These four-character idioms give vivid images and they are rhythmic in sound and balanced in structure. When describing beautiful scenery, Chinese people tend to use literary words, especially four-character idioms in a sequence, to realize a rhythmic sound, a balanced structure and an intensified meaning, while English writers tend to give a more specific and informational description. After these changes, the translation of this sentence becomes " 绵延起伏的山峰、蜿蜒曲折的河流、银珠飞溅的瀑布和碧波粼粼的海水使其更加蔚为壮观 ". The Chinese expression with idioms is more in line with the emotional and persuasive style of introductions to scenic spots, a style more familiar to Chinese readers.

③ The plant covering of the park varies from microscopic algae in hot spring runoffs to forest trees.

| 森林树木 |

| 参天大树 |

覆盖着公园的植物从温泉口边的微小藻类到森林树木应有尽有。

The same thing happens in the third example. The literal meaning of the phrase "forest trees" is "森林树木", but this expression is sort of flat in Chinese. For a vivid expression, this translation could be replaced here with "参天大树". The entire sentence then is translated as "覆盖着公园的植物，从温泉口边的微小藻类到森林中的参天大树，应有尽有". The phrase "参天大树" refers to big trees with branches stretching up to the sky and it is easy for readers to picture a sharp contrast between microscopic algae and great trees, one being tiny and the other gigantic. And the two four-character words "参天大树" and "微小藻类" are rhythmic in sound and balanced in structure. In addition , "参天大树"

is a word that has a subtle positive connotation in comparison with the neutral word "森林树木". Therefore, the translation of "参天大树" fits well with the general appreciative tone of the context.

④ Dainty, rare and less conspicuous plants bloom in secretive woodland environments.

林间偏僻的地方　　不起眼的奇花异草

在秘密的森林环境中，稀有、不那么显眼的植物绽放着娇艳的花朵。

In the fourth example sentence, there are two places where translation is somewhat difficult and needs to be carefully considered. The first is the noun "plants" modified by adjectives "rare and less conspicuous" and the other is "secretive woodland environments". With the literal meaning, the original "rare and less conspicuous plants" could be translated as "稀有、不那么显眼的植物" which appears wordy and flat in Chinese. To achieve a better effect, the translation can be modified as "不起眼的奇花异草" that is much concise and rhythmic. In the same way, "secretive woodland environments" can be literally translated as "秘密的森林环境", which, however, sounds awkward. Then the translation can be modified as "林间偏僻的地方" as the English word "secretive" still means "偏僻的" here in the context. Compared with the initial version, the revised one is more more concise, literary and idiomatic.

↳ 3. Parallel Texts

Here are the original and the translated texts for comparison. Each sentence in the original, in fact, needs to be understood accurately before a faithful translation.

Yellowstone national park

The Yellowstone National Park is the oldest and the best known park of the United States. Yellowstone has lots of unusual geologic phenomena. Hundreds of miles of clear streams flow from the park's mountains and plateaus. The Grand Canyon of the Yellowstone is a colorful gorge 30.6 kilometers long. It is a remarkable display of the work of weathering and other erosive forces. The brilliant walls of red, pink, yellow, buff, lavender and white are its crowning glory. Rugged ridges, sinuous rivers, white cascades and emerald green waters enhance its spectacular character.

The plant covering of the park varies from microscopic algae in hot spring runoffs to forest trees. The Yellowstone is 90% forested. In season, wild flowers splash the landscape with colors. Dainty, rare and less conspicuous plants bloom in secretive woodland environments. Yellowstone has a large fauna, typifying the native animals of the Rocky Mountain region. The bird list includes 237 species as permanent residents and seasonal migrants. Waterfowl are especially abundant on the lakes and streams. The park waters are stocked with a variety of fishes, and the native black-spotted trout is eagerly sought by fishermen.

黄石国家公园

　　黄石国家公园是美国最古老、最著名的公园。黄石公园有许多不同寻常的地质现象。清澈的溪流从公园的山脉和高原流淌出来，绵延数百英里。黄石大峡谷是一个30.6千米长的五彩峡谷。它是风化及其他侵蚀力作用下的杰作。那由红色、粉红色、黄色、暗黄色、淡紫色和白色组成的光彩夺目的峭壁，正是它最美之处；绵延起伏的山峰、蜿蜒曲折的河流、银珠飞溅的瀑布和碧波粼粼的池水使其更加蔚为壮观。

　　覆盖着公园的植物，从温泉口边的微小藻类到森林中的参天大树，应有尽有。黄石公园里，90%为林区。每逢花季，公园里野花齐放，五彩缤纷。林间偏僻的地方，不起眼的奇花异草竞相绽放。黄石公园的动物群数量庞大，乃是落基山脉地区原生动物的典型代表。这里有237种常驻鸟和候鸟。湖边与河边水鸟不计其数。公园的水域里聚集着各种鱼类，当地的黑花鲑鱼是渔民们孜孜以求的目标。

4. Translation Skills Summarized

When it comes to translation, there are two main stages: comprehension and expression. Comprehension is the analysis of the source text and the accurate comprehension is the precondition of translation. After that, the translator restructures his understanding of the source text into the target language, which is the stage of expression. Expression is the result of comprehension, but an accurate comprehension does not necessarily ensure a successful expression. So, expression is also a key factor in translation.

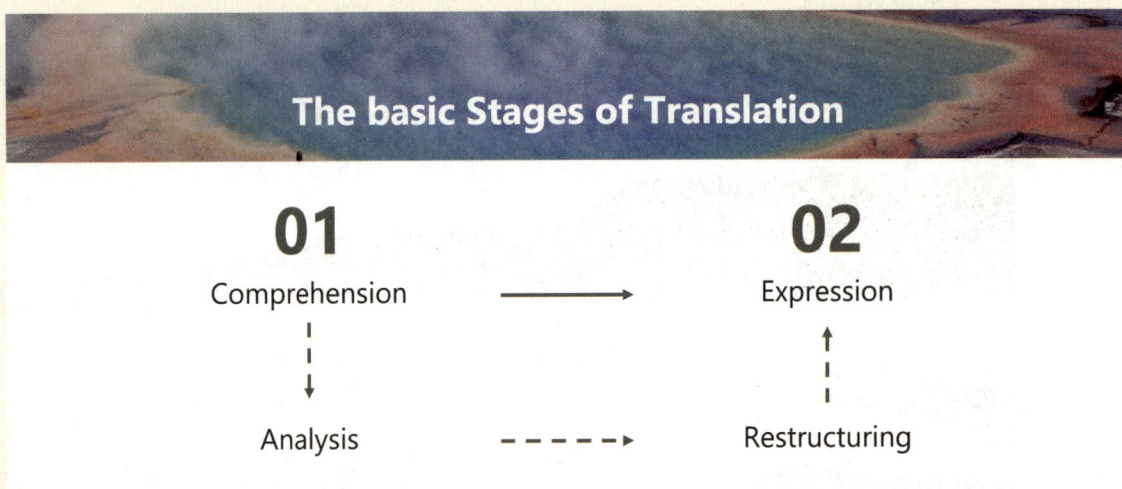

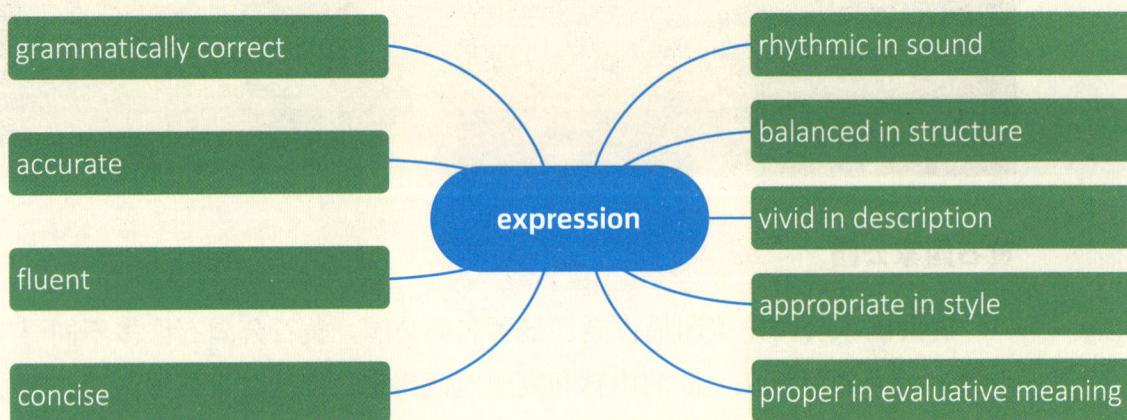

The basic Stages of Translation

01 Comprehension ⟶ **02** Expression

Comprehension ⋮ ↓ Analysis ⤳ Restructuring ⋮ ↑ Expression

grammatically correct

accurate

fluent

concise

expression

rhythmic in sound

balanced in structure

vivid in description

appropriate in style

proper in evaluative meaning

The previous examples illustrate that a good translation should be grammatically correct, accurate, fluent and concise. Moreover, there are other important elements in a good translation, such as being rhythmic in sound, balanced in structure, vivid in description, appropriate in style and proper in evaluative meaning. The translation should not be confined entirely to the dictionary meaning, so the translator should choose words flexibly and appropriately according to the context. The stage of expression is actually a process of restructuring and recreation.

5. Cultural Expressions

As the best-known national park of America, Yellowstone is rich in landforms with lakes, canyons, rivers, basins and mountain ranges. The representative attractions include Yellowstone Lake, Grand Canyon, Yellowstone River, West Thumb Basin, Rocky Mountain, etc.

Yellowstone is known for its abundant geothermal resources like multiple geysers and hot springs. Among them, Old Faithful Geyser and Grand Prismatic Spring are especially famous.

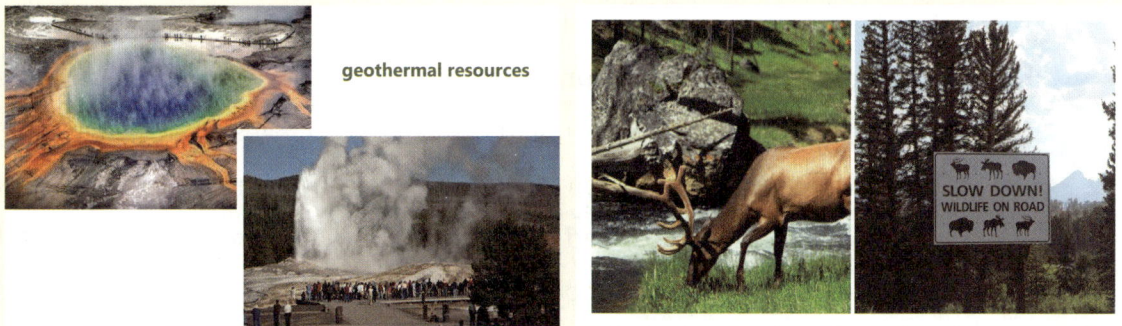

geothermal resources

As the largest wildlife reserve in America, Yellowstone is home to a large number of wild animals. The park is the centerpiece of the Greater Yellowstone Ecosystem, the largest remaining nearly-intact ecosystem in the northern temperate zone.

6. Questions for Discussion

1) What are the main landforms in Yellowstone National Park? Please name some famous representative scenic spots in each of these landforms.

2) What aspects should be considered in the stage of expression in E-C translation?

III The River Thames

↳ 1. Cultural Background

The River Thames lies off the north-western coast of Continental Europe. With a total length of 210 miles, it is the longest river entirely in England and the second after the River Severn. It rises in the **Cotswolds**[①] in southwest England and flows through the Midlands of England to London and out into the North Sea. While it is best known for flowing through London and it has always played a central role in the life of the capital city. Its rich history **encompasses**[1] all aspects of London's life——economic, social, political and cultural. It also flows alongside other towns and cities, including Oxford, Reading, **Henley-on-Thames**[②] and Windsor.

The Thames flows rather slowly, which is very **favorable**[2] for water transportation. Along its course are 45 **navigation**[3] locks with accompany weirs. Its **catchment**[4] area covers a large part of Southeastern and a small part of Western England. Ocean-going ships can sail up it as far as London and small ships can sail up it for further 138 km. The river contains over 80 islands, and having both seawater and freshwater **stretches**[5], it has a variety of wildlife and a number of adjoining Sites of Special Scientific Interest, with the largest being in the remaining parts of the North Kent Marshes and covering 5,449 **hectares**[6].

The river has supported human activity from its source to its **mouth**[7] for thousands of years, providing **habitation**[8], water power, food and drink. It has also acted as a major highway both for international trade through the Port of London, and internally along its length and connecting to the British **canal**[9] system. Its **strategic**[10] position has seen it at the center of many events and fashions in British history, earning it a description by John Burns as "**Liquid**[11] History". It has been a physical and political boundary over the centuries and generated a range of river crossings. In more recent time the river has become a major **leisure**[12] area supporting tourism and pleasure outings as well as the sports of

◇◇◇◇◇◇◇

① Cotswolds 科茨沃尔德丘陵地带，位于英国西南部。

② Henley-on-Thames 泰晤士河畔亨利镇。

rowing, sailing, kayaking, and punting. The river has had a special appeal to writers, artists, musicians and film-makers and is well represented in the arts.

The River Thames is famous throughout the world for its history, its culture and its amazing variety of wildlife, **archaeology**[13] and scenery. If you ask a Londoner what is the City's greatest **asset**[14] or the thousands of boaters in cruisers up and down the length of the river, they will come up with **a myriad of**[15] reasons why a day on or near the Thames is a great experience.

Words and Expressions:

1 encompass /ɪnˈkʌmpəs/ v. 包含，包括；涉及（大量事物）

2 favorable /ˈfeɪvərəbl/ adj. 有利的；有助于……的

3 navigation /ˌnævɪˈgeɪʃn/ n. 航行；导航

4 catchment /ˈkætʃmənt/ n. 流域，排水区

5 stretch /stretʃ/ n. 一片（土地或水域）；伸展，舒展；一段（时间）

6 hectare /ˈhekter/ n. 公顷（土地丈量单位，等于 1 万平方米或约 2.5 英亩）

7 mouth /maʊθ/ n. 入海口；河口

8 habitation /ˌhæbɪˈteɪʃn/ n. 居住；住所

9 canal /kəˈnæl/ n. 运河；水道

10 strategic /strəˈtiːdʒɪk/ adj. 战略性的

11 liquid /ˈlɪkwɪd/ adj. 液体的；液态的

12 leisure /ˈliːʒər/ n. 休闲；空闲；闲暇

13 archaeology /ˌɑːrkiˈɑːlədʒi/ n. 考古学

14 asset /ˈæset/ n. 有价值的人（或事物）；资产，财产

15 a myriad of 无数的；大量的：表示数量非常多，形容事物或人群数量庞大

2. Translation Examples Explained

In E-C translation, the linguistic differences between the two languages are an unavoidable topic. This section will discuss the linguistic contrasts and introduce the techniques useful to deal with those differences by translating a short passage about the Thames River. Here is the passage containing eight sentences, each of which is marked with numbers.

---

① *The Thames River is the second longest and most important river in Britain.* ② *The Thames, 338 km (210 miles) long, flows eastward out of the Cotswold Hills and weaves through the metropolis of London.* ③ *While it is best known for flowing through London, the river also flows alongside other towns and cities, including Oxford, Reading, Henley-on-Thames, and Windsor.* ④ *Its catchment area covers a large part of South Eastern and a small part of Western England and the river is fed by 38 named tributaries.* ⑤ *It provides water to the city of London and is used to carry commercial freight.* ⑥ *With its waters varying from freshwater to seawater, the Thames supports a variety of wildlife* in a number of adjoining Sites of Special Scientific Interest with the largest being in the North Kent Marshes and covering 5,449 hectares. ⑦ *Rowing and sailing clubs are common along the Thames, which is navigable to such vessels.* ⑧ *Major annual events include the Henley Royal Regatta and The Boat Race, while the Thames was used during two Summer Olympic Games.*

---

④ Its catchment area covers a large part of South Eastern and a small part of Western England and the river is fed by 38 named tributaries.

这 河　　　38 叫得上名字的支流
　条　　　　　条

First, take a look at the fourth sentence. The word "the" can be translated as "这" and "river" as "河", which sounds strange because there is a missing measure word "条". This Chinese measure word (量词) has no English equivalent. The same is true when translating the latter part "38 named tributaries." It is necessary to add the Chinese measure word "条" again and then we have the translation as "38条叫得上名字的河流".

---

⑥ With its waters varying from freshwater to seawater, the Thames supports a variety of wildlife ...

多 野生动物
　种

---

⑧ ...while the Thames was used during two Summer Olympic Games.

两 夏季奥运会

届

Similarly in Sentence 6, when translating "a variety of" as "多" and "wildlife" as "野生动物", we add a Chinese measure word "种" here to get the translation "多种野生动物". There is one more example in Sentence 8. To get the accurate Chinese translation of "two Summer Olympic Games", the measure word "届" should be added between "两" and "夏季奥运会".

As shown in the above examples, measure words that often appear in Chinese are rarely and infrequently used in English. So, it is necessary to add measure words in E-C translation, which is caused by the difference in the two languages.

③ While it is best known for flowing through London, the river also flows alongside other towns and cities, including Oxford, Reading, Henley-on-Thames, and Windsor.

Plural

这条河以横贯伦敦而闻名，它也流经其他多个城镇，包括牛津、雷丁、亨利河温莎。

The third sentence shows another difference between English and Chinese. The phrase "towns and cities" can be simply translated into "城镇". However, the words "towns" and "cities" are plural and the meaning of the plural do not come out in such translation. In order to highlight the plural meanings in the English original, we need to add the Chinese word "多个" here.

uncountable

⑤ It provides water to the city of London and is used to carry commercial freight.
⑥ With its waters varying from freshwater to seawater, the Thames supports a variety of wildlife...

plural

它为伦敦提供淡水，运送货物。泰晤士河的水域既有淡水也有海水，为多种野生动物提供了栖息地……

The translation of the fifth sentence also involves the inflection form of the noun. In this sentence, the English word "water" is used as an uncountable noun, but in its plural form in the next sentence. This deserves special attention since Chinese nouns do not have such inflectional forms. In dictionary, "water" is used as an uncountable noun referring to a material, i.e., "水" in Chinese; but when used in the plural form it means "a large area of sea or river", i.e., "水域" in Chinese. The two examples tell that the English noun can be singular or plural. Therefore, in translation, we often add some Chinese words to reproduce the plural meaning of English words.

⑤ It provides water to the city of London and is used to carry commercial freight.

| provide + ~s: third person singular | use + ~ed: passive |

它为伦敦提供淡水，被用来运送货物。

Like the nouns, verbs in English may be used in different forms to indicate tense and voice. For example, in the fifth sentence, the word "provide" is used in the third person singular with the letter "s" added to its end. Usually, there is no need to translate such tense meaning. The word "use" is changed to its passive form with "~ed" added. To translate the passive voice, we can use the Chinese "被" structure which, however, is not used as frequently as in English. Therefore, the English passive voice is often conversed into active structures in Chinese.

the simple present tense

⑧ Major annual events include the Henley Royal Regatta and The Boat Race, while the Thames was used during two Summer Olympic Games.

use → was used: past passive

泰晤士河在两届夏季奥运会期间使用过，现在每年的主要赛事包括亨利皇家赛艇比赛河牛津剑桥划船比赛。

In the eighth example, the word "include" is used in its simple present tense, which can be emphasized by adding the Chinese word "现在". The word "use" here takes the form of the past passive, which can be translated into a Chinese active and meanwhile can be conveyed into the grammatical meaning of the past tense with the use of words like "过".

⑥ With its waters varying from freshwater to seawater, | the Thames supports a variety of wildlife | in a number of adjoining Sites of Special Scientific Interest || with the largest being in the North Kent Marshes ||| and covering 5,449 hectares.

泰晤士河的水域由淡到咸，| 为多种野生动物提供了栖息地，| 与具有特殊科学价值的保护区紧密相邻，| 其中最大的位于北肯特沼泽的剩余部分，| 占地5449公顷。

Sentence 6 illustrates another contrast. The core parts of the sentence are the main clause: "the Thames supports a variety of wildlife." But there is an adverbial before it and an even longer adverbial after it. This long adverbial can be divided further into two parts before the word "with" and the "with" part can be divided even further into two parts before the word "and." When the whole sentence is translated into Chinese, these long and multi-layered English adverbials are divided and conversed into verbal phrases, to form a running sequence of short verbal clauses in Chinese.

This English sentence and its translation illustrate a typical contrast between English and Chinese on the sentence level. That is, the English sentence is more like a tree. Its core parts—subject, predicate and object—form the trunk; and the non-core parts—attributes, adverbials and complements—are like leaves of the tree. On the other hand, the typical Chinese sentence structure is more like a bamboo, formed by a parallel of short verbal clauses occurring one after another.

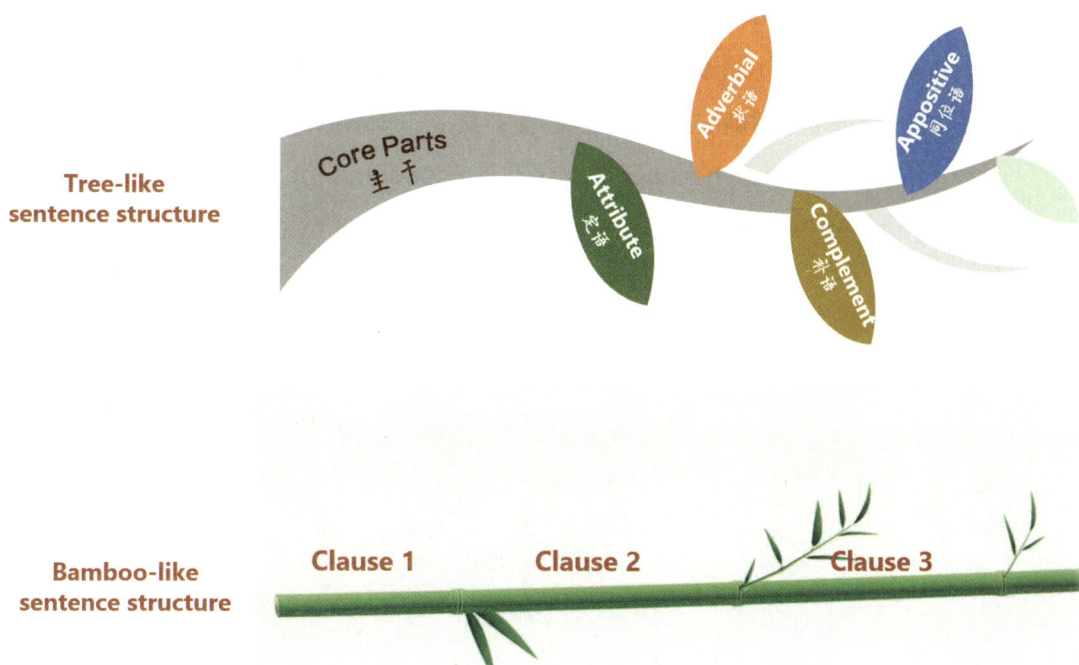

Tree-like sentence structure

Core Parts 主干

Adverbial 状语
Appositive 同位语
Attribute 定语
Complement 补语

Bamboo-like sentence structure

Clause 1　　Clause 2　　Clause 3

Another linguistic contrast at the sentence level is the use of conjunctive words. As in Sentence 3, there are three conjunctions, which make the connection between different parts of the sentence clear. We can keep all of them in the translation. However, when reading the translation, readers may find that the Chinese conjunctives "尽管" and "和" can be omitted, as Chinese speakers tend to imply rather than clearly indicate the relationship within or between clauses. The same is true for Sentence 4. The first "and" is kept but the second is omitted in the Chinese translation. This and the previous examples show that connective words are used rather less frequently in Chinese than that in English, which is a contrast between English and Chinese called hypotaxis (形合) vs. parataxis (意合).

③ While it is best known for flowing through London, the river also flows alongside other towns and cities, including Oxford, Reading, Henley-on-Thames, and Windsor.

④ Its catchment area covers a large part of South Eastern and a small part of Western England and the river is fed by 38 named tributaries.

~~尽管~~这条河以横贯伦敦而闻名，它也流经其它多个 城~~和~~镇，包括牛津、雷丁、亨利~~和~~温莎。它的集水区覆盖了英格兰东南部的大部分地区~~和~~西部的小部分地区，~~并且~~这条河支流众多，叫得上名字的就有三十八条。

The last contrast is the order of clauses within a sentence. There are two clauses in Sentence 3. Clause a is the main clause that carries the focus of the whole message; Clause b is an attributive clause used to modify "the Thames." When following the original order, we get the translation "划船俱乐部和帆船俱乐部在泰晤士河沿岸很常见，泰晤士河可行驶赛艇和帆船等水上交通工具。" However, this translation sounds odd to most Chinese speakers because Clause b is a condition for what happens in Clause a and is expected to appear before it, a temporal order favored by Chinese speakers.

3a Rowing and sailing clubs are common along the Thames, 3b navigable to such vessels.

3a 划船俱乐部和帆船俱乐部在泰晤士河沿岸很常见，
3b 泰晤士河可行驶赛艇和帆船等水上交通工具。

3b 泰晤士河可行驶赛艇和帆船等水上交通工具，
3a 划船俱乐部和帆船俱乐部在泰晤士河沿岸很常见。

The same is true for Sentence 8. Clause a speaks about the current state and is put in the beginning as the focus of the whole message. This order can be retained as in the first version. But to Chinese speakers, what happened in the past is expected to appear before what happens now, the same as the chronological order in Sentence 3. These two examples show that it is necessary to adjust the order of clauses in consideration of the linguistic preferences of the target language.

> 8a Major annual events include the Henley Royal Regatta and The Boat Race, 8b while the Thames was used during two Summer Olympic Games.
>
> 8a 现在每年的主要赛事包括亨利皇家赛艇比赛和牛津剑桥划船比赛 8b 泰晤士河在两届夏季奥运会期间使用过。
>
> 8b 泰晤士河在两届夏季奥运会期间使用过，8a 现在每年的主要赛事包括亨利皇家赛艇比赛和牛津剑桥划船比赛。

3. Parallel Texts

Here are the original and the translated texts for comparison. Each sentence in the English text is translated into Chinese, with consideration of the linguistic differences.

The River Thames

The Thames River is the second longest and most important river in Britain. The Thames, 338 km (210 miles) long, flows eastward out of the Cotswold Hills and weaves through the metropolis of London. While it is best known for flowing through London, the river also flows alongside other towns and cities, including Oxford, Reading, Henley-on-Thames, and Windsor. Its catchment area covers a large part of South Eastern and a small part of Western England and the river is fed by 38 named tributaries. It provides water to the city of London and is used to carry commercial freight. With its waters varying from freshwater to seawater, the Thames supports a variety of wildlife in a number of adjoining Sites of Special Scientific Interest with the largest being in the North Kent Marshes and covering 5,449 hectares. Rowing and sailing clubs are common along the Thames, which is navigable to such vessels. Major annual events include the Henley Royal Regatta and The Boat Race, while the Thames was used during two Summer Olympic Games.

泰晤士河

泰晤士河是英国第二长河，也是英国最重要的河。泰晤士河全长 338 公里（210 英里），发源于科茨沃尔德丘陵，向东迂回流经伦敦市区。这条河以横贯伦敦而闻名，它也流经其它多个城镇，包括牛津、雷丁、亨利和温莎。它的集水区覆盖了英格兰东南部的大部分地区和西部的小部分地区，这条河支流众多，叫得上名字的就有三十八条。它为伦敦提供淡水，运送货物。泰晤士河的水域既有淡水也有海水，为多种野生动物提供了栖息地，与具有特殊科学价值的众多保护区紧密相邻，其中最大的位于北肯特沼泽，占地 5 449 公顷。泰晤士河可行驶赛艇和帆船等水上交通工具，划船俱乐部和帆船俱乐部在泰晤士河沿岸很常见。泰晤士河在两届夏季奥运会期间使用过，现在每年的主要赛事包括亨利皇家赛艇比赛和牛津剑桥划船比赛。

4. Translation Skills Summarized

The linguistic contrasts of two languages mentioned above, along with the translation techniques from English to Chinese, are as follows. First, the Chinese language has a part of speech called measure words that, however, are rarely and infrequently used in English. Therefore, it is essential to add measure words in Chinese translation. Second, the English nouns and verbs do have inflectional changes, but there are no plural forms, tense forms and voice changes for Chinese words. So, we often need to add Chinese words to indicate the plural, tense and voice meanings in English.

English		Chinese
∅		measure words
plural	Add words	∅
tense		∅
voice		∅
tree-like sentence structure	Divide	bamboo-like sentence structure
hypotaxis	Omit connectives	parataxis
most important ideas first	Adjust the order	temporal order

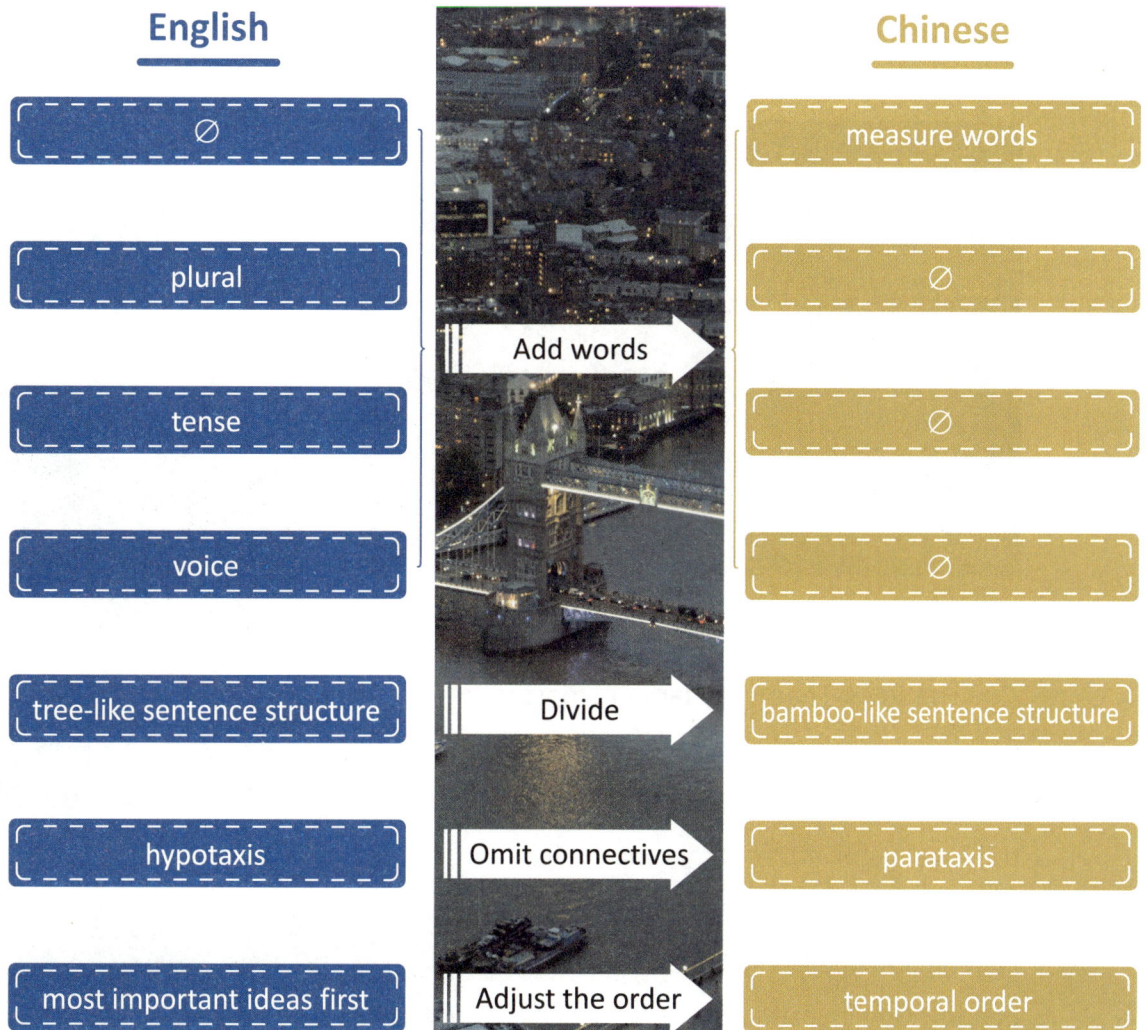

Another contrast is that the typical English sentence structure is like a tree with many branches and leaves, while the typical Chinese sentence structure is like a bamboo. So, it's very common to divide a long, multi-layered tree-like English sentence into several short and parallel Chinese clauses in E-C translation.

Moreover, English speakers emphasize hypotaxis and use more connectives, whereas Chinese speakers prefer parataxis and use connectives less frequently. So, we often need to omit connectives in Chinese translation.

Last, English speakers often present their most important idea in the first clause of a sentence, and then support it in the following clause. However, Chinese speakers prefer to arrange clauses by time order and speak what happens first in the beginning. So, the order of clauses is often to be adjusted in E-C translation.

5. Cultural Expressions

Tower Bridge

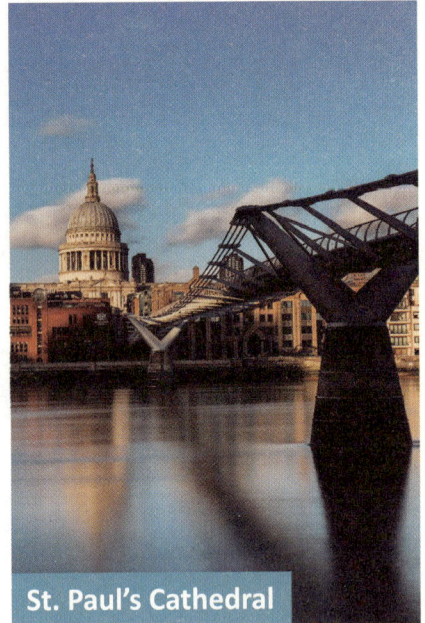
St. Paul's Cathedral

The River Thames is famous mostly because it flows through London, with many attractions on both sides. If we take a cruise from the sea into London, the first major attraction is the famous Tower Bridge. It is close to the Tower of London and opens and closes to let ships pass by. Going upstream, we can see the St. Paul's Cathedral on the right side. And then we can see the Big Ben and Houses of Parliament, and Palace of Westminster,

Big Ben and Houses of Parliament

on the right side. On the left side we have the London Eye. Continue to go upstream, and we will find the Buckingham Palace on the right side. It is the palace where the Queen/King lives and where the Changing of the Guard attracts tourists from all over the world.

London Eye

Buckingham Palace

6. Questions for Discussion

1) What are the main cities and towns through which the Thames flows? Please name some famous scenic spots along the river.

2) What are the main language differences between Chinese and English?

IV Exercises

Section A. True or false

_____ 1) Comprehension is an unimportant stage in translation.

_____ 2) The Mississippi has been called "Father of Waters".

_____ 3) The Yellowstone National Park is the oldest and the best-known park of the United States.

_____ 4) Rising in Lake Itasca, the Mississippi flows southward more than 3,700 kilometers.

译文：密西西比河从依塔斯卡湖升起，向南流经 3 700 多公里。

_____ 5) English sentence structure is like a baboo, while the typical Chinese sentence structure is like a tree with many branches and leaves.

Section B. Multiple choice

_____ 1) With endless green prairies and spectacular mountain ranges, Yellowstone is the very best of North American wilderness.

A. 有着无边的绿色大草原和壮丽的山脉，黄石公园是北美大陆最美公园。

B. 有着无垠草原与崇山峻岭的黄石公园堪称北美大陆最美公园。

C. 黄石公园有着无尽的绿色草原和壮观的山脉，是北美荒野中最好的。

_____ 2) The Grand Canyon is an unearthly sight and its most spectacular feature is Redwall limestone (石灰岩) cliff.

A. 科罗拉多大峡谷是一道超凡脱俗的风景，壮丽之处在于"红墙"石灰石悬崖。

B. 科罗拉多大峡谷是一道怪异的风景，特别之处在于"红墙"石灰石悬崖。

C. 科罗拉多大峡谷是一道神奇的风景，其特征是"红墙"石灰石悬崖。

_____ 3) The investigation moves to these slabs (平板；厚片) of rock flanking (在……侧面) the Rockies, known as the Flatirons (原指"熨斗").

    A. 调查来到与落基山侧面相接的名为熨斗形山岩石群。

    B. 调查来到与落基山侧面相接的岩石群，被称为熨斗。

    C. 调查转移到与落基山侧面相接的岩石群，被称为熨斗。

_____ 4) The Mississippi has several mouths in which water flows.

    A. 密西西比河有好几个嘴巴，水从这里流入。

    B. 密西西比河有好几个河口，水从这里流入。

    C. 密西西比河有好几个出口，水从这里流入。

_____ 5) The majestic Rockies (落基山) tower high above the American West.

    A. 雄伟的落基山脉像塔楼一样在美国西部。

    B. 壮丽的落基山塔高于美国西部。

    C. 雄伟的落基山脉高耸在美国西部。

V Test

↳ Section A. Multiple choice (5 items*4 points=20 points)

_____ 1) River Thames flows eastward through London and finally empties into the North Sea.

    A. 泰晤士河向东流过伦敦，最后入北海时河水已经干涸了。

    B. 泰晤士河向东流经伦敦，最后流入北海。

    C. 泰晤士河向东流经伦敦，最后使北海变得干涸。

_____ 2) The Rockies are the longest chain in North America and the third longest in the world.

    A. 在北美，落基山的山脉链条非常长，居于世界第三。

    B. 落基山是北美最长山脉，位居世界第三。

    C. 落基山是北美最长的山脉链，也是世界上第三长的山脉链。

_____ 3) Just 25 square miles in area, this pocket-sized British Crown Dependency is big on sunshine, serenity and history.

    A. 这个面积仅 64 平方公里的袖珍小岛为英国的皇家属地，阳光充足、分外宁静、历史悠久。

B. 这个面积仅有 64 平方公里的口袋大的小岛为英国的皇家属地，然而阳光足、安静、历史久。

C. 面积只有 64 平方公里，这个口袋大小的英国王室属地非常依赖阳光、宁静和历史。

_____ 4) Isle of Wight is one of those places which invites us to stop and appreciates nature's gifts.

A. 怀特岛令我们驻足于此，感受大自然的鬼斧神工。

B. 怀特岛就是一个令我们停在这里和欣赏大自然的馈赠的地方。

C. 怀特岛是邀请我们停下来欣赏大自然的礼物的地方之一。

_____ 5) In the Lake District (湖区), the main attractions are the lakes and mountains carved by glacial erosion (冰川侵蚀；冰蚀) and providing dramatic and inspiring scenery.

A. 湖区最吸引人的景点是由冰川侵蚀雕刻的湖泊和山脉，提供戏剧性和启发灵感的风景。

B. 湖区最吸引人的景点是被冰川侵蚀的湖泊和山脉，提供戏剧性和启发灵感的风景。

C. 冰蚀形成的湖泊和山脉是湖区最吸引人的景点，景色优美，令人叹为观止。

↳ Section B. Sentence translation (5 items*6 points=30 points)

1) In the early days, the Mississippi was the most important means of transportation for people and commercial goods, and now it is still one of the major in-land carriers of freight.

2) Yellowstone Park has numerous recreational activities, including hiking, camping, boating, fishing and sightseeing.

3) Guernsey (根西岛) is the second largest of the Channel Islands (海峡群岛). For those who've called this island home, Guernsey has long been a safe harbor, a place of pride and inspiration.

4) The United States has varied geographical features with large mountains, round topped hills, big plains, dry deserts and low basins.

5) Despite its small area, the island of Great Britain can be divided into two major natural regions: the highland zone, an area of high hills and mountains in the north and west; and the lowland zone, a south and east area consisting mostly of rolling plains.

Section C. Paragraph translation (50 points)

The mainland of the United States of America is situated in the south of North American Continent. On the north it shares a land boundary with Canada, which runs along the 49th parallel of north latitude and across four of the five Great Lakes. Its southern land neighbors Mexico and waters bounded by the Gulf of Mexico. To the east of the mainland is the Atlantic Ocean, and its west coast is washed by the Pacific Ocean. Stretching 4,500 kilometers from east to west and 2,500 kilometers from north to south, the mainland of the United States offers almost every variety of physical feature and climate. Including the States of Alaska and Hawaii, the country covers an area of 9.37 million square kilometers, ranking fourth in the world.

Unit 2
FESTIVALS

I Christmas

1. Cultural Background

Christmas means **Christ's Mass** [①], a church service, and it is the festival which celebrates the birth of Jesus Christ, the founder of Christianity. Historians disagree on when the real Jesus was actually born, but it is probable that he was not born on 25 December; that date was chosen by the Christian Church because it was more-or-less in the middle of winter and it could be used to substitute the old European mid-winter **pagan**[1] festival. The modern celebration of Christmas is, though, a **fusion**[2] of Christian and pagan.

The modern celebration of Christmas, with a Christmas tree, presents, and images and symbols like **sleighs**[3] and **reindeer**[4], is a 19th century invention. It was Victoria's husband, Prince Albert, who introduced the German custom of the Christmas tree. Religious customs like singing **carols**[5] and putting up a **crib**[6] in public places and churches or performing **Nativity**[7] plays in schools have existed for many centuries. For most people who celebrate Christmas, the holiday season is an occasion for gatherings of family and friends, **feasting**[8], and giving gifts.

Words and Expressions:

1 pagan /ˈpeɪɡən/ *adj.* 异教徒的

2 fusion /ˈfjuʒən/ *n.* 融合；结合

3 sleigh /sleɪ/ *n.* 雪橇

4 reindeer /ˈreɪnˌdɪr/ *n.* 驯鹿

5 carol /ˈkærəl/ *n.* 圣诞颂歌

6 crib /krɪb/ *n.* 圣诞马槽（表现耶稣诞生的情景）

7 Nativity /nəˈtɪvəti/ *n.* 耶稣降生；圣诞

8 feast /fiːst/ *v.* 尽情享用（美味佳肴）

◇◇◇◇◇◇◇

① Christ's Mass 指为纪念"耶稣基督 (Jesus Christ)"诞生所举行的弥撒仪式。弥撒在英语中称为 Mass，是天主教中的重要圣礼仪式；直到 16 世纪初宗教改革的一千多年间，包括英国在内的大多数欧洲国家都信仰天主教。在耶稣的生日举行的纪念弥撒，就称为 Christ's Mass；后来逐渐合并成 Christmas 这个单独的词语。

⌐ 2. Translation Examples Explained

When translating a text, identifying the core parts of a sentence can help with correct and quick understanding, and facilitate effective translation expressions. This section is to explore how to identify the core parts of a sentence by translating a short passage about Christmas roots. Below is the passage with five sentences serving as the focus of discussion.

Christmas traditions can be traced back to old Winter Solstice (冬至) festivals in northern Europe. Centuries before the birth of Jesus Christ, early Europeans were celebrating light and birth in the darkest days of winter around December 21st, the winter solstice. ①People rejoiced during this time, looking forward to longer days and extended hours of sunlight. ②Fathers and sons would drag home the biggest yule log they could find and set it on fire until it burned out. ③It was believed that each spark from the fire represented a new pig or calf that would be born in the next year. ④Also dragged inside were evergreens, the one plant that could make it through a Norse winter. ⑤Evergreens are sign of strength that prove life persisted in this dark time.

For as long as a yule log burned about 12 days, feasting and revelry (狂欢) reigned supreme (大行其道). This celebration gave the name Yuletide (圣诞季), and the 12 days the log burned gave birth to the 12 days of Christmas.

Let us look at the first example.

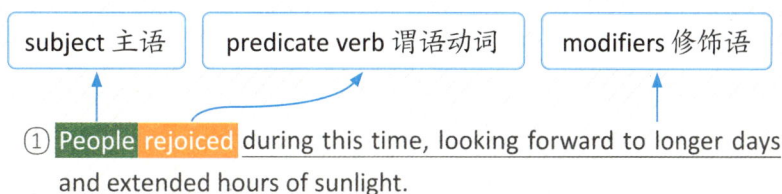

| subject 主语 | predicate verb 谓语动词 | modifiers 修饰语 |

① People rejoiced during this time, looking forward to longer days and extended hours of sunlight.

在此期间，人们欢心喜悦，期盼更长的白天和更充足的日光。

What is the main idea? To find the answer, we can simply ask ourselves two questions. The first question is "what is the action or state of being in this sentence?" And this question will lead us to the predicate verb (谓语动词). Right there we see the past-tense verb "rejoiced." So, the action is "rejoice," meaning feeling happy or pleased. Once we have located the verb, we can ask the next question: "Who or what is doing the action or in that state of being?" And this will lead us to the subject. Obviously, it is "People" who feel happy celebrating the winter solstice (冬至). So, the core parts of the sentence are "People rejoiced". They consist of a subject and an intransitive verb (不及物动词), a basic sentence structure in English. Other elements like "during this time" and "looking forward to longer days and extended hours of sunlight" are just modifiers (修饰语). They only provide additional information about one of the core parts.

To translate this sentence into Chinese, we can first translate the core parts and then add the additional information.

Here comes the second sentence. What is the main idea?

| compound subject 复合主语 | compound predicate 复合谓语 | object 宾语 |

② Fathers and sons would drag home the biggest yule log they could find and set it on fire until it burned out.

父子们会把他们能找到的最大的圆木拖回家点燃，直到它燃尽为止。

As we just learned, the main idea of a sentence is carried by the subject and the predicate verb that form the core parts of a sentence. Here in this sentence, the subject is "fathers and sons," involving two participants. Like the subject, the predicate also involves two actions: "drag" and "set on fire." The two verbs share the same modal "would" and are joined together by the conjunction "and". Since this sentence consists of more than one subject and one verb, we say it has a compound subject (复合主语) and a compound predicate (复合谓语).

Now we know the subject and the predicate verb, but "Fathers and sons would drag and set on fire" does not express a complete meaning since the object (宾语) is missing. In this sentence, the action verbs "drag" and "set on fire" are both transitive (及物的). It means they require an object to provide essential information about the receiver of the action, namely, to whom or what the action was done. The object often follows an action verb (行为动词).

In this sentence, the object of the action verb "drag" is "log," and that of the phrasal verb "set on fire" is "it". The two verbs actually share the same object since the pronoun "it" simply refers back to the word "log" mentioned earlier. So, the core parts of this sentence are "Fathers and sons would drag log and set it on fire." Based on the core parts, we can translate this sentence into Chinese as: "父子们会把他们能找到的最大的圆木拖回家点燃，直到它燃尽为止."

"Subject + predicate verb + object" is another basic sentence structure we can depend on to identify the core parts of an English sentence.

formal / grammatical subject 形式主语	passive verb 被动动词	clause as logical subject 主语从句作主语

③ It was believed that each spark from the fire represented a new pig or calf that would be born in the next year.

人们相信，篝火上的每朵火苗都代表着一头来年新生的猪或牛。

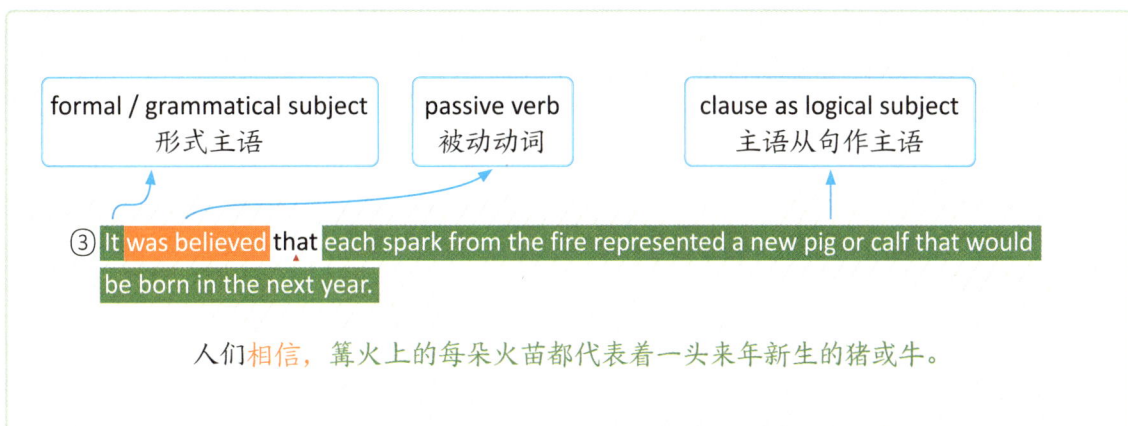

Now, please read the third sentence. What is the action? The action is "believe," but this verb is in its passive form. So "was believed" is the predicate verb.

In a passive sentence, the subject is not doing the action but being acted upon by the action. And the agent (施动者) that does the action is often omitted.

To identify the subject of this sentence, we can simply ask "what or who is believed?" The pronoun "it" is the subject, but it is only the grammatical or formal subject (形式主语). To put it another way, although the pronoun "it" occupies the position of the subject, it still needs a subsequent word, phrase or clause as the real subject to specify the actual content it contains.

In this sentence, the real subject or the logical subject is the clause introduced by "that": "each spark from the fire represented a new pig or calf that would be born in the next year". This clause clarifies the meaning of the pronoun "it".

In English, it is common practice to use the pronoun "it" as the grammatical subject when the logical subject is a clause.

However, when translating sentences like this into Chinese, we can do exactly the opposite. That is, we can first put the that-clause back to the subject position, replacing the grammatical subject "it"; and then change the sentence into the active voice, adding the omitted agent (省略掉的施动者). This makes it easier for us to translate it into Chinese as: "人们相信，篝火上的每朵火苗都代表着一头来年新生的猪或牛".

Here is the fourth sentence. What are the core parts?

```
┌─────────────────────────────────────────┐
│  subject and predicate in inverted order │
│            主谓倒装                       │
└─────────────────────────────────────────┘
```

④ Also dragged inside were evergreens, the one plant that could make it through a Norse winter.

一并被拖回家的还有常青树，一种能够撑过斯堪的纳维亚冬天的植物。

Based on what we have discussed earlier, we can find the subject and the verb with ease. Obviously, the subject is "evergreens" and the verb "were dragged" is in its passive form. You may find that in this sentence, the predicate verb comes before the subject. This is done to emphasize the verb. And we call this type of sentence an inverted sentence (倒装句).

The core parts of this sentence are "evergreens were dragged" that means "常青树被拖." Combining other additional information together, we can translate this sentence into Chinese as: "一并被拖回家的还有常青树，一种能够撑过斯堪的纳维亚冬天的植物".

Finally, here comes the last sentence. To reduce it to the core parts, let us first locate the subject and the main verb.

```
┌──────────────────┐   ┌──────────────────┐
│ linking verb 系动词 │   │ Predicative 表语  │
└──────────────────┘   └──────────────────┘
```

⑤ Evergreens are symbols of strength that prove life persisted in this dark time.

常青树是坚韧的象征，它证明生命在黑暗时期得到了延续

In this sentence, the subject is "Evergreens", but the predicate verb is not an action verb but a linking verb (系动词) "are". It links the subject to the noun "symbols", the "predicative (表语)" to describe the subject.

"Subject + Verb +Predicative" is the third basic sentence structure we can depend on to identify the core parts of a sentence. With the core parts "Evergreens are symbols", we can have a quick understanding of the basic meaning of the sentence: "常青树是象征." Then adding other additional elements, we can translate the whole sentence into Chinese as: "常青树是坚韧的象征，它证明了生命在黑暗时期得到了延续".

↳ 3. Parallel Texts

Here are the original and the translated texts for comparison. When dealing with each sentence in the original text, it is essential to understand its core parts correctly.

Christmas

Christmas traditions can be traced back to old Winter Solstice festivals in northern Europe. Centuries before the birth of Jesus Christ, early Europeans were celebrating light and birth in the darkest days of winter around December 21st, the winter solstice. People rejoiced during this time, looking forward to longer days and extended hours of sunlight. Fathers and sons would drag home the biggest yule log they could find and set it on fire until it burned out. It was believed that each spark from the fire represented a new pig or calf that would be born in the next year. Also dragged inside were evergreens, the one plant that could make it through a Norse winter. Evergreens are symbols of strength that prove life persisted in this dark time.

For as long as a yule log burned about 12 days, feasting and revelry reigned supreme. This celebration gave the name Yuletide, and the 12 days the log burned gave birth to the 12 days of Christmas.

圣诞节

圣诞传统的来源可追溯到北欧古老的冬至节日庆典。早在耶稣出现的几个世纪以前，早期欧洲人在 12 月 21 日左右的冬至——冬天最漆黑的日子里——庆祝光与新生。在此期间，人们欢心喜悦，期盼更长的白昼和更多的阳光。父子们会把他们能找到的最大的原木拖回家点燃，直至燃烧殆尽。人们相信，篝火上的每朵火苗都代表着一头来年新生的猪或牛。一并被拖回家的还有常青树，一种能够撑过斯堪的纳维亚冬天的植物。常青树是坚韧的象征，它证明生命在黑暗时期得到了延续。

一根原木燃尽大概需要 12 天左右，在此期间宴会和狂欢大行其道。这个庆典被称为"圣诞季节"，而原木燃烧的这 12 天也演变为圣诞节的 12 天节日。

4. Translation Skills Summarized

In this lesson, we have learned the origins of Christmas and the way to identity the core parts of an English sentence, particularly by the three basic sentence structures: SV, SVO, and SVP. Those basic structures also have variations. As the following two examples show, they can either use an active or passive voice.

S + V	S + V + O	S + V + P

active / passive voice

active: People celebrate Christmas on December 25.

passive: Christmas is celeberated on December 25.

Or they can be in a natural or inverted order.

S + V	S + V + O	S + V + P

natural or inverted order

natural: Many people wear Santa hats on Christmas Eve.

inverted: There are many people wearing Santa hats on Christmas Eve.

expletive 虚词，填补词

Here, the first sentence is in a natural order, but it can be inverted by placing the word "There" at the beginning, as is shown in the second sentence. Note that in the second sentence, the word "There" is only an expletive (虚词、填补词) that has no meaning and is not grammatically related to the rest of the sentence. Actually, the core parts of this sentence are almost the same with that of the first one; they are "people are wearing hats."

Despite all those variations, the three basic structures are helpful when we want to identify the core parts of English sentences.

But why is it important to know the core parts of an English sentence? One crucial reason is that it helps us understand the most important idea of sentences.

As we know, English sentences tend to be longer and more complex than Chinese sentences. In some extreme cases, a sentence may run through several lines, a paragraph or even pages.

For many students, it is a serious challenge to grasp the accurate meaning of a long sentence, let alone translate it into Chinese. But no matter how long a sentence is, it grows from the core parts.

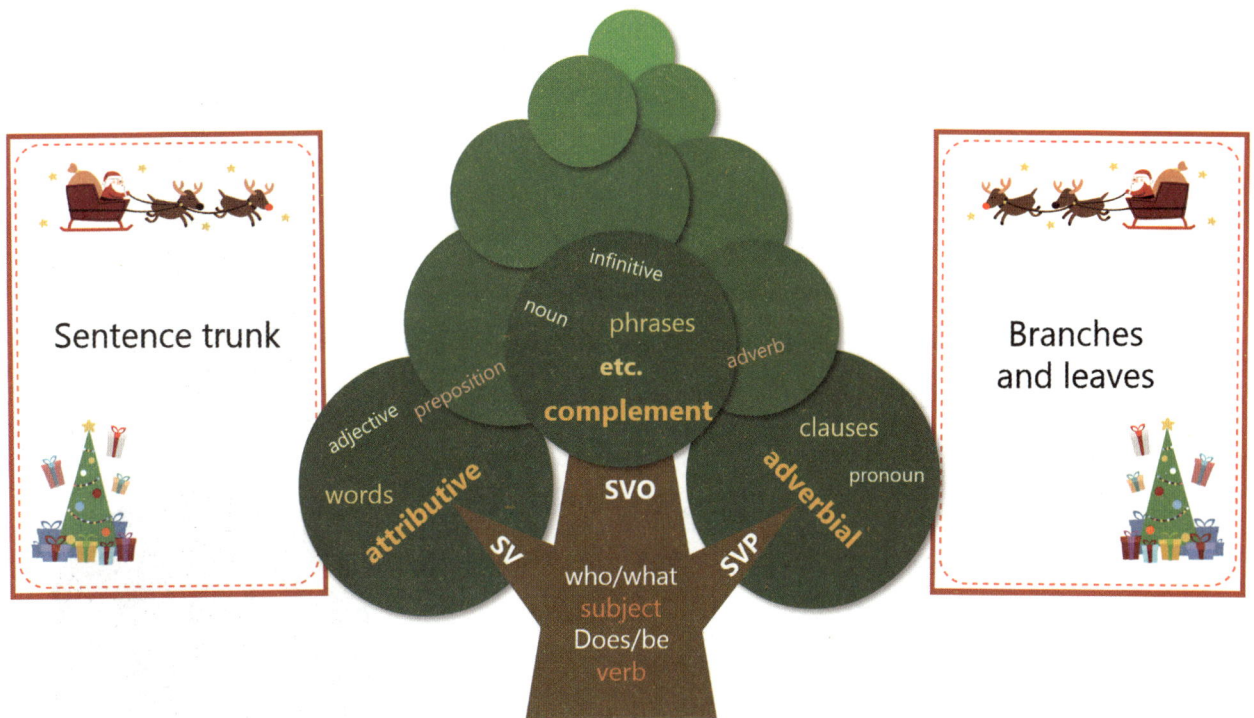

Sentence trunk

Branches and leaves

infinitive
noun phrases adverb
etc.
preposition complement
adjective clauses
words attributive SVO pronoun
SV adverbial
who/what SVP
subject
Does/be
verb

If we compare an English sentence to a tree, then the core parts of the sentence are like the trunk (树干) of the tree. They tell who or what does or is and constitute the basic meaning of a sentence.

As we add one or more modifiers, such as words, phrases, or clauses to the core parts, the sentence tree grows with branches and leaves. Those branches and leaves bring additional information to the sentence trunk. This is how a sentence expands. And the three basic structures "SV", "SVO," and "SVP" we are talking about today lay the foundation for sentence expansion.

If we want to get the basic meaning of a sentence, the quickest way is to cut all the modifying branches and leaves but retain the trunk of the tree, that is, the core parts of a sentence.

After we have grasped the basic meaning of the sentence, we can start to sort out (梳理) all the modifying elements and clarify their relationship with those core parts.

To sum up, identifying the core parts of a sentence is the starting point for effective comprehension. Once we are able to identify the core parts, we are well on our way to becoming proficient readers and translators.

5. Cultural Expressions

...n learn some useful cultural ...brations of Christmas. The ...ons would accumulate over time: perhaps beginning with the yule log, followed by the Christmas tree and finally evolving into the way they are today.

Modern Christmas traditions often include decorating Christmas trees, hanging Christmas stockings and evergreen wreaths, exchanging greeting cards and gifts, sharing meals with family and friends, going to church, and singing songs about Santa Claus.

Decorating Christmas trees

Church caroling

Hanging Christmas stockings and evergreen

Exchanging greeting cards and gifts

Sharing meals with family and friends

Nowadays, as Christmas is widely celebrated by people around the world, it has developed its own characteristics in different countries.

In China, Christmas is often treated as a new way of entertainment. A tradition that is becoming more and more popular is giving apples on Christmas Eve. Those apples are called "平安果", meaning "peace apples". Peace apples carry messages such as "Merry Christmas" or "平安", and are wrapped up in colored paper for sale.

They are called peace apples because the Chinese word for apple, "pingguo", sounds similar to the Chinese word for Christmas Eve, "pinganye", meaning "a peaceful or quiet evening" which has been translated from the carol "Silent Night".

Giving peace apples is a Chinese way of celebrating Christmas. It is a successful trans-cultural practice that proves it is possible to localize (本地化) a western festival like Christmas. This also tells us that we can take western festivals as a new way of cultural expression, that is, to incorporate Chinese cultural elements into such a festival instead of accepting everything without questioning.

↳ 6. Questions for Discussion

1) Can you compare the similarities and differences between Christmas and the Spring Festival? You may want to list a few examples to support your views.

2) Can we compare the core parts of an English sentence to the skeleton of a man? Please illustrate your points with examples.

II Halloween

⤷ 1. Cultural Background

If you like the Harry Potter stories, you might be interested in tales of ghosts, **ghouls**[1], **witchcraft**[2] and magic. Halloween is based on a combination of the old **Celtic**[3] New Year and the Christian festival of **All Saints' Day** ①. It is the traditional end of the harvest season in European agriculture when people **slaughtered**[4] their **livestock**[5] to store for the winter. The ancient Celts also believed that the end of October was when the boundaries between the living and the dead broke down and sickness came to crops and animals.

Today, people do not view the holiday as just one day any more. It is an entire month or even a season long celebration, and as a result, even more and more people are taking part in Halloween activities. During the holiday, houses are often decorated with the types of elements around Halloween. Halloween imagery includes themes of death, evil and **mythical**[6] monsters.

Words and Expressions:

1 ghoul /guːl/ *n.* （传说中的）盗墓食尸鬼

2 witchcraft /ˈwɪtʃˌkræft/ *n.* 巫术；（尤指）妖术，魔法

3 Celtic /ˈkɛltɪk/ *adj.* 凯尔特人的；凯尔特语的

4 slaughter /ˈslɔːtər/ *v.* 屠宰；宰杀

5 livestock /ˈlaɪvstɑːk/ *n.* 牲畜；家畜

6 mythical /ˈmɪθɪkl/ *adj.* 神话的；虚无的

◇◇◇◇◇◇◇

① All Saints' Day 万圣节，一般认为源于古代凯尔特人的秋天祭典，也称"鬼节"。10 月 31 日被凯尔特人认为是秋季的结束，11 月 1 日是冬季的开始，也被视作新年伊始。凯尔特人相信故人亡魂会在新年前回到故地，在活人身上寻生灵以获得唯一再生的希望。如今，万圣节的宗教色彩已比较淡薄，反而是充满了喜庆的意味。人们打扮古怪，参加化装舞会；各家准备好南瓜灯和糖果；儿童要逐家索要糖果，不给的人会被认为不够慷慨。朋友、家人间互寄贺卡祝万圣节快乐，也是每年十月间流行的习俗。

2. Translation Examples Explained

When translating a sentence, its subject is of great importance for translating both the sentence's core parts and the entire sentence. This section will explore how to recognize and translate rather complex subjects by translating a passage about the roots and celebrations of Halloween. Below is the passage, with four underlined sample sentences being the focal point.

> *Halloween, which falls on October 31, is a traditional festival popular among English-speaking countries. Originally the festival was dedicated to praising autumn harvest. ①In addition, it also serves as remembering the dead as it is believed that all ghosts rise from the Underworld on Halloween. People light bonfires and lanterns to frighten evil spirits and guide the souls of dead relatives and friends back home.*
>
> *Today, the original spirit of the festival has been replaced by rejoicing and revelry. ②Making pumpkin lanterns, trick-or-treating, playing pranks, having costume parties, visiting haunted attractions, telling scary stories are traditional Halloween activities. ③It is popular for cinemas to show horror films and for bookshops to sell more ghost stories around this time. Children dress up as witches, vampires, ghosts, monsters, or characters from movies. They go from house to house, knocking at doors and asking "trick or treat?" ④If you are at home on Halloween, it is a good idea to have a bowl of small presents or sweets to offer to anyone who knocks on your door. Without treat, kids will play tricks on them.*

01

Zero translation (零翻译)

In addition, <u>it</u> also serves as remembering the dead as <u>it</u> is believed that all ghosts rise from the Underworld on Halloween.

Keeping the position in the end

此外，这也是个祭祀亡魂的日子，据说这天鬼魂都会从地下造访人间。

In the subordinate clause (从句) of the first example, we can find "it" comes in the subject position followed by the predicate (谓语) "is believed". But what is replaced by the anticipatory (引导词) "it" in the initial position since it refers to nothing? That is the real subject in the form of a subject clause which is postponed till the end. Meanwhile, the subject clause brings up the topic and the statements on it. In the translation practice, we tend to neglect the anticipatory and keep the subject clause as in the original.

Next, let us see what the subject is in the following sentence.

02

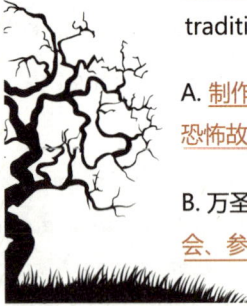

Making pumpkin lanterns, trick-or-treating, playing pranks, having costume parties, visiting haunted attractions, telling scary stories are traditional Halloween activities.

A. 制作南瓜灯、挨家挨户要糖果、恶作剧、举行化装舞会、参观闹鬼景点、讲恐怖故事和看恐怖电影是万圣节的传统活动。

B. 万圣节的传统活动包括制作南瓜灯、挨家挨户要糖果、恶作剧、举行化装舞会、参观闹鬼景点、讲恐怖故事和看恐怖电影。

It bears the "SVP" structural pattern with a compound subject (复合主语), which includes five activities in the form of the gerunds (动名词) listed. For this sentence we have two options. We can translate this long subject following the original order (顺译) as Version A; the other option is to translate it in the reverse order (逆译). What is the difference between the two?

In Version B the subject "万圣节活动" refers back to the subject of the previous sentence, which also discusses the festival. By doing so, better cohesion (衔接) is built between this and the previous sentence in the Chinese translation. In addition, the word "包括" emphasizes the diversity of the celebrations while the verb "是" in the above version can not do so.

03

Zero translation

It is popular for cinemas to show horror films and for bookshops to sell more ghost stories around this time.

A. 电影院流行在万圣节期间放映恐怖片，书店流行在万圣节期间摆卖更多的鬼故事书。

B. 万圣节期间流行在电影院放映恐怖片，在书店摆卖更多的鬼故事书。

The original spirit of the festival | ② Making pumpkin lanterns...telling scary stories

As for the third sentence, what are the subjects? Like the previous two examples, "it" fills the position of the subject, while the conjunction "and" connects two coordinating subjects of to-infinitives. There are two possible ways to translate this sentence. One way is to, as in Version A, move the sense subjects (意义上的主语) "电影院" and "书店" to the initial positions to serve as the subjects in two clauses. The other way is to move the adverbial of time (时间状语) "万圣节期间" to the beginning of the sentence so it will function as the topic in the Chinese version. Meanwhile, the sense subjects are both converted to the adverbials of place (地点状语).

In Version B, the topic served by the adverbial of time (万圣节期间) is in line with those in the previous sentences in this paragraph. This helps to create a better cohesion among the three straight sentences, focusing our reader's attention on the big topic — Halloween.

04

Zero translation

If you are at home on Halloween, it is a good idea to have a bowl of small presents or sweets or to offer to anyone who knocks on your door.

A. 如果万圣节那天你在家，一个不错的建议是在碗里装些小礼物或者糖果来打发那些敲门的人。

B. 如果万圣节那天你在家，在碗里装些小礼物或者糖果来打发那些敲门的人是一个不错的建议。

Let us move on to the fourth one. In the principal clause (主句) we can find the "SVC" structure with "it" as the subject. Since "it" is more of the subject in the form (形式主语), we cannot help but look for the real subject, which is served by the to-infinitive (不定式), a long and complex structure. In translating it, we can follow or reverse the sentence order. By following the original order, as in Version A, don't translate "it" but use the English predicative (表语) as the subject in the Chinese translation, while keeping the real subject, the to-infinitive structure, in the end of the translation.

In contrast, we can reverse the original order, as in Version B, to put the to-infinitive as a long subject in the Chinese translation. In this context, we think both versions are acceptable.

3. Parallel Texts

Here we can compare the source text and its Chinese translation. Please focus on the bold parts.

Halloween

Halloween, which falls on October 31, is a traditional festival popular among English-speaking countries. Originally the festival was dedicated to praising autumn harvest as it marks the end of autumn. ① In addition, it also serves as remembering the dead as **it** is believed **that all ghosts rise from the Underworld on Halloween.** People light bonfires and lanterns to frighten evil spirits and guide the souls of dead relatives and friends back home.

Today, the original spirit of the festival has been replaced by rejoicing and revelry. ② **Making pumpkin lanterns, trick-or-treating, playing pranks, having costume parties, visiting haunted attractions, telling scary stories** are traditional Halloween activities. ③ **It** is popular **for cinemas to show horror films and for bookshops to sell more ghost stories around this time.** Children dress up as witches, vampires, ghosts, monsters, or characters from movies. They go from house to house, knocking at doors and asking "trick or treat? ④ If you are at home on Halloween, **it** is a good idea **to have a bowl of small presents or sweets to offer to anyone who knocks on your door.** Without treat, kids will play tricks on them.

万圣节

10 月 31 日的万圣节是流行于英语国家的传统节日。最初，这个节日是为了赞颂秋收，因为它宣告秋天即将结束。此外，这也是个祭祀亡魂的日子，据说**这天鬼魂都会从地下造访人间**。人们燃起篝火、点上灯笼来驱赶恶灵，引导逝去的亲朋好友魂归故里。

如今，这个节日最初的精神已完全被纵情欢乐所替代。万圣节活动包括**制作南瓜灯、挨家挨户要糖果、恶作剧、举行化装舞会、参观闹鬼景点、讲恐怖故事和看恐怖电影**。万圣节期间流行**在电影院放映恐怖片，在书店摆卖更多的鬼故事书**。孩子们扮成巫婆、吸血鬼、幽灵、怪兽或电影人物，挨家挨户敲门，说"不给糖就捣蛋！"如果万圣节那天你在家，**在碗里装些小礼物或者糖果来打发那些敲门的人是一个不错的建议**。不给的话，孩子们就会捉弄主人。

4. Translation Skills Summarized

As is shown in the chart, we can see how we often handle complex subjects in English sentences in E-C translation practice.

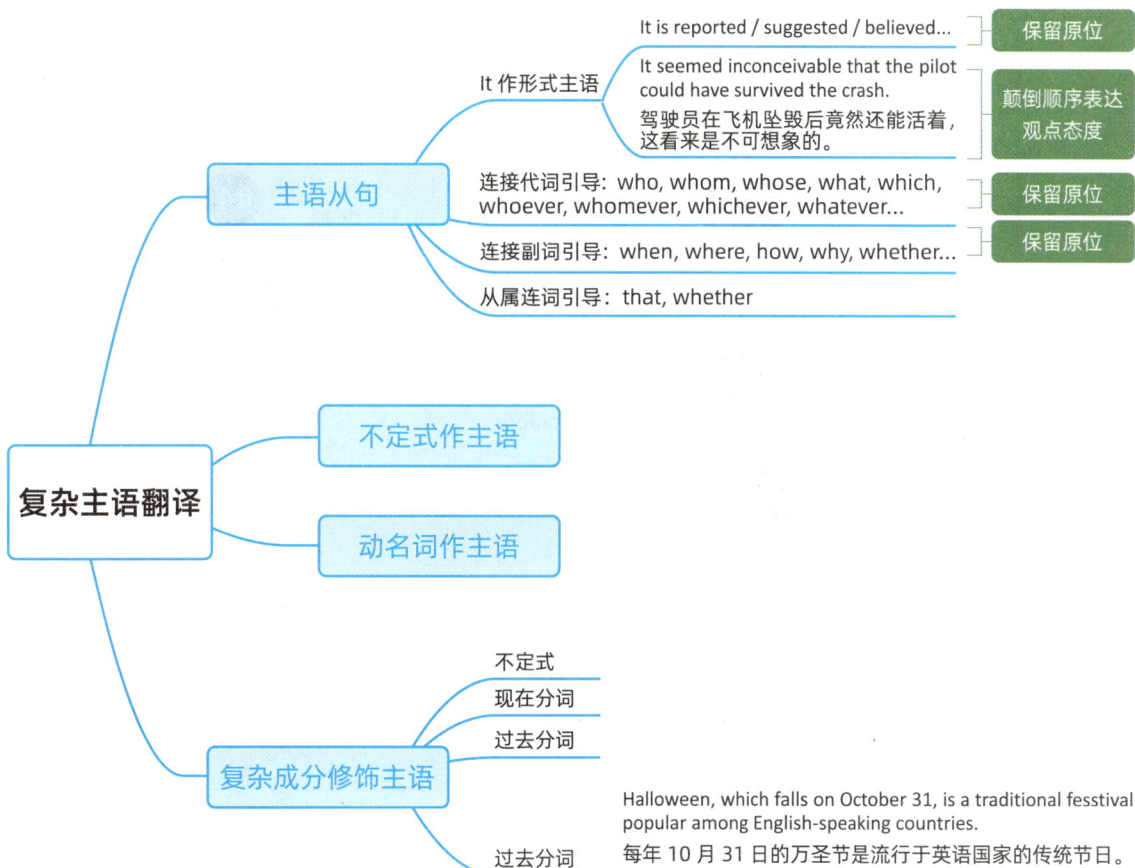

Basically, whether the subject remains where it is in the original is the major concern in E-C translation. They can retain the position in the beginning in most cases, but if the logical connection or coherence and cohesiveness are expected to be highlighted, or the predicate on attitude and cognition to be emphasized, we can make the options other than that.

5. Cultural Expressions

Halloween is a festival of historical significance and worldly amusement. Halloween is thought to have originated around 4,000 B.C., and borrowed traditions from different festivals, as is shown in the evolution of the festival.

1. The Evolution of the Festival

0 1 The Roman Feralia Festival
commemorating the dead

0 2 The Roman Pomona Festival
honoring the goddess of fruit and trees

0 3 The Celtic（凯尔特人的）Samuin Festival
meaning "summer's end" and the bulk of origins of Halloween traditions

0 4 The Catholic All Saint's Day
starting around 800 by a church to try to replace Samuin

Halloween is where death (winter) takes over from the life-giving fall harvest, hence the mixtures of black and orange come at the festival.

2. The Colors of Halloween

Black   death, gloom and the foreboding night.

fortitude, survival and power, the harvest, and the colors of fall.   **Orange**

The custom of wearing costumes or masks comes from the Celtic（凯尔特人的）tradition of the young impersonating (扮演) evil spirits, by dressing up in white costumes with blackened faces or masks in an attempt to placate (安抚) these spirits.

3. Costumes

"Trick or Treat" has a short history. In the 19th century Scotland and Ireland, there were some records of children travelling door-to-door, praying for souls or performing for money or cakes on All Hallows' Eve. However, the tradition is a short step from the medieval (中世纪的) practice of souling, in which beggars went door to door on October 31 to pray for souls in return for food. The food given was often a Soul Cake, which was a small round cake that represented a soul being freed when the cake was eaten. Today "Trick or Treat" means "give us a treat or we'll pull a prank (恶作剧) on you."

4. Trick or Treat

According to the Irish legend, Jack-O'-Lanterns are named after a man named Jack.

5. Jack-O'-Lanterns

This crafty fellow fooled the devil on numerous occasions and, as a result, his soul was condemned to hang about the Earth for all eternity (永远). Jack, barred from both heaven and hell, put the burning ember given to him by Beelzebub into the very first "Jack-O'-Lanterns", in order to ward off (避开) any more encounters with the evil.

↳ 6. Questions for Discussion

1) Is "horror" the most distinctive feature of Halloween or not? Please support your view with details.

2) What is the role of the subject in an English sentence? Please explain it with the analysis of an English sentence.

III Exercises

Section A. True or false

_____ 1) Christmas trees are usually made of evergreens and decorated with colored lights and ribbons.

_____ 2) Originally, Halloween was dedicated to praising autumn harvest and it also served as remembering the dead.

_____ 3) The main structure of the sentence "He who does not advance loses ground" is "He does not advance."

_____ 4) In the sentence—The only man who is really free is the one who can turn down an invitation to dinner without giving any excuse—the main sentence structure is "SV".

_____ 5) In the sentence—The Christmas season, also called the festive season, or the holiday season, is an annually recurring period recognized in many Western and Western-influenced countries that is generally considered to run from late November to early January—the main structure is "The Christmas season is a period".

Section B. Multiple choice

_____ 1) Other decorations such as lights and wreaths of evergreen and signs wishing a "Merry Christmas" can be found inside and outside of many homes.

　　A. 像彩灯和常绿花环这类的装饰和祝愿"圣诞快乐"的标签能在许多家庭的里里外外被找到。

　　B. 像彩灯和常绿花环这类的装饰和祝愿"圣诞快乐"的标签在许多家庭的里里外外都可以找到。

　　C. 其它装饰，如光线、常绿花环和祝愿"圣诞快乐"的标签，在许多家庭的里里外外都可以找到。

_____ 2) Some people who are friends or relatives and live great distances from each other may not be much in contact with each other during a year, but will usually exchange greeting cards and often Christmas letters telling their family news.

　　A. 是朋友或亲戚且相距甚远的人们，可能整年中联系不多，但经常会交换贺卡和圣诞书信，告知家人的近况。

　　B. 一些距离较远的朋友或亲戚可能整年中联系不多，但经常会交换贺卡和圣诞贺信，告知家人的新闻。

　　C. 一些距离较远的亲朋好友可能整年中联系不多，但经常会交换贺卡和圣诞书信，告知家人的近况。

_____ 3) During their first winter, over half of the settlers died of starvation or epidemics, and those who survived began sowing in the first spring.

　　A. 在第一个冬天，半数以上的移民都死于饥饿和传染病；人们活下来，并在第一个春季开始播种。

　　B. 在第一个冬天，半数以上的移民都死于饥饿或传染病；人们活下来，并在第一个春季开始散播疾病。

　　C. 在第一个冬天，半数以上的移民都死于饥饿或传染病；活下来的人们在第一个春季开始播种。

_____ 4) But as cooking varies with families and with the regions where one lives, it is not easy to get a consensus on the precise kind of stuffing for the turkey.

　　A. 但烹饪技艺因家不同、因地而异，在火鸡填充材料上也就很难取得一致。

　　B. 但烹饪技艺常因家庭和地区的不同而各异，这很难取得一致，在火鸡填充材料上。

　　C. 但烹饪技艺常因家庭和人们居住的地区的不同而各异，应该用什么填料填充火鸡也就很难取得一致。

_____ 5) Finally, the fields produced a yield rich beyond expectations, and therefore it was decided that a day of thanksgiving to the Lord be fixed.

　　A. 后来，田地获得了意外的丰收，所以大家决定要选一个固定的日子来感谢上帝。

　　B. 后来，田地获得了意外的丰收，所以要选一个固定的日子来感谢上帝被决定下来。

　　C. 后来，田地获得了意外的丰收，所以要选一个固定的日子来感谢上帝，这被决定下来。

Section A. Multiple choice (5 items*4 points=20 points)

_____ 1) It might be a good idea to detox after the indulgences of Christmas.

A. 在圣诞节的放纵之后，戒去毒瘾或许是个不错的主意。

B. 在圣诞节的放纵之后排排毒或许是个不错的主意。

C. 这或许是个不错的主意，在圣诞节的放纵之后排排毒。

_____ 2) There are varying opinions as to the origin of Valentine's Day.

A. 有许多种说法，关于情人节的起源。

B. 关于情人节的起源有许多种说法。

C. 这些是关于情人节起源的多种说法。

_____ 3) On the night of October 31st, it has become a tradition for millions of children to dress up as fun or scary characters and shout "Trick-or-Treat" to collect candies.

A. 10 月 31 日晚上，这已成为传统，数以百万计的孩子乔装打扮成有趣或恐怖的角色，喊着 "不给吃就捣蛋"，讨要糖果。

B. 10 月 31 日晚上，数以百万计的孩子乔装打扮成有趣或恐怖的角色，喊着 "不给吃就捣蛋"，讨要糖果，这已成为传统。

C. 10 月 31 日晚上，数以百万计的孩子乔装打扮成有趣或恐怖的角色，喊着 "不给吃就捣蛋"，讨要糖果。

_____ 4) During this period, it was believed that the boundaries between our world and the world of the dead were weakened, allowing spirits of the recently dead to cross over and possess the living.

A. 在这期间，这被认为，我们的世界和死者的世界之间的界限被削弱，允许刚刚死去的鬼魂穿越生活。

B. 在这期间，人们认为，我们的世界和死者的世界之间的界限被削弱，允许刚刚死去的鬼魂穿越生活。

C. 在这期间，人们认为，我们和死者世界之间的界限被削弱，刚刚死去的鬼魂可以穿越并附着于活人身上。

_____ 5) What almost all the holidays have in common whether they are local, regional or national is that they provide an opportunity for families and friends to get together to visit, eat, exchange good wishes and enjoy each other's company and hospitality.

A. 英国的节日无论是全国性的还是地方性的，都能给各个家庭提供相聚的机会。

B. 这些节日，无论是地方性的、区域性的还是全国性的，相同之处在于都能够让亲朋好友有机会聚在一起，游历不同地方，享受美食，互祝安康，相互陪伴，各尽地主之谊。

C. 这些节日相同之处在于，无论是地方性的、区域性的或全国性的，都能够让亲朋好友有机会聚在一起，游历不同地方，享受美食，互祝安康，相互陪伴，各尽地主之谊。

Section B. Sentence translation (5 items*6 points=30 points)

1) It was my first round playing Santa and bringing Christmas presents to other children.

2) People decorate their houses with glittering paper chains, gold and silver and brightly colored, and special electric lights which only come out at this time of the year.

3) If you are at home on Halloween, it is a good idea to have to have a bowl of small presents or sweets to offer to anyone who knocks on your door.

4) In winter's twilight, the lower branches were parted, and with the first strokes of the saw the scent of pine pitch rose like incense in nature's cathedral.

5) The Scots, who live in Scotland, in the north of British Isles, take small notice of Christmas, but celebrates instead at New Year, which they call Hogmanay (新年前夜).

Section C. Paragraph translation (50 points)

The Christmas season, also called the festive season, or the holiday season, is an annually recurring period recognized in many Western and Western-influenced countries that is generally considered to run from late November to early January. Christmas window displays and Christmas tree lighting ceremonies when trees decorated with ornaments and light bulbs are illuminated are traditions in many areas.

Unit 3
LIFE
CEREMONIES

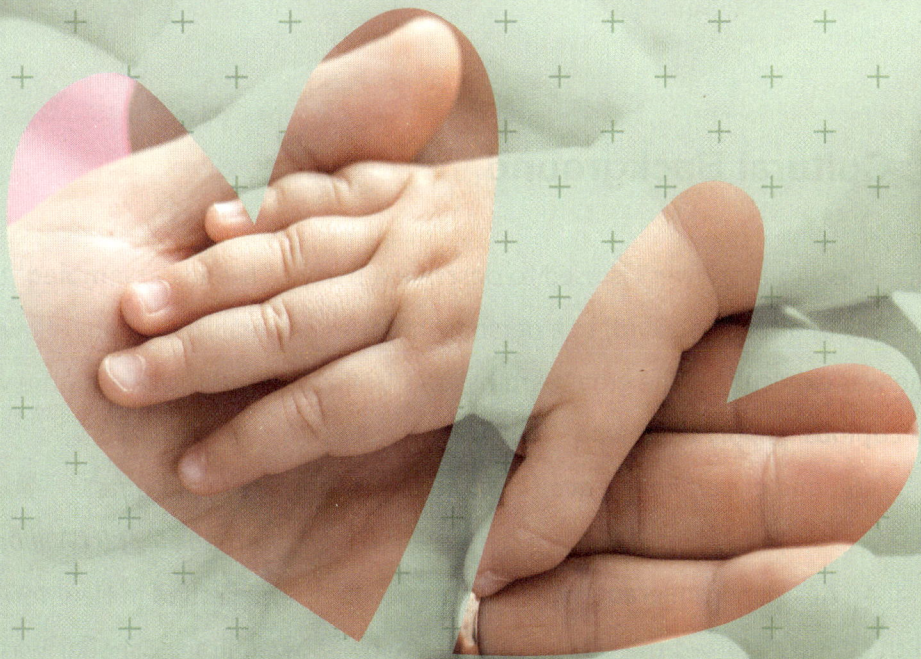

I

Baby Shower

In the play *As You Like It* by William Shakespeare, he describes the seven stages of life:

"All the world's a stage. And all the men and women merely players. They have their exits and their entrances. And one man in his time plays many parts. His acts being seven ages."

From infancy to adulthood, from birth to death, life comes and goes in orbit, and the seven ages or stages are always marked by memorable events. Today we are beginning the life journey to catch a glimpse of the important events throughout it.

In Britain and America, the diverse celebrations or ceremonies on the milestones in one's life somehow impart cultural traditions and religious rituals. This unit will cover four important events throughout the life. They are the baby shower in America, the graduation ceremony, the wedding ceremony and the funeral. Meanwhile, we are going to learn to handle tense meanings, voices (语态) and sentence objects in E-C translation.

↳ 1. Cultural Background

The word "shower" is used to describe a party of friends **assembled**[1] to **present**[2] gifts (usually of a specified kind) to a person; "her friends organized a baby shower for her when she was expecting". The great Bard himself, William Shakespeare used the word to **convey**[3] "a **copious**[4] supply **bestowed**[5]".

"He and myself have travail'd in the great shower of your gifts".

Timon of Athens: Act 5 (William Shakespeare)

An Austrian **immigrant**[6] named Franz Schauer, who settled in New York during the late 18th century, started the tradition of the Baby Shower. Franz Schauer was a **silversmith**[7], **engraver**[8] and **merchant**[9] looking for his fortune[①] in America.

◇◇◇◇◇◇◇

① seek one's fortune 外出寻找发财机会；外出闯荡；闯世界。

There is little information about Schauer; however, his name is mentioned in a book that was published in 1759. The book contained pictures of "plates from drawings by Susanna Sophia Betzin and engraved by von Franz Schauer". It was the first book to have hand-colored plates drawn by a woman. This leads us to believe that the origin of Baby Showers **commenced**[10] sometime after 1759, but well before 1800. Schauer specialised in silver engravings but he was also a merchant. Selling his silver was his main **priority**[11] and it was Schauer who came up with the brilliant idea to encourage the wealthy upper classes of New York to give silver gifts to newborn babies.

The tradition of giving gifts to new babies dated back thousands of years to the ancient Romans and Ancient Egyptians. Franz Schauer no doubt **capitalised**[12] on this tradition by encouraging sales of his silver merchandise that could be personalized by engraving! The tradition of giving Showers for wealthy mothers-to-be started in America and the popularity of this type of party **steadily**[13] grew as the wealth of people increased, especially following WWII. It has now become an American tradition, which is being adopted across Europe, especially in the UK.

Words and Expressions:

1 assemble /əˈsembl/ v. 聚集；集合

2 present / prɪˈzent / v. 赠送；致以（问候等）

3 convey /kənˈveɪ/ v. 表达；表示；传达

4 copious adj. 丰富的；充裕的

5 bestow v.（将……）给予；授予；献给

6 immigrant /ˈɪmɪɡrənt/ n.（外来）移民

7 silversmith /ˈsɪlvərsmɪθ/ n. 银匠；银器商

8 engraver /ɪnˈɡrevə-/ n. 雕刻师；雕刻工

9 merchant /ˈmɜːrtʃənt/ n. 商人；批发商

10 commence /kəˈmens/ v. 开始发生；开始

11 priority /praɪˈɔːrəti/ n. 优先事项；重点

12 capitalise /ˈkæpɪtəlaɪz/ v. 利用；用……以牟利

13 steadily /ˈstedəli/ adv. 稳定地；稳步地

2. Translation Examples Explained

Please read the following passage. It is a brief introduction to the baby shower. While reading it, you'd better pay more attention to the tense of the bold parts.

> ① *Traditionally, baby showers **were** given only for the family's first child, and only women **were** invited.* ② *The original intent **was** for women to share wisdom and lessons on the art of becoming a mother.* ③ *Over time, it **has become** common to hold them for subsequent or adopted children. According to etiquette, because the party centers on gift-giving, the baby shower is typically arranged and hosted by a close friend rather than a member of the family, since it is considered rude for families to beg for gifts on behalf of their members.* ④ *There is no set rule for when or where showers **are to be held**.* ⑤ *Generally a baby shower is held one to two months prior to the due date to allow the parents to buy any much needed items that they **did not** receive during the shower. The number of guests and the style of entertainment are determined by the host. Most hosts invite only women to baby showers, although there is no firm rule requiring this. Showers typically include food but not a full meal.*

> Attaching the Chinese adverb "过去" to the compound predicate verbs to indicate the simple past tense.
>
> ① Traditionally, baby showers <u>were</u> given only for the family's first child, and only women <u>were</u> invited.
>
> 传统上来说，迎婴聚会过去只为家中的第一个孩子而办，并且只邀请女性参加。

Please take a look at the first example. The word "traditionally" indicates the act in the past, and the origin of the custom is thus stressed. We can even anticipate the dynamic change of it over time. In accordance with the time signal of the past, we are supposed to add the Chinese adverb "过去" to reproduce the simple past tense of the English sentence in the Chinese translation.

Zero translation

② The original intent was for women to share wisdom and lessons on the art of becoming a mother.

起初的目的是让女性们分享初为人母的智慧和经验教训。

Then let us move on to the next example. The source text (原文本) here introduces the "original" purpose of baby showers, which implies the evolution of the custom later on. On the other hand, since in the first example the simple past tense has already been translated and emphasized by adding the Chinese word "过去" and the Chinese word "起初"（original）in this sentence also indicates a past practice, we do not need to add another time word to translate "was" any more. This method is called zero-translation.

Attaching the Chinese adverb "已经" to the predicate verb to indicate the influence of the evolving tradition.

③ Over time, it has become common to hold them for subsequent or adopted children.

随着时间的推移，给其他的孩子或是收养的孩子开迎婴聚会已经变得很平常。

Unlike the first two examples, the time signal expression "over time" portrays how the tradition has evolved. We are expected to convey and underline the evolution of the event in the Chinese version, so the Chinese adverb "已经" is better added in this context.

> Adding the Chinese adverb "将要" before the predicate verb (谓语动词) to indicate the intent for the future.

④ There is no set rule for when or where showers <u>are to be held.</u>

关于何时何地<u>将要</u>举办迎婴聚会没有特别的规定。

This sentence refers to a future event with the pattern "be + to infinitive". We'd better translate the meaning of the future tense by placing the adverb "将要" before the predicate Chinese verb "举办".

⑤ Generally a baby shower <u>is</u> held one to two months prior to the due date to allow the parents to buy any much needed items that they <u>did not</u> receive during the shower.

> Adding the Chinese adverb "未曾" to specify what did not happen at the baby shower.

通常，迎婴聚会在产前一到两个月举办，以便给准爸爸、准妈妈时间购买那些他们迫切需要却<u>未曾</u>在迎婴聚会上收到的物品。

In the last instance the words "generally" and the predicate "is held" in the simple present tense indicate when a baby shower often takes place, whereas the verb "did" refers to what was yet to be prepared for childbirth at the baby shower. We can see a striking contrast between the present and the past. But because of the lack of tense changes of Chinese verbs, we can only rely on the Chinese adverb "通常" to indicate the current practice of an American baby shower. For the same reason, the Chinese adverb "未曾" is added in the translation to emphasize the grammatical meaning of the simple past tense in the English original.

↳ 3. Parallel Texts

Here we can compare the source text and its translation. Please focus on the bold parts we've practiced. You may be wondering what has caused the differences in expressing tense meanings in the two languages.

The Baby Shower

Traditionally, baby showers **were** given only for the family's first child, and only women **were** invited. The original intent **was** for women to share wisdom and lessons on the art of becoming a mother. Over time, it **has become** common to hold them for subsequent or adopted children. According to etiquette, because the party centers on gift-giving, the baby shower is typically arranged and hosted by a close friend rather than a member of the family, since it is considered rude for families to beg for gifts on behalf of their members. There is no set rule for when or where showers **are to be** held. Generally a baby shower **is** held one to two months prior to the due date to allow the parents to buy any much needed items that they **did not receive** during the shower. The number of guests and the style of entertainment are determined by the host. Most hosts invite only women to baby showers, although there is no firm rule requiring this. Showers typically include food but not a full meal.

迎婴聚会

传统上来说，迎婴聚会**过去**只为家中的第一个孩子举办，并且只邀请女性参加。起初的目的**曾**是让女性们分享为人母的智慧和经验教训。随着时间的推移，给其他的孩子或是收养的孩子开迎婴聚会**已经**变得很平常。根据礼节，由于派对以送礼为主，一般由准妈妈的好友而不是家庭成员来安排和主持，因为对家庭来说代表家人讨要礼物有些无礼。关于何时何地**将要**举办迎婴聚会并没有特别的规定。通常迎婴聚会在产前一到两个月举办，以便给准爸爸、准妈妈时间购买那些他们迫切需要却**未曾**在迎婴聚会上收到的物品。客人数量和游戏方式由主人决定。虽然没有明确规定男士不能参加，但大多数主人只邀请女士来参加迎婴聚会。通常迎婴聚会上会摆上食物，但绝非正餐。

4. Translation Skills Summarized

Please take a close look at the following chart. From the chart, we can see how the two languages differ and by what means the differences can be maximally bridged to reproduce tense meanings in E-C translation.

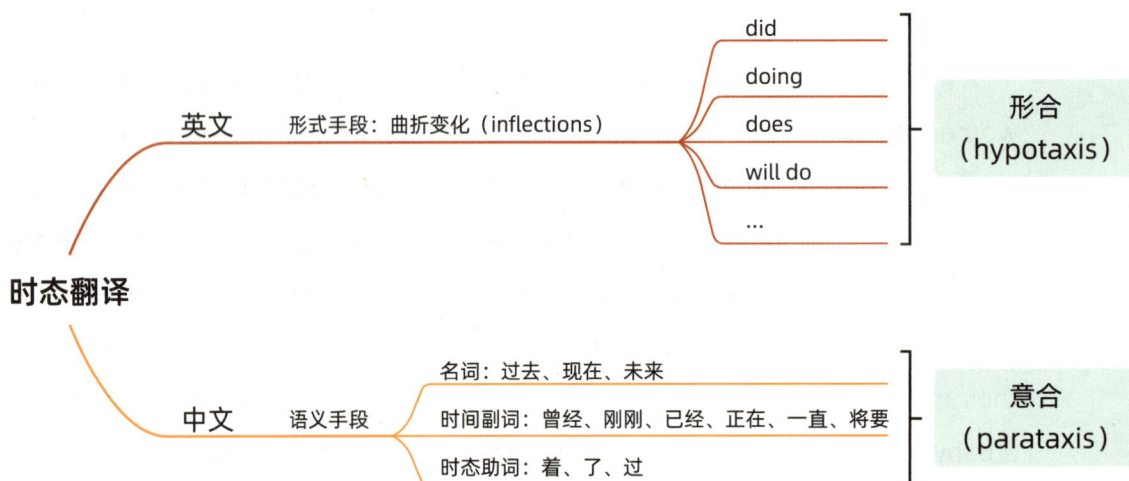

The next table shows how tense meanings are basically realized in English and Chinese. However, we should know that the choices of tense expressions in E-C translation may not coincide with each other as is shown in the table. We'd better make a case-by-case decision in reproducing tense meanings in E-C translation.

时间／状态	简单体	进行体	完成体	完成进行体
现在时	do/does	am/is/are doing	has/have done	has/have been doing
过去时	did	was/were doing	had done	had been doing
将来时	will/shall do	will/shall be doing	will/shall have done	will/shall have been doing

With the above examples, we can see the tense-meaning translation is optional (可选择的) in the translation process. So, in what cases must the tense meanings in English be retained in the Chinese translation? There is no hard and fast rule but we should take full account of these two points. First, it is when the time order of the actions or the finished state is highlighted that we should use the tense-related expressions in Chinese. Second, translators should pay close attention to tense use in context rather than translate tense meanings mechanically. Only by properly translating tense meanings can the Chinese version be faithful and expressive.

5. Cultural Expressions

Here we can play a game. Can you tick off the Do's and Don'ts at the baby shower? Some of the activities at the party are in question. Why?

Cultural Expressions — Do's and Don'ts

To shower the new-born with water

To make a wish list of baby items

To have fun with the games

To have a feast

To give gifts and open gifts

To share the diaper cake

A baby shower is never to throw the baby in the bath and more often than not the woman is still pregnant. When it comes to the food and drinks at the baby shower, it is more likely to be light snacks than a heavy meal that is served. By the way, don't take a bite on the diaper cake, which might look delicious, but is inedible (无法食用)!

Anyhow, the baby-related celebrations are not unique to Americans. In China, we have a similar custom, that is, the one-month-old birthday (满月). Can you figure out the differences?

The baby shower often takes place one or two months before the baby is delivered to celebrate the expected birth of a child or the transformation (蜕变) of a woman into a mother, while the one-month-old birthday tends to fall one month after the baby is born.

The close friends of the mother play the role to throw the party at home, at the workplace, or somewhere else, while in China the family where the child was born hosts the banquet at home or more formally at the restaurant with a bounteous dinner (盛宴).

Baby showers are often women-only social gatherings and the female friends are invited to share the experiences in child upbringing, whereas the one-month-old birthday in China is a great union for the relatives and the friends of the family to share the joy of the beginning of the tender new life.

The theme of the baby shower is giving gifts often ticked off from the wish list of the parents-to-be and purchased by the guests. Unwrapping presents is a common activity at baby showers, however, in China we prefer to join in the feast and enjoy the livelier atmosphere.

When it comes to the activities at the baby shower, the baby-themed activities are amusing, such as bingo and food-tasting, whereas the Chinese tend to give gifts, typically red envelops in return for the gifts handed out on the birth of the child.

Based on what we've learned about the baby shower, let's have a review of some baby-related expressions below.

expecting a baby/being in the family way	怀孕
due date	预产期
going into labor	分娩
throwing the baby out with the bath water	丢弃不想要的东西的同时失去宝贵的东西

↳ 6. Questions for Discussion

1) Is the baby shower full of blessings? Please support your view with details.
2) In what case is it advisable to translate tense meanings? Please explain it with an English sentence.

II Graduation Ceremony

1. Cultural Background

Exploring Graduation Traditions Around the World

Graduation marks the end of an **academic**[1] journey and the **onset**[2] of a new chapter in life. It's an event celebrated around the world, varying to an **eminent**[3] degree from culture to culture. But as diverse as these traditions are, they all express the same core values – achievement, **anticipation**[4], and **reverence**[5] for **scholarly**[6] development.

Understanding the Significance of Graduation Traditions

Understanding the **significance**[7] of graduation traditions is crucial in exploring the core of these traditions. Traditions are cultural practices that are passed down from generation to generation. They **embody**[8] collective wisdom, shared values, and community identity. In the context of graduation, these traditions **showcase**[9] the significance of educational growth and the transition into a new phase of life.

Graduation ceremonies are not merely events to mark the completion of a course or degree. They are rich in history and symbolism, representing the **culmination**[10] of years of hard work, **dedication**[11], and personal growth. The traditions associated with graduation serve as a **reminder**[12] of the importance of education and its value in society.

The Role of Graduation in Various Cultures

Graduation signifies diverse meanings in different cultures. In many, it represents an **attainment**[13] of knowledge and signifies maturity. It also **commemorates**[14] the passage of time and the promise of a future beyond academics. In every place, though, the graduation tradition speaks to a larger narrative of cultural value placed on education and academic progression.

For example, graduation is seen as a **rite**[15] of passage in some cultures, marking the transition from **adolescence**[16] to adulthood. It is a time when individuals are recognized for their accomplishments and ready to take on new **societal**[17] responsibilities. In other cultures, graduation is a celebration of family and community, where the achievements of the graduates are seen as a collective success.

Furthermore, graduation traditions vary in their rituals and customs. Some cultures emphasize the importance of wearing specific **attire**[18], such as caps and gowns, to symbolize the achievement and honor of completing a degree. Others **incorporate**[19] religious or spiritual **elements**[20] into the ceremony, highlighting the connection between education and personal growth.

1 academic /ˌækəˈdemɪk/ *adj.* 学术的；学业的

2 onset /ˈɑːnset/ *n.* 开端；发生

3 eminent /ˈemɪnənt/ *adj.* 卓越的；杰出的

4 anticipation /ænˌtɪsɪˈpeɪʃn/ *n.* 期望；预期

5 reverence /ˈrevərəns/ *n.* 尊敬；崇敬

6 scholarly /ˈskɑːlərli/ *adj.* 学术性的；有学问的

7 significance /sɪɡˈnɪfɪkəns/ *n.* 重要性；重大；意义

8 embody /ɪmˈbɑːdi/ *v.* 具体表现；体现

9 showcase /ˈʃəʊkeɪs/ *v.* 使展现；使亮相 *n.* 展示（本领、才华或优良品质）的场合

10 culmination /ˌkʌlmɪˈneɪʃn/ *n.* 顶点；巅峰；高潮

11 dedication /ˌdedɪˈkeɪʃn/ *n.* 献身；奉献

12 reminder /rɪˈmaɪndər/ *n.* 提示；帮助记忆的记号

13 attainment /əˈteɪnmənt/ *n.* 成就；造诣；达到；获得

14 commemorate /kəˈmeməreɪt/ *v.* 纪念；庆祝；作为……的纪念

15 rite /raɪt/ *n.* 仪式；典礼

16 adolescence /ˌædəˈlesns/ *n.* 青春；青春期

17 societal /səˈsaɪətl/ *adj.* 社会的

18 attire /əˈtaɪər/ *n.* 服装；衣着

19 incorporate /ɪnˈkɔːrpəreɪt/ *v.* 包含；吸收；使并入

20 element /ˈelɪmənt/ *n.* 要素；基本部分；典型部分

2. Translation Examples Explained

In E-C translation, attention to the verb's voice ensures accurate understanding of the agent (施行者) and receiver of the action, avoids unclear translation, and accords with Chinese expression habits. This section will explore the differences in verb voice usage between the two languages.

> *The college graduation ceremony celebrates the achievements of the graduating seniors and represents the culmination of the academic experience. ①Commencement is a festive and joyous occasion at which **family and guests are invited** to celebrate the accomplishments of the graduating class in addition to the faculty, staff and trustees joining in the tradition of conferring degrees. ②At the graduation ceremony, students dress up in **special graduation caps and clothing that are made just for this purpose.** ③In addition to appropriate attire, **women are requested to wear dark dress shoes and men to wear white shirts and dark shoes.** It is more than a sacred ritual but also heartiest celebrations for the graduating class at a major milestone in life.*

01

Commencement is a festive and joyous occasion at which family and guests are invited to celebrate the accomplishments of the graduating class in addition to the faculty, staff and trustees joining in the tradition of conferring degrees..

passive voice ➜ active sentence (被动转主动)
Subject ➜ Object (主语转宾语)

毕业典礼是一个喜悦的时刻，除了教职员工和校董事会参加, 还会邀请家人和朋友来祝贺毕业生所取得的成就。

Let us focus on the voice conversion in translating the three highlighted segments. Please look at Segment 1, "family and guests are invited". It is natural to use passive voice in English for two reasons. First, the emphasis falls on the action "welcome". Second, the agent is self-evident, the "university or graduate", so it is not necessary to mention it. If we keep the passive in Chinese, the sentence is "家人和朋友被邀请来祝贺毕业生所取得的成就"，which reads awkwardly. Thus, the English passive is usually translated into Chinese active through two steps. First, shift the subject to the object. Second, structure the sentence without the subject in Chinese. Then, the properly translated version is "邀请家人和朋友来祝贺毕业生所取得的成就".

02

At graduation ceremony, students dress up in special graduation caps and clothing that are made just for this purpose.

> passive voice ➜ passive sentence
> (被动转被动："为……所")

在毕业典礼上，学生们穿戴上专门**为**此**所**缝制的毕业帽和服装。

> "遭/受……"
> "被……"
> "给……"

Please look at Segment 2, "special graduation caps and clothing that are made just for this purpose". Whether in Chinese or in English, the semantic (语义的) relation between "special graduation caps and clothing" and "made" is "being done". Such English passive can be translated into Chinese passive by using the phrase "为……所". Apart from that, there are other similar Chinese characters to translate English passives, such as: "遭/受……", "被……", and "给……".

Segment 3 emphasizes the action, "request", and has removed the agent "the university" as it is self-evident in the context. In translating the sentence, the subject in the English original is moved to the object position (宾语位置) in the Chinese translation, therefore, we don't say "女生被（大学）要求……". Instead, we just say "要求女生……" And by doing so, the English passive is converted to a subjectless active sentence in Chinese: "还要求女生穿深色正装鞋，（要求）男生穿白衬衫和深色皮鞋".

03

In addition to appropriate attire, women are requested to wear dark dress shoes and men to wear white shirts and dark shoes.

> passive voice ➜ active sentence (被动转主动)
> Subject ➜ Object (主语转宾语)

除了正式的学位服，还**要求女生**穿深色正装鞋，（**要求**）**男生**穿白衬衫和深色皮鞋。

3. Parallel Texts

Please compare the original and the translation. You may see clearly that English passive sentences are translated into Chinese sentence structures in different ways.

Graduation Ceremony

The college graduation ceremony celebrates the achievements of the graduating seniors and represents the culmination of the academic experience. ① Commencement is a festive and joyous occasion at which **family and guests are invited to** celebrate the accomplishments of the graduating class in addition to the faculty, staff and trustees joining in the tradition of conferring degrees. ② At the graduation ceremony, students dress up in **special graduation caps and clothing that are made just for this purpose.** ③ In addition to appropriate attire, **women are requested to wear dark dress shoes and men to wear white shirts and dark shoes.** It is more than a sacred ritual but also heartiest celebrations for the graduating class at a major milestone in life.

毕业典礼

大学毕业典礼是为了庆祝毕业生顺利完成学业，也象征着他们取得了学术上的造诣。毕业典礼是一个喜悦的时刻，除了教职员工和校董事会参加，还会**邀请家人和朋友**来祝贺毕业生所取得的成就。在典礼上，学生们穿戴上专门**为此所**缝制的毕业帽和毕业服。除了正式的学位服，**还要求女生**穿深色正装鞋，（**要求**）**男生**穿白衬衫和深色皮鞋。这不仅是一项神圣的仪式，也是毕业生最热闹的庆祝活动，它是学生生涯结束的里程碑。

4. Translation Skills Summarized

Generally speaking, there are three ways to translate English passives into Chinese. First, we can translate English passives into Chinese passive sentences, often by using "被/给……", "（遭）受……" and "为……所……", like what we have learned in the second sentence. Second, we can translate English passives into Chinese sentence structures like "把……", "由……" and "使……". For example, "Most letters from his wife are read to him by the nurse in the hospital." The Chinese version is "他妻子写给他的信件，大多数是由医院里的护士念给他听的".

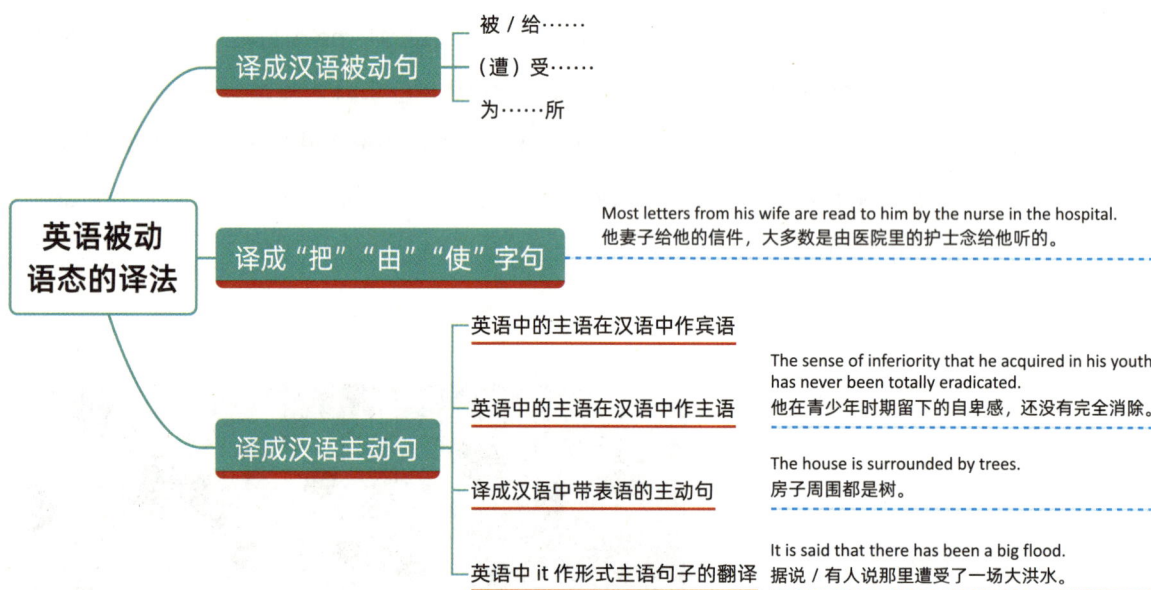

译成汉语被动句
- 被 / 给……
- （遭）受……
- 为……所

英语被动语态的译法

译成"把""由""使"字句
Most letters from his wife are read to him by the nurse in the hospital.
他妻子给他的信件，大多数是由医院里的护士念给他听的。

译成汉语主动句
- 英语中的主语在汉语中作宾语
  The sense of inferiority that he acquired in his youth has never been totally eradicated.
  他在青少年时期留下的自卑感，还没有完全消除。
- 英语中的主语在汉语中作主语
  The house is surrounded by trees.
  房子周围都是树。
- 译成汉语中带表语的主动句
- 英语中 it 作形式主语句子的翻译
  It is said that there has been a big flood.
  据说 / 有人说那里遭受了一场大洪水。

But in most instances, English passive voices are translated into Chinese active structures. There are four ways to do so. First, we can move the subject in English sentences to the object positions in Chinese sentences, like the translation of the first and the third sentences. Second, we can keep the subject in English sentence as the subject in the Chinese sentence, but in active structure. For example, "The sense of inferiority that he acquired in his youth has never been totally eradicated." The Chinese version is "他在青少年时期留下的自卑感，还没有完全消除". Third, English passive is translated into Chinese active with predicative (表语). For example, "The house is surrounded by trees." The Chinese version is "房子周围都是树". Last, if the English sentence uses the formative subject "it", it is usually translated into Chinese active without a subject or with uncertain subjects like "大家", "有人" and "我们". For example, "It is said that there has been a big flood." The Chinese version is "据说/有人说那里遭受了一场大洪水".

Why is there voice converting in most cases when translating English into Chinese? Different thinking modes contribute to the difference in voice preference. As we know, passive voice uses things and objects as the sentence subject, emphasizing the recipients (接受者) of actions rather than the actors themselves and underlining the observation and analysis of nature rather than humans. This fits with the thinking mode of objectivity (客体型思维) preferred by the mainstream western cultures. Thus, passive voice is used frequently in the English language.

By contrast, active forms use human agents as the subject, stressing the feelings and thoughts of humans, as well as the harmony of human and nature. This coheres well with the thinking mode of subjectivity (主体型思维) that is popular in the traditional Chinese culture; therefore, active sentence structures are used widely in the Chinese language. This is why in many cases we need to convert English passive sentences into Chinese active structures in E-C translation.

↳ 5. Cultural Expressions

Below are some cultural expressions that can be useful for talking about graduation ceremonies in Western countries.

Wearing academic robes dates back to the 12th century when the first universities came into being in Europe. During this time, most scholars were clerics (牧师), who tended to wear clerical gowns (牧师服) and plainly colored garb (纯色制服), generally black. Long gowns could have been necessary for warmth in the unheated, drafty (透风的), medieval church buildings.

And the caps fought off bad weather when clerics ventured outdoors. Today, the caps are the most iconic (标志性的) component of academic dress.

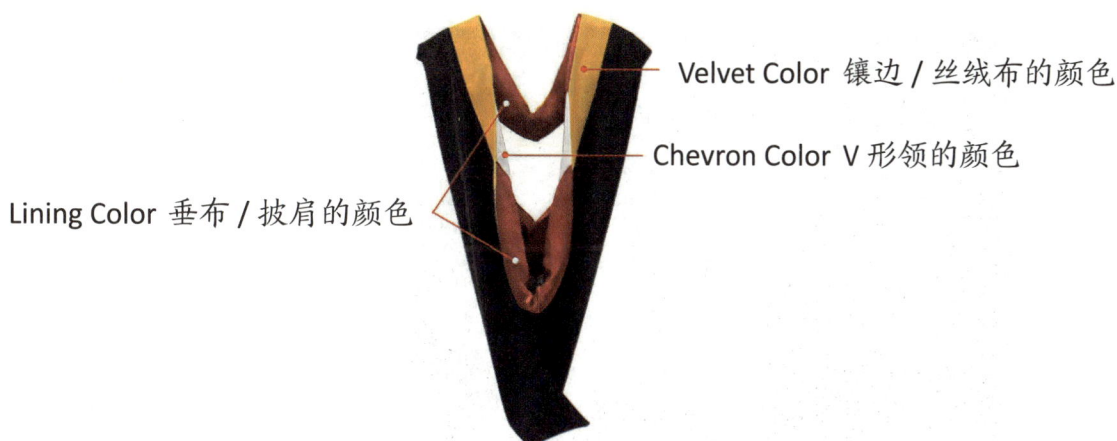

Velvet Color 镶边 / 丝绒布的颜色

Chevron Color V 形领的颜色

Lining Color 垂布 / 披肩的颜色

hooding ceremony 带帽仪式

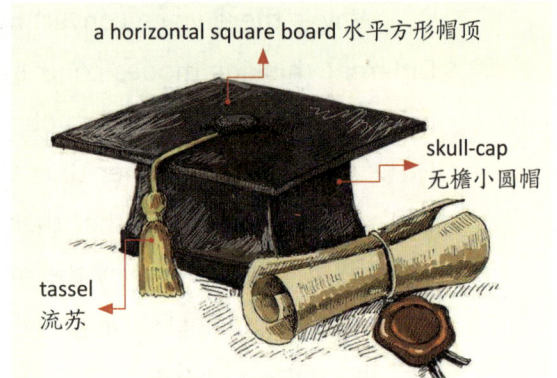

a horizontal square board 水平方形帽顶

skull-cap
无檐小圆帽

tassel
流苏

academic cap 学位帽

They serve to indicate students' school, degree and field of study through their length, color of the lining (垂布/披肩), of the chevron, and of the binding (镶边), also called velvet (丝绒布). Professors place the cap on the student as a symbol of passage from students to masters.

The academic cap consists of a horizontal square board fixed upon a skull-cap, with a tassel (流苏) attached to the centre. It originated from a biretta (四角帽) worn by scholarly clergies who were famous for their superiority and intelligence. It is also called mortarboard (灰泥板), because of its similarity in shape to the mortarboard used by brick masons (砌砖工) to hold mortar. The cap should be worn flat on the head and parallel to the floor. The front point of the cap should be centred on the forehead.

The tassel was originally designed to decorate graduate caps only 40 or 50 years ago. Prior to the ceremony, the tassel is expected to fall on the right side. In the ceremony, the tassel should be moved to the left side after the diploma is received. The gesture of moving the tassel from one side to another symbolizes an individual's passage from a candidate to a graduate. This custom is practiced in educational institutes worldwide now.

the front point centred on the forehead

flat on the head parallel to the floor

Throwing graduate caps into the air is a tradition started by the Naval Academy in 1912. Prior to 1912, graduates of the academy were required to serve two years in the fleet as midshipmen (海军少尉候补军官) before becoming Navy officers, therefore they still needed their hats. But the class of 1912 received their officer hats from the time of graduation, thus their hats were no longer needed, leaving graduates free to toss their hats into the air and not worry about getting hats back. Soon this tradition caught on at other institutes throughout the country and the whole world. Now the tossing is regarded as a symbolic gesture at the end of scholar achievements.

6. Questions for Discussion

1) What is the symbolic meaning of turning the tassel from the left side to the right side at the graduation ceremony?
2) Why is passive voice used frequently in English but not in Chinese?

III Wedding Ceremony

↳ 1. Cultural Background

A wedding ceremony may take place anywhere, but often in a church, courthouse, or outdoor venue. The ceremony may be dictated by the couple's religious practices. The most common non-religious form is derived from a simple Anglican ceremony in the *Book of Common Prayer*, and can be performed in less than ten minutes, although it is often extended by inserting music or speeches. Brides may choose any color, although black is strongly discouraged by some as it is the color of mourning in the West. Uncooked rice is sometimes thrown at the newlyweds as they leave the ceremony to symbolize fertility. The wedding party may form a receiving line at this point, or later at a wedding reception, so that each guest may briefly greet the entire wedding party. Drinks, snacks, or perhaps a full meal, especially at long receptions, are served while the guests and the wedding party mingle. Often, best men and/or maids of honor will toast newlyweds with personal thoughts, stories, and well-wishes; sometimes other guests follow with their own toasts. If dancing is offered, the newlyweds first dance together briefly.

↳ 2. Translation Examples Explained

Please read this passage and then focus on the translation of objects and predicatives in English sentences into Chinese.

The Western custom of a bride wearing a white wedding dress came to symbolize purity in the Victorian era. ①When the guests arrive for a wedding, the ushers' duty is **to hand out the correct books, flowers and the order of service**. *They also ensure* **that the guests are seated in the correct places.** *②Traditionally, the side on which people sit depends on* **whether they are friends or family of the bride or of the groom**. *During the ceremony, the bride and the groom make their marriage vows. ③Marriage vows are* **what a couple promise to each other during a wedding ceremony.** *④In Western culture, these promises have traditionally included* **the notions of affection, faithfulness, unconditionality, and permanence**. *⑤After the wedding ceremony, the bride, the groom, the officiant, and two witnesses generally go off to a side room to sign the wedding register which* **makes it legal to be married and a wedding certificate will be issued**.

① When the guests arrive for a wedding, the ushers' duty is <u>to hand out the correct books, flowers and the order of service</u>. They also ensure <u>that the guests are seated in the correct places.</u>

T1：迎宾员的职责是正确发放婚礼小册子、鲜花及仪式顺序表。【顺译√】

T2：正确发放婚礼小册子、鲜花及仪式顺序表是迎宾员的职责。【逆译】

In the first sentence, the infinitive "to hand out the correct books, flowers and the order of service" is the predicative. We can translate it in two ways. As in T1 (Translation 1), we can keep the predicative at the end just as it is in the English original. Alternatively, we can translate the predictive and move it to the beginning of the Chinese translation as in T2. However, T2 moved to the end the original subject "the ushers" (迎宾员), which is also the subject of the following sentence in the original. This breaks the cohesive link (衔接) between the two sentences, so T2 is not a good translation in this context.

For the same reason, we'd better retain the order of the object clause led by "that" in the translation as where it is in the English original.

② Traditionally, the side on which people sit depends on <u>whether they are friends or family of the bride or of the groom.</u>

T1：习惯上，宾客坐哪边取决于他们是新郎还是新娘的亲朋好友。【顺译】

T2：习惯上，新娘和新郎的亲朋好友分列而坐。

【逆译√】

be moved to the beginning in the Chinese sentence

In the second sentence, there also exists an object clause, which is after the conjunction "whether". When we translate the object clause without changing its position in the sentence, we will find that T1 sounds a little bit awkward in Chinese because it is unnecessarily lengthy and complex. However, when the object clause is moved to the sentence beginning as in T2, the Chinese translation is simpler and clearer.

③ Marriage vows are <u>what a couple promise to each other during a wedding ceremony.</u>

T1：这（婚礼誓言）是新人在婚礼上对彼此所作出的承诺。【顺译√】

T2：新人在婚礼上对彼此作出承诺，即是婚礼誓言。

【逆译】

In Sentence 3, you will find a predicative as in Sentence 1. The predicative is led by the "what". Will the translation method be different? This sentence begins with "marriage vows", with which the previous sentence ends. To keep the coherence in the English original, we'd better translate the predicative clause (表语从句) directly without changing its position in the original.

④ In Western culture, these promises have traditionally included <u>the notions of affection, faithfulness, unconditionality, and permanence.</u>

T1：在西方文化中，这些承诺包括如下观念：互重互爱、忠贞不渝、毫无保留、海枯石烂。【顺译】

T2：<u>互重互爱、忠贞不渝、毫无保留、海枯石烂</u>往往是西方新郎新娘对彼此的承诺。【逆译√】

Please look at the fourth sentence. Have you found any differences between this and the previous sentence? In this sentence, the object consists of four nouns with rich and condensed meanings. Usually, we can translate such a long and complex object following its original sentence order, as shown in T1; however, if we want to emphasize the meanings of the four nouns, we can move them to the beginning of the translated Chinese sentence, as shown in T2.

⑤ After the wedding ceremony, the bride, the groom, the officiant, and two witnesses generally go off to a side room to sign the wedding <u>register which makes it legal to be married</u> and a wedding certificate will be issued.

婚礼后，新娘、新郎、主婚人和两名证婚人会来到侧房签署婚姻登记。<u>经过这项程序，新人的婚姻合法，并被颁发结婚证书。</u>

Can you find the translation of "it" in the Chinese sentence?

Let us move to the last sentence. We will focus on the formal object (形式宾语) "it" after the verb "makes". In English, such formal objects are used mainly to achieve a structural balance (结构平衡); in contrast, there is no formal object in Chinese. In most circumstances, the formal object "it" can be omitted in translation without losing its meaning or affecting structural fluency in the Chinese translation.

3. Parallel Texts

Below are the original and the translated texts. Please read them in comparison while observing the translation of the English objects and predicatives into Chinese.

The Wedding Ceremony

The Western custom of a bride wearing a white wedding dress came to symbolize purity in the Victorian era. When the guests arrive for a wedding, the ushers' duty is ① **to hand out the correct books, flowers and the order of service**. They also ensure ② **that**

the guests are seated in the correct places. Traditionally, the side on which people sit depends on ③ **whether they are friends or family of the bride or of the groom**. During the ceremony, the bride and groom make their marriage vows. Marriage vows are ④ **what a couple promise to each other during a wedding ceremony**. In Western culture, these promises have traditionally included ⑤ **the notions of affection, faithfulness, unconditionality, and permanence**. After the wedding ceremony, the bride, the groom, the officiant, and two witnesses generally go off to a side room to sign the wedding register which ⑥ **makes it legal to be married and a wedding certificate will be issued**.

婚礼仪式

按照西方习俗, 新娘要穿上白色婚纱。从维多利亚时代开始, 白色婚纱象征着纯洁。客人到达婚礼现场时, 迎宾员的职责是①**正确发放婚礼小册子、鲜花及仪式顺序表**。另外, 他们还负责②**引导宾客正确入座**。习惯上, ③**习惯上, 新娘和新郎的亲朋好友分列而坐**。婚礼上, 新娘和新郎宣读婚姻誓言。④**这是新人对彼此所作出的承诺**。⑤**互敬互爱、忠贞不渝、毫无保留、海枯石烂往往是西方新郎新娘对彼此的承诺**。婚礼后, 新娘、新郎、主婚人和两名证婚人会来到侧房签署婚姻登记。⑥**经过这项程序, 新人的婚姻合法, 并被颁发结婚证书**。

4. Translation Skills Summarized

The types of objects and predicatives as well as the recommended translation methods have been listed in the figure.

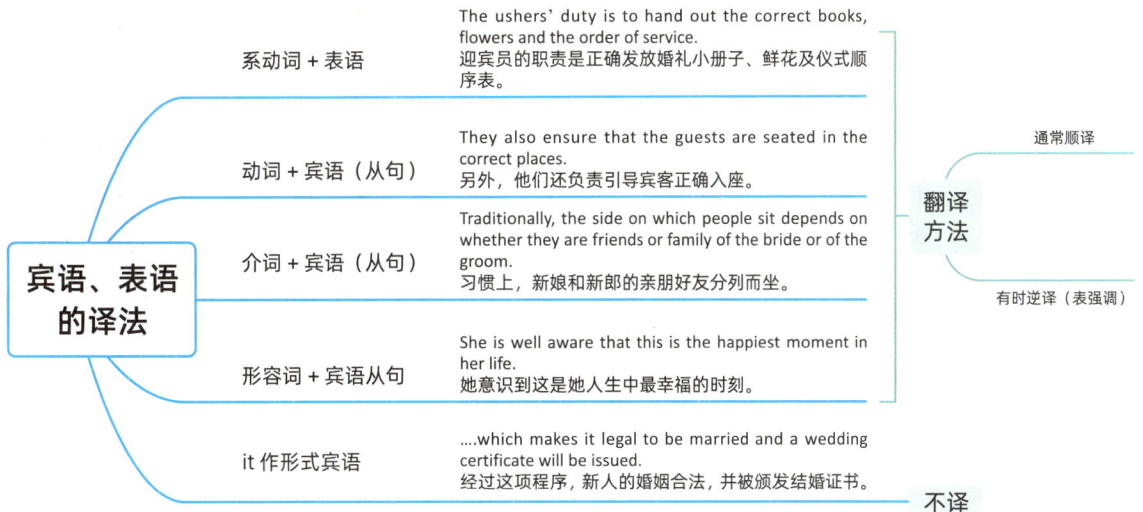

	系动词 + 表语	The ushers' duty is to hand out the correct books, flowers and the order of service. 迎宾员的职责是正确发放婚礼小册子、鲜花及仪式顺序表。	
宾语、表语的译法	动词 + 宾语（从句）	They also ensure that the guests are seated in the correct places. 另外，他们还负责引导宾客正确入座。	通常顺译
	介词 + 宾语（从句）	Traditionally, the side on which people sit depends on whether they are friends or family of the bride or of the groom. 习惯上，新娘和新郎的亲朋好友分列而坐。	**翻译方法**
	形容词 + 宾语从句	She is well aware that this is the happiest moment in her life. 她意识到这是她人生中最幸福的时刻。	有时逆译（表强调）
	it 作形式宾语	....which makes it legal to be married and a wedding certificate will be issued. 经过这项程序，新人的婚姻合法，并被颁发结婚证书。	不译

To sum up, there are three methods "顺译", "逆译", and "不译" in translating objects and predicatives. The majority of objects and predicatives can be translated without changing their positions to keep the coherence and cohesion of the original. This is called "顺译" and it is more widely applied in E-C translation, as the two languages are similar as to where the object and predicative appear in the sentence .

However, sometimes we may not keep the position of the sentence object or predicative of the original; instead, we may use "逆译" to emphasize the meaning of the object of the original. When meeting across the formal object "it", we usually omit it without affecting the readability of the original.

5. Cultural Expressions

proposal 求婚

engagement ring 订婚戒指

get engaged 订婚

wedding ceremony 结婚典礼

maid of honor/bridesmaid 伴娘

bride 新娘

groom 新郎

engagement ring 订婚戒指

best man 伴郎

pageboy 陪伴新娘的男童

wedding party 婚礼派对

Useful Cultural Expressions

wedding ceremony 结婚典礼

bridesmaid 伴娘

engagement ring
订婚戒指

get engaged
订婚

bride
新娘

groom
新郎

wedding ceremony 结婚典礼

best man 伴郎

pageboy 陪伴新娘的男童

wedding party 婚礼派对

↳ 6. Questions for Discussion

1) Can you give your own examples for the three methods "顺译" "逆译" and "不译" in translating objects and predicatives?

2) Do you know other customs of foreign wedding ceremonies?

Ⅳ Exercises

↳ Section A. True or false (5 items)

_____ 1) A baby shower is to throw the baby in the bath.

_____ 2) Many other couples have also tied the knot in the same church.

_____ 3) Translators should pay close attention to tense use in the context rather than translating tense meanings mechanically.

_____ 4) In most circumstances, the formal object (形式宾语) "it" can be omitted in translation without losing its meaning or affecting structural fluency in the Chinese translation.

_____ 5) In most instances, English passive voices are translated into Chinese active structures.

↳ Section B. Multiple choice (5 items)

_____ 1) Archbishop (大主教) Anders married the couple in front of their guests. Thousands of roses decorated in and outside the church.

A. 大主教安德斯在双方宾客的见证下宣布两人结为夫妻，那天教堂内外布满了玫瑰。

B. 大主教安德斯当着宾客的面娶了那两人，教堂内外布满了玫瑰。

C. 大主教安德斯过去在双方宾客的见证下宣布两人结为夫妻，教堂内外曾经布满了玫瑰。

_____ 2) Key themes in the western feminist wedding included doing away with the engagement ring, choosing not to be "given away like property" and wearing a color other than white.

A. 不要订婚戒指、不愿"像私有财产一样被肆意赠送"、不穿白色婚纱，是西方女权主义婚礼上的主题。

B. 西方女权主义婚礼上的主题包括：不要订婚戒指、不愿"像被交付的私有财产一样"、不择白色婚纱作为礼服。

C. 西方女权主义婚礼是以不要订婚戒指、不愿"像私有财产一样馈赠"、不选白色婚纱作为礼服为主题的。

_____ 3) Graduating students think it important that they attend the degree conferment.

     A. 毕业生认为参加学位授予很重要。

     B. 毕业生认为，这是重要的：他们参加学位授予。

     C. 对即将毕业的学生来说，他们参加学位授予这是很重要的。

_____ 4) If the friends are very close, you will probably be admitted to speak to them after hearing of the death.

     A. 如果你与朋友的关系十分亲密，他们在听到噩耗后，多半会听你倾诉。

     B. 如果你与朋友的关系十分亲密，他们在听到噩耗后，你可能会被允许向他们倾诉。

     C. 如果你与朋友的关系十分亲密，他们在听到噩耗后，你可能将会被允许向他们倾诉。

_____ 5) Academic regalia (学位服) recalled medieval times when scholars were clerics (牧师) who wore robes, hoods and capes (披肩) to shield themselves from European winters.

     A. 学位服想起中世纪的牧师学者们，他们为了保护自己免受欧洲冬天的侵袭，身穿着长袍、戴兜帽、肩裹披肩。

     B. 学位服让人想起中世纪的牧师学者们，那时为了抵御欧洲寒冷的冬天，他们穿了长袍、戴兜帽、披着披肩。

     C. 学位服让人想起中世纪的牧师学者们，那时为了抵御欧洲寒冷的冬天，他们身穿长袍、头戴兜帽、肩裹披肩。

Ⅴ Test

Section A. Multiple choice (5 items*4 points=20 points)

_____ 1) In this Scottish tradition, the bride, groom, or both are taken out on the day before their wedding, plied with alcohol, and covered in treacle (糖浆), ash, feathers, and flour by friends and family.

    A. 按照苏格兰传统，在婚礼前一天，亲朋好友会拉新娘、新郎或两人同时出去喝酒，给他们涂满糖浆、泥灰、羽毛、面粉之类的东西。

    B. 按照苏格兰传统，在婚礼前一天，新娘、新郎或两人都会被拉出去，被灌酒，然后被亲朋好友涂满糖浆、泥灰、羽毛、面粉之类的东西。

    C. 按照苏格兰传统，新娘、新郎两人都会被带出去喝酒，并被亲戚和朋友涂满糖浆、泥灰、羽毛、面粉之类的东西。

_____ 2) A baptism was a formal ceremony which was given only for the family's first child.

    A. 过去，受洗礼是一种正式的仪式，只为家中的第一个孩子举行。

    B. 受洗礼是一种正式的仪式，被给予家中的第一个孩子。

    C. 受洗礼是一种只为家中的第一个孩子举行的正式的仪式。

_____ 3) After the ceremony, students take pictures of each other and will show each other these pictures a few nights later at the graduation party.

    A. 典礼后，学生们互相拍照，并将在几天后的毕业舞会上分享。

    B. 典礼后，学生们将互相拍照，并在几天之后举行的毕业舞会上分享。

    C. 典礼后，学生们互相拍照，并将要分享在几天之后举行的毕业舞会上。

_____ 4) Traditionally, the side on which people sit depends on whether they are friends or family of the bride or of the groom.

    A. 习惯上，新娘和新郎的亲朋好友分列而坐。

    B. 习惯上，宾客坐哪边取决于他们是新郎还是新娘的亲朋好友。

    C. 习惯上，宾客的座位取决于他们是新郎的亲朋好友还是新娘的亲朋好友。

_____ 5) The original intent of baby showers was for women to share wisdom and lessons on the art of becoming a mother.

A. 迎婴聚会的最初目的过去是为了让女性们分享为人母的智慧和经验教训。

B. 迎婴聚会的最初目的是让女性们分享为人母的智慧和经验教训。

C. 迎婴聚会的最初目的曾经是让女性们分享为人母的智慧和经验教训。

Section B. Sentence translation (5 items*6 points=30 points)

1) After the wedding ceremony, the bride, the groom, the officiant, and two witnesses generally go off to a side room to sign the wedding register which makes it legal to be married and a wedding certificate will be issued.

2) In addition to appropriate attire, women are requested to wear dark dress shoes and men to wear white shirts and dark shoes.

3) Over time, it has become common to hold baby showers for subsequent or adopted children.

4) A commencement speech is typically given by a notable figure in the community or a graduating student.

5) There is no set rule for when or where showers are to be held.

Section C. Paragraph translation (50 points)

The wedding was more of a business transaction than anything else, as the "giving away" referred to a transfer of property. "In Britain, as in many places, women had long been considered essentially the property of men, first their fathers and then their husbands," according to *Times* (《泰晤士报》).

Unit 4
DRINKS AND FOOD

Ⅰ Pubs In Britain

1. Cultural Background

In the eyes of British people, pubs, like Chinese teahouses, are an indispensable part of the local culture.

The British pub culture has a long history of more than a thousand years. It originated in the churches of the **Middle Ages**[①]. The original form of the pub was similar to that of the Chinese inn, which was to provide a place for people on the way to get some rest and food. Now the traditional pub in the UK usually refers to the pub and bar.

Pubs are places for leisure in Britain, where people can take part in various activities besides drinking and chatting. As early as the sixteenth century, English **vagabond acts**[1] often played in the middle of pub yards, and many popular bands first started their concerts in local pubs.

Words and Expressions:

vagabond acts 流浪艺人表演

2. Translation Examples Explained

In this section, we are going to learn the pub culture in Britain. Meanwhile, we are going to learn the technique of sorting out additional sentence elements (理清枝叶) to achieve a clear understanding and translation.

What is a pub? A pub is an establishment licensed to sell alcoholic drinks. It functions as a social center for folks, offering them opportunities to meet and relax.

Samuel Pepys, a 17th-century politician notable for his decade-long diary, described the pub as "the heart of England".

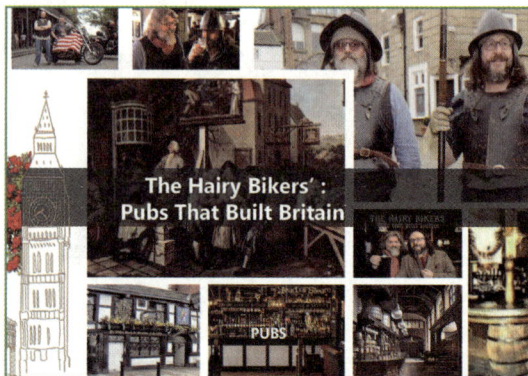
The Hairy Bikers': Pubs That Built Britain

---

① Middle Ages: 中世纪是文艺复兴时期人文主义者对欧洲中古时期的统称，时间从公元 476 年到公元 1453 年。

The Hairy Bikers, the most popular foodie duo (美食二人组) in the UK, made a fifteen-episode series for BBC exploring the history of great British pubs. The audiences are informed that pubs have been at the center of the British communities, rich and poor, for over a thousand years. That's why this show can hold the title *Pubs That Built Britain* (《造就英国的酒吧》).

How many pubs are there in the UK?

The following passage briefly introduces about British pubs. When translating it, please pay special attention to the numbered sentences with a focus on additional sentence elements.

Pubs in Britain

①*Owing to the uncertainty of the weather, outdoor activities are not a feature of British life.* ②*Their place of public entertainment is partly filled by what are colloquially known as "pubs", public houses.* ③*People consider pubs the main source of secular recreation and entertainment.* Pub culture is designed to promote sociability in a society known for its reverse. ④*Standing at the bar for service gives you a chance to chat with others waiting to be served.* ⑤*There are approximately 60,000 pubs with distinctive British characteristics in the UK.* The traditional British pubs are the best places in which the visitors can sample the local culture. There is a saying that "If you haven't been to a pub, you haven't been to Britain."

① Owing to the uncertainty of the weather, outdoor activities are not a feature of British life.

Please look at the first sentence. We have learned in the previous lecture that the core parts of an English sentence carry its basic meaning. Here it is quite easy for us to identify the core parts: "activities are not a feature", which is a "Subject + Verb + Predicative" sentence pattern. However, the core parts are only the skeleton of the sentence, carrying a basic but incomplete idea. When we translate it as "户外活动不是特色", we may feel the meaning is incomplete. It leaves us much room to wonder, such as "Which café?", "What kind of feature?", and "For what reason we draw this conclusion?" So, more information needs to be added to make the meaning rich and complete.

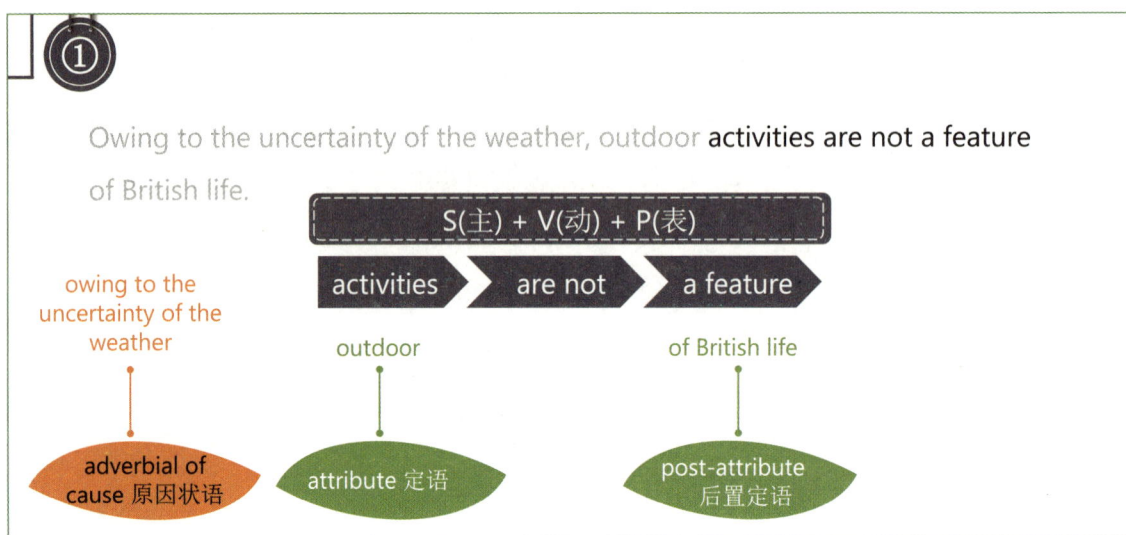

①

Owing to the uncertainty of the weather, outdoor **activities are not a feature of British life.**

S(主) + V(动) + P(表)

activities ➤ are not ➤ a feature

owing to the uncertainty of the weather

adverbial of cause 原因状语

outdoor

attribute 定语

of British life

post-attribute 后置定语

Firstly, the adjective "outdoor" serves as an attribute to modify "activities". Then a prepositional phrase "of British life" is used as a post-attribute, adding descriptive details to the word "feature". Another prepositional phrase introduced by "owing to" tells us the reason why the British life is not outdoor-oriented. Finally, we have a sentence consisting of the core parts and the non-core, additional elements. The additional elements make the meaning of the sentence rich and complete but at the same time make the sentence longer and more complex. This means we need to sort out various, layered, and embedded non-core elements before we come to a good understanding and translation.

Given our careful analysis, we can translate the sentence as: 由于天气多变，户外活动并不是英国人生活的一个特色.

② Their place of public entertainment is partly filled by what are colloquially known as "pubs", public houses.

The core parts are "place is filled", which consists of a subject and a verb, meaning " 地方被占满 ". The limited and incomplete meaning may make us wonder "in which place?", "how this place is filled?", etc. Analyzing the additional sentence elements helps us to better understand this long and complex sentence.

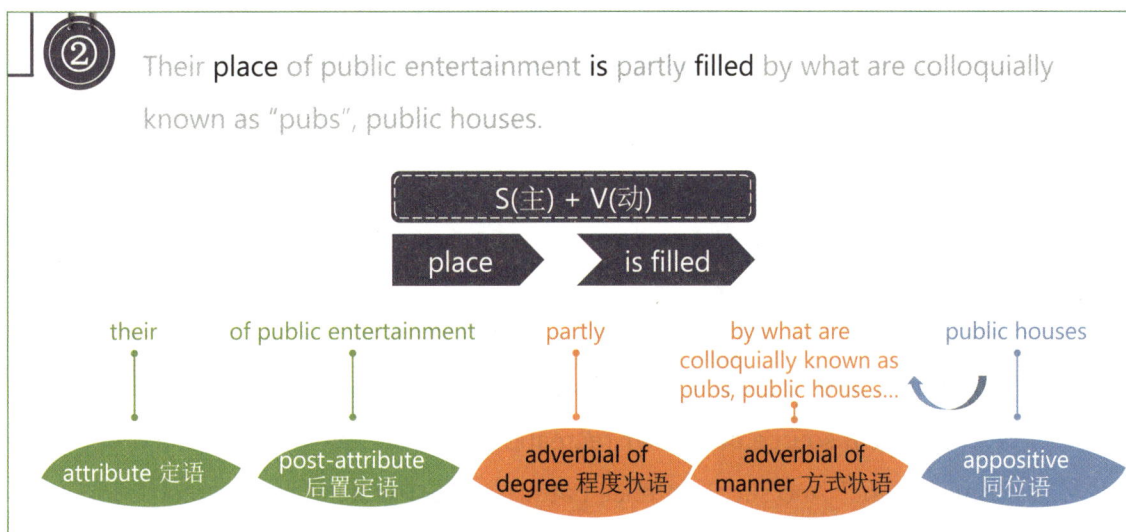

② Their **place** of public entertainment **is** partly **filled** by what are colloquially known as "pubs", public houses.

S(主) + V(动)

place → is filled

their	of public entertainment	partly	by what are colloquially known as pubs, public houses...	public houses
attribute 定语	post-attribute 后置定语	adverbial of degree 程度状语	adverbial of manner 方式状语	appositive 同位语

The word "their", an attribute, refers to the British people mentioned before. The prepositional phrase "of public entertainment" serves as a post-attribute to modify the "place". Both attributes give us more information about the sentence subject.

To modify the verb, the adverb "partly" is used, showing to what degree this place is filled.

Then, the "what-" clause following the word "by" serves as an adverbial explaining in what way the action of the verb "be filled" is carried out. Then we know it is the pubs that partly constitute the entertaining place of British. Please notice the last noun phrase, "public houses". It follows the noun "pubs", to describe it in another way. In other words, "pubs" refer to "public houses". The two play the same grammatical role and function in this sentence. We call the latter one "public houses" the appositive (同位语) of the former one.

After combining the various added elements with the core parts, we can translate the whole sentence as: 他们的娱乐场所部分被俗称为 " 酒吧 " 的公共场所占据 .

③ People consider pubs the main source of secular recreation and entertainment.

What are the core parts? "People consider pubs". So the core meaning is " 人们认为酒吧 ". But do you think the sentence sounds unfinished? People cannot just "consider pubs". They have to draw a complete conclusion after consideration. What do people really think about the pubs?

③

People consider pubs the main source of secular recreation and entertainment.

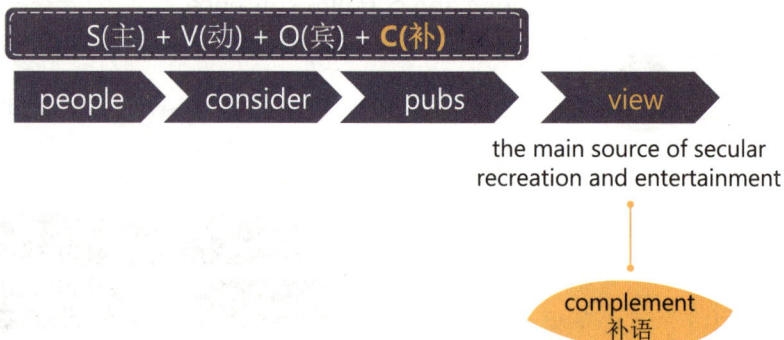

S(主) + V(动) + O(宾) + **C(补)**			
people	consider	pubs	view

the main source of secular recreation and entertainment

complement
补语

Thus, something about people's view on pubs needs to be supplemented, that is to say, "the main source of secular recreation and entertainment". We name this added part "complement". And such sentence pattern — "Subject+ Verb + Object + Complement" — is quite often used in English.

After adding the complement, we finally have a sentence which communicates a whole and complete idea effectively. Then we translate it as: 人们将酒吧视作世俗消遣和娱乐的主要来源 .

④ Standing at the bar for service gives you a chance to chat with others waiting to be served.

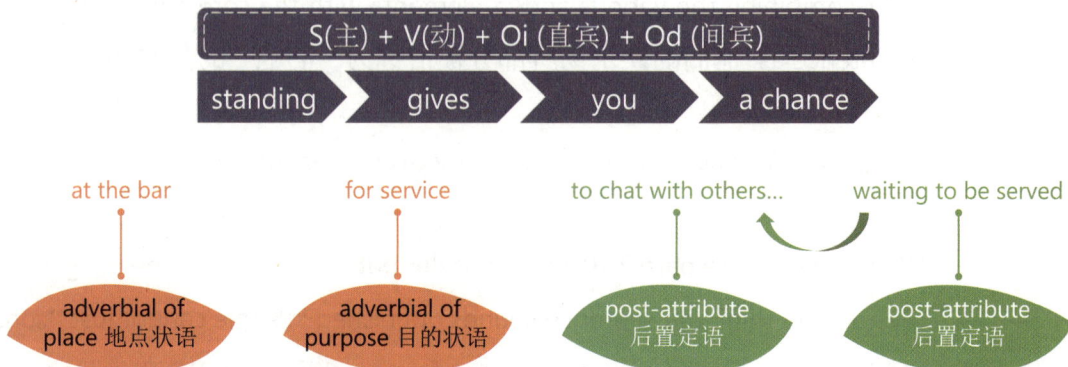

④ Standing at the bar for service **gives you a chance** to chat with others waiting to be served.

S(主) + V(动) + Oi (直宾) + Od (间宾)			
standing	gives	you	a chance

at the bar

for service

to chat with others...

waiting to be served

adverbial of place 地点状语

adverbial of purpose 目的状语

post-attribute 后置定语

post-attribute 后置定语

The core parts are: "standing gives you a chance". As you see, two prepositional phrases "at the bar" and "for service" respectively clarify the place you stand and the purpose of standing there. Then, please notice the preposition "to" and its following statement "chat with others waiting to be served". The whole part forms a long post-attribute describing the type of the chance, with which you can have a talk with others. Note again in that long attribute, the words "waiting to be served" were put behind "others" as a modifier indicating what kind of people you will chat with. Such structural analysis helps us to grasp the main idea and at the same time sort out layers of rich and supplementary information. This is essential to understanding and translating the English text. Finally, we have this Chinese translation after combing all the additional sentence elements: 站在吧台边等候，给了你与其他等待之人交谈的机会．

⑤ There are approximately 60,000 pubs with distinctive British characteristics in the UK.

Please look at the fifth sentence. We have learned a similar "there + be" structure previously, knowing that it is an inverted sentence. The word "there" is only an expletive (填补词) that has no meaning and is not grammatically related to the rest part. The real core parts of this sentence are "pubs are in the UK", following a regular "Subject + Verb + Predicative" structure.

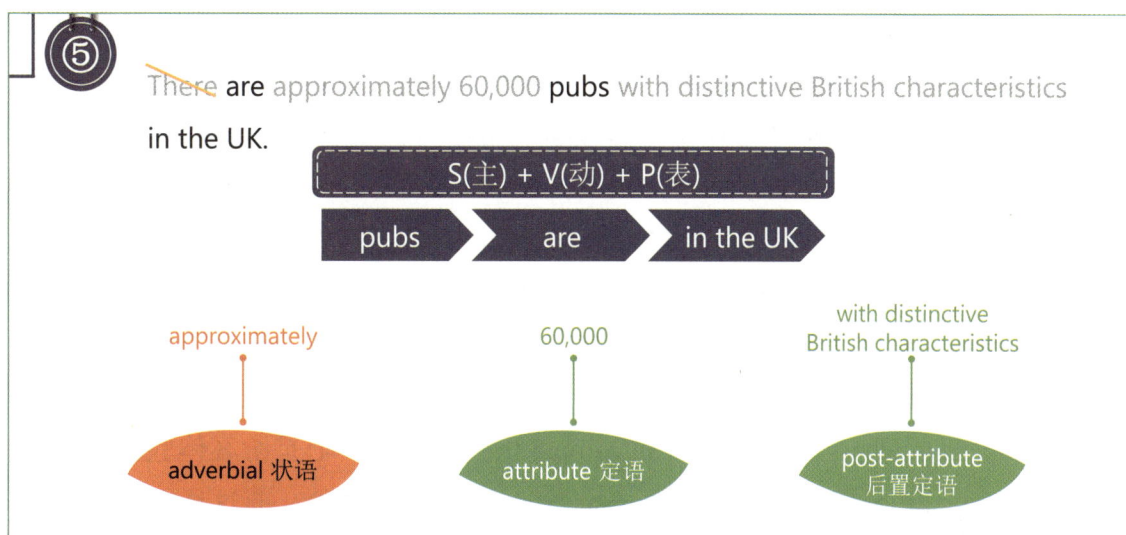

⑤ There are approximately 60,000 pubs with distinctive British characteristics in the UK.

S(主) + V(动) + P(表)		
pubs	are	in the UK

approximately	60,000	with distinctive British characteristics
adverbial 状语	attribute 定语	post-attribute 后置定语

However, the core parts do not make enough sense, because everybody knows we are talking about the pubs in the UK in this passage. So, what does this sentence drive us to? In this case, the additional information is quite necessary. Two attributes are used to modify the "pubs". Then we know the characteristics and the number of the pubs. But the number "60,000" cannot be an exact one because of their yearly increase or decline. Therefore, an adverb "approximately" is used to show that it is an estimated number. These additional elements carry more detailed, layered meanings and should be sorted out for a better understanding and translation.

This is the Chinese translation of Sentence 5: "在全英国，大约有六万个各具特色的英式酒吧".

3. Parallel Texts

Please compare the source text and its translation and review how additional sentence elements were sorted out and translated.

Pubs in Britain

Owing to the uncertainty of the weather, outdoor activities are not a feature of British life. Their place of public entertainment is partly filled by what are colloquially known as "pubs", public houses. People consider pubs the main source of secular recreation and entertainment. Pub culture is designed to promote sociability in a society known for its reverse. Standing at the bar for service gives you a chance to chat with others waiting to be served. There are approximately 60,000 pubs with distinctive British characteristics in the UK. The traditional British pubs are the best places in which the visitors can sample the local culture. There is a saying that "If you haven't been to a pub, you haven't been to Britain."

英国酒吧

由于天气多变，户外活动并不是英国人生活的一个特色。他们的公众娱乐场所部分被俗称为"酒吧"的地方所占据。人们将酒吧视作世俗消遣和娱乐的主要来源。在因保守而闻名的英国社会里，酒吧文化的形成是为了促进社会交往。站在吧台边等候，给了你与其他等候之人交谈的机会。在全英国，大约有六万个各具特色的英式酒吧。传统英式酒吧是游客体验本土文化的最佳之处。有这样一种说法：你如果没有去过酒吧，那就等于没有到过英国。

↳ 4. Translation Skills Summarized

We have learned how an English sentence is constructed. The core parts act like the tree trunk while the additional sentence elements are branches and leaves. The core parts carry the fundamental meaning of a sentence while the additional sentence elements contribute greatly to a complete meaning. We can add such information in many forms: attributes, adverbials, complements, appositives, etc.

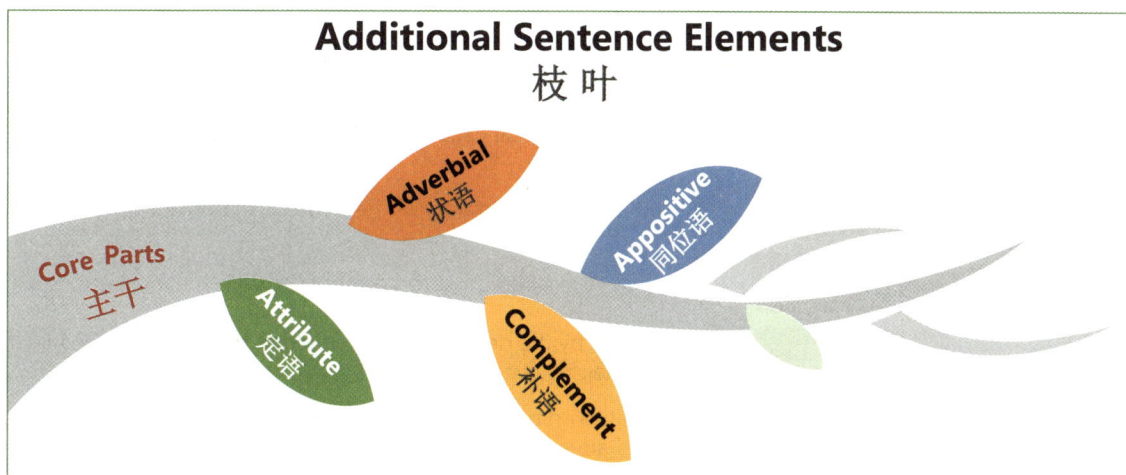

Additional Sentence Elements
枝 叶

Adverbial 状语
Appositive 同位语
Core Parts 主干
Attribute 定语
Complement 补语

The attribute refers to the word, phrase or sentence used to describe the quality or character of somebody or something. In this list, examples derived from our passage show many possibilities for us to learn. You may discover that the shorter attributes are often prepositions, such as local culture, computer games, and closing time; while the longer ones are more likely to be postpositions. For example, "The traditional British bars are the best places in which the visitors can sample the local culture."

Attribute 定语	描述名词或代词的修饰语（可前置或后置）
Adj. 形容词（短语）	• local culture; soft drinks • It's a traditional bar, old-styled and delicately decorated.
N. 名词（短语）	• computer games; a variety of entertainment
Prep. Phrase 介词短语	• It's not a feature of British life.
Infinitive 不定式（短语）	• order something to drink
V-ed 动词-ed分词（短语）	• a society known for its reverse
V-ing 动词-ing形式（短语）	• closing time; a bell hanging behind the counter
Attributive clause 定语从句	• The traditional British bars are the best places in which the visitors can sample the local culture.

The adverbial is an important sentence element functioning like the adverb to modify other expressions, including verbs, adjectives, adverbs, prepositional phrases, and sentences. Various forms of adverbials can be used in a sentence to elucidate time, place, manner, cause, purpose, degree, condition, concession, accompanying, etc. Below are some topic-related examples.

Adverbial 状语	修饰动词、形容词、副词、介词短语或整个句子的成分（位置灵活）
	The adverbials of time/ place/manner/ cause/purpose/degree/condition/ concession/ accompanying, etc.
Adv. 副词（短语）	• be partly filled; be colloquially known
Prep. Phrase 介词短语	• owing to the uncertainty of the weather; in pubs
Infinitive 不定式（短语）	• Pub culture is designed to promote sociability in a society.
V-ed 动词-ed分词（短语）	• Shocked by the decline rate of the old pubs, they raised money to save their beloved.
V-ing 动词-ing形式（短语）	• The landlord may agree to offer you a free drink, hoping that you would advertise it.
Adverbial clause 状语从句	• You may be asked for identification before you enter.

The complement is the expression to complete the meaning of another part of the sentences. It can be divided into two categories. The object complement is necessarily attached to the sentence's object providing further descriptions. Here is an example: "They've kept their pubs fun and entertaining." The subject complement, equal to the predicative, is an illustration of the sentence subject. For instance, "Stout" is a heavy dark beer. Complements usually play very important roles in English sentences, as their absence may lead to broken sentences.

Complement 补语	描述和说明主语或宾语的情况，如性质、状态
❶ S (主) + V(动) + O(宾) +C(补)	❷ S(主) + V(动) + P(表) /(C补)
Object complement 宾语补语	Subject complement 主语补语
• They've kept their pubs fun and entertaining.	• "Stout" is a heavy dark beer.
• The BBC series has made it a household name.	• This pub looks cool and trendy.

An appositive is a word, phrase or sentence placed next to another noun or pronoun to rename it or to describe it in another way. For instance, the appositive noun, "travelers" is used in the example "We travelers should follow the local rituals." Another similar example is that "you three can go for a drink." Please read the following examples for a thorough study.

Appositive 同位语	当两个或以上具有相同语法地位、指代同一事物时，后项（解释项）即前项的同位语。
N. 名词（短语）	• We travelers should follow the local rituals in the pubs. • be known as "pubs", public houses
Pron. 代词	• They all serve draught beer.
Num. 数词	• You three can go for a drink in the nearest pub.
Adj. （名词化）形容词	• Tom the taller is the landlord and Nike the shorter is the bartender.
Appositive clause 同位语从句	• In this news, we're told the message that 30 pubs are closing everyday.

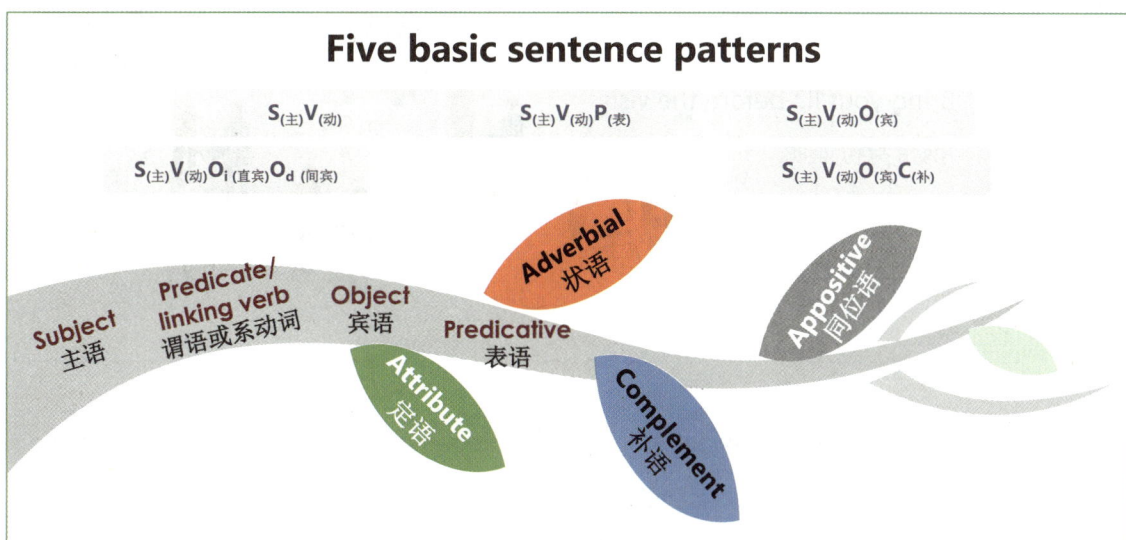

Five basic sentence patterns

$S_{(主)}V_{(动)}$　　　　$S_{(主)}V_{(动)}P_{(表)}$　　　　$S_{(主)}V_{(动)}O_{(宾)}$

$S_{(主)}V_{(动)}O_{i\,(直宾)}O_{d\,(间宾)}$　　　　$S_{(主)}V_{(动)}O_{(宾)}C_{(补)}$

Subject 主语　Predicate/linking verb 谓语或系动词　Object 宾语　Predicative 表语　Adverbial 状语　Attribute 定语　Complement 补语　Appositive 同位语

This time the tree map reveals almost all the sentence elements, from the core parts to various additional sentence elements. When you build an English sentence, there is a key point you need to know — an English sentence, no matter how long it is, you have to follow one of the five basic sentence patterns and then expand the sentence with additional elements. That is the essence of the English sentence construction.

The non-core, additional elements of a sentence usually provide rich and supplementary information but also make the sentence long and complex. Therefore, sorting our additional sentence elements is a key method to understand and translate long sentences in English.

5. Cultural Expressions

For you who have never been there, there are some basics to know before visiting a pub. People over 18 years old can be allowed to order a drink in pubs, so make sure you bring your ID with you before you visit a pub. Bar staff, like security guards at the entrance, the bartender and the landlord are responsible to check if you have reached the legal drinking age. You may have to pay when you enter a pub, with the entrance fees ranging from £1 — £25.

Before entering a pub

- Legal drinking age
  ≥ 18 years old 法定饮酒年龄

- Bring your ID before the visit
  携带身份证明

Security guard 保安

bartender 酒保
landlord 店主

Then how do you order a drink? Traditionally, pubs have no waiters or table service, so you have to go to the bar, pay for your drink and carry it to your seat.

Then what to order? Beer must be the best-selling type in the UK. Usually there are two types of beers you can choose from: bottled or draught (生啤). Draught means fresh beer from the tap of a barrel. If you are asking for a draught, you need to tell the bartender how much you want. Use the measurement "pint" to order how much beer you want.

Order at the bar

Bottled 瓶装啤酒

Draught 生/鲜啤酒

Tap 龙头

Pint – a unit of volume 品脱－体积单位

Some popular types are: Wheat beer, Lager, India Pale Ale, Stout, Bitter, etc. They have different ways of brewing with different degrees of alcohol or bitterness. An easier way to estimate the taste is to look at the color of the beer — the darker the color, the bitter the taste.

Order at the bar

Wheat beer

小麦啤酒

Lager

拉格啤酒

India Pale Ale

印度淡色艾尔啤酒

Stout

世涛啤酒

Bitter

苦味啤酒

You can check the IBU number（国际苦味指数）— The larger the number, the bitterer; or the ABV number（酒精体积分数）— the larger the number, the stronger its aftertaste.

Order at the bar

HOUSE BEERS
- SOUTHERLITE   9 IBU's , 4% ABV
- CUCUMBER GOSE 9 IBU's, 4% ABV
- WARLOCK   39 IBU's, 4.52% ABV
- PEACH FACE   38 IBU's, 6.1% ABV
- PALES FROM THE CRYPT
                 72 IBU's, 6.5% ABV

IBU
International Bittering Unit
苦度 / 国际苦味指标

ABV
Alcohol by Volume
酒精度数

When ordering the beer, you may say: "Can I get one pint of Lager?" or "I think I'll try two pints of IPA." Sometimes you may ask: "What do you have on taps?" or "What do you recommend?"

Order at the bar

Can I get/have one pint of Lager?

I'll try two pints of IPA.

What do you have on taps?

What do you recommend?

In addition to beers, British pubs indeed serve a large selection of drinks: cider, spirits, wines, cocktails, and soft drinks.

cider 西打酒	•	an alcoholic beverage made from the fermented juice of apples
spirits 烈酒	•	strong alcoholic drinks such as whisky and vodka
wine 葡萄酒	•	an alcoholic drink made from fermented grapes
cocktail 鸡尾酒	•	an alcoholic mixed drink
soft drinks 软饮料	•	a cold, non-alcoholic beverage or carbonated drink

Many pubs have a long tradition of serving food, as they originated from inns and hotels. They mainly serve plain but good-quality food: burgers, steaks, sandwiches, fish and chips, pickled eggs, salted crisps, pork scratchings, peanut cockles, lasagna, etc. Thus, a reputable pub is also a good place for you to taste traditional British food.

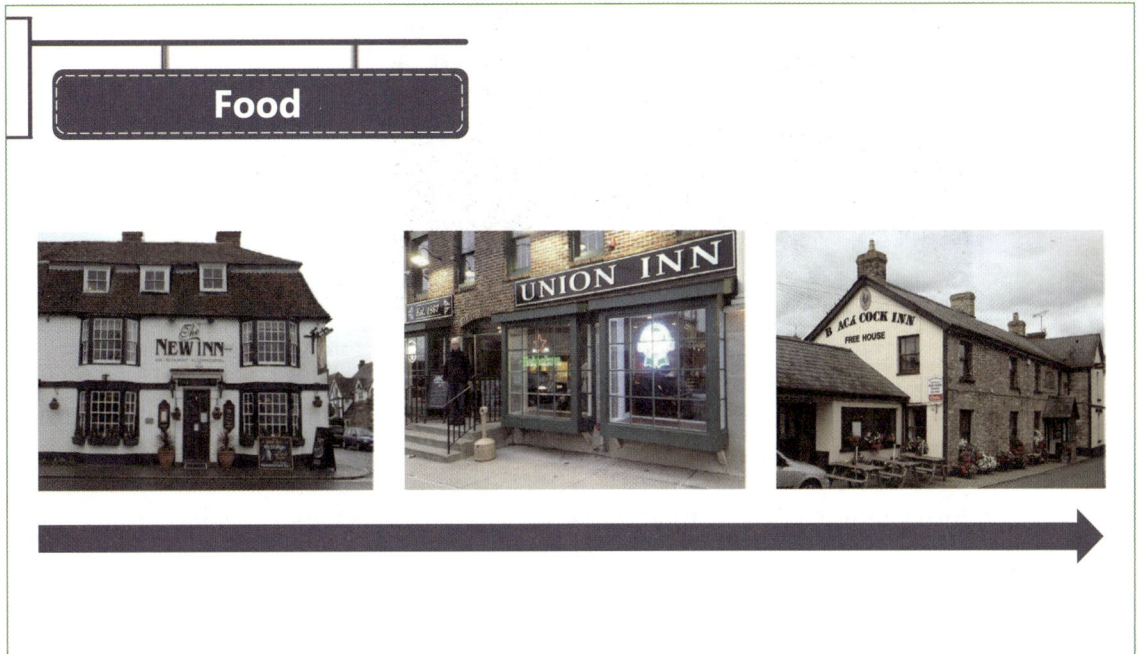

Food

Food

curry 咖喱	lasagna 千层面	burgers 汉堡
salted crisps 焗薯片	pickled eggs 腌鸡蛋	sausages 香肠
pork scratchings 炸猪皮	peanut cockles 花生海扇	steaks 牛排

Games

- buying a round of drinks 轮庄买酒
- table football 桌式足球
- snooker 斯诺克
- slot machines 游戏机
- having pub quizzes 猜谜游戏
- Dominoes 多米诺骨牌
- skittles 滚球撞柱
- dart 飞镖

For time-killing, pubs are ideal places to relax, socialize, or buy a round of drinks. Traditional games like darts, skittles, dominoes, snooker, and table football are played. Modern games such as computer games and VR games are provided.

6. Questions for Discussion

1) Why do people say that "If you haven't been to a pub, you haven't been to Britain"?

2) What are the forms of the additional sentence elements in English? What functions do they make respectively?

II Afternoon Tea

1. Cultural Background

It was the British who first developed afternoon tea as a cultural custom. The habit of drinking tea in England began in 1661. An afternoon tea is mainly divided into low tea and high tea. Leisured aristocrats or the upper class generally eat low tea, which generally refers to the afternoon tea after lunch, not far from lunch time. The tea usually contains sandwiches and small pancakes. The working class, on the other hand, consume high tea. High tea usually refers to a meal served before dinner, usually with meat.

2. Translation Examples Explained

In this section, we are going to learn the afternoon tea culture in Britain. Meanwhile, we are going to learn the techniques of dealing with attributive elements in E-C translation.

> ### *What is Afternoon Tea?*
> ①*Afternoon Tea is a tea-related ritual, introduced in Britain in the early 1840s.* ②*It evolved as a light meal to stem (阻止) the hunger and anticipation of a dinner at 8 p.m.*
> ③*Afternoon Tea is a snack that is traditionally composed of finger sandwiches, scones with clotted cream and jam, sweet pastries, cakes, and of course, tea.*
> *Afternoon Tea initially developed as a private social event for ladies of the affluent (富裕 的) classes. It was only when Queen Victoria engaged in the Afternoon Tea ritual that it became a formal occasion on a larger scale, known as "tea receptions".*
> ④*These royal receptions could have as many as two hundred guests with an "at home" invitation to visit between 4 p.m. and 7 p.m., during which they could come and go as they pleased; this was the genesis (起源) of the Afternoon Tea as we know it.*

> ① Afternoon Tea is a tea-related ritual, introduced in Britain in the early 1840s.

From the previous sections, we know that in an English sentence, there are many modifying elements that can cause translation difficulty, and among them, the most challenging one may be attributive elements (定语) — they are the words, phrases, or clauses that modify the nouns in an English sentence.

In this sentence, the nouns modified by attributives are the subject and the predicative, "tea" and "ritual." What modifies "tea" is the noun "afternoon." What modifies "ritual" is the adjective "tea-related" and the participle phrase (分词短语) "introduced in Britain in the early 1840s".

As we can see from this sentence, English attributives are put in places different from those in Chinese. Chinese attributives, either short or long, are usually placed before the nouns they modify. In contrast, English attributives can precede or follow the nouns they modify. In most cases, prepositive (前置的) attributives are short and simple, creating no translation barriers. When translating, we can simply keep their original sequence. Like in this sentence, the prepositive noun and adjective can be directly translated in their original sequence: "下午茶是一种与茶相关的仪式."

Although English attributives can be both prepositive and postpositive, most of them are postpositive (后置的). Those postmodifiers (后置修饰语) are often longer and more complex than premodifiers (前置修饰语), often causing difficulty in the E-C translation process. How shall we deal with the participle in this sentence? Here, we will show three ways. Below are three methods.

First, we can follow the Chinese linguistic preference to use the Chinese "……是……的……" structure and move it to the place before its head noun: "下午茶是19世纪40年代初传入英国的一种与茶相关的仪式。" In doing so we have adjusted the order of the postpositive attributive.

Or, to reproduce the grammatical characteristics of the original sentence, we can first translate the main clause, repeat the head noun, and then place the postpositive modifier before it: "下午茶是一种与茶相关的仪式，一种在19世纪40年代初传入英国的仪式。" By repeating the head noun, we actually divided one "modifying + modified" structure into two. The translation technique "division (拆分)" helps to avoid an extremely long Chinese premodifier when we move the participle phrase ahead of its head noun.

The third way is to consider the participle phrase as a shortened attributive clause "which was introduced in Britain in the early 1840s". Then, we can translate the whole sentence into Chinese in a way as if we had two parallel independent clauses: "下午茶是一种与茶相关的仪式，（它）在19世纪40年代初传入英国". In doing so we have turned a participle phrase to a full clause. This is a method called "adjusting the linguistic level (调整语言层级)."

The three Chinese translations reflect different ways dealing with postpositive attributives. Let us make a comparison and see which one is your favorite.

　　a. 下午茶是 19 世纪 40 年代初传入英国的一种与茶相关的仪式。

　　b. 下午茶是一种与茶相关的仪式，一种在 19 世纪 40 年代初传入英国的仪式。

　　c. 下午茶是一种与茶相关的仪式，（它）在 19 世纪 40 年代初传入英国。

---

② It evolved as a light meal to stem the hunger and anticipation of a dinner at 8 p.m.

As we can see, the attributive elements in this sentence are the adjective "light" and the to-infinitive structure (不定式结构).

To translation this sentence, we can also use the two techniques mentioned earlier: "division" and "adjusting the adjustment of linguistic levels."

We can first divide the sentence into three sense groups (意群): "It evolved as a light meal" "to stem the hunger" "and anticipation of a dinner at 8 p.m."

Then, we can translate as if the two infinitive phrases were two clauses, "(it is) to stem the hunger" and "(it is) to stem the anticipation of a dinner at 8 p.m." That is, we adjust their linguistic levels (调整语言层级), making them parallel to "it evolved as a light meal."

In doing so, we can have a Chinese translation characteristic of a Chinese sentence, which consists of a series of short, simple clauses, parallel in structure and without connectives: " 它逐渐演变成一种简餐，用来消除饥饿，抑制对 8 点晚餐的期望 ".

---

③ Afternoon Tea is a snack that is traditionally composed of finger sandwiches, scones with clotted cream and jam, sweet pastries, cakes, and of course, tea.

The attributive elements in the third sentence are "afternoon" and the clause following the head noun "snack."

To translate it, we can simply place all the attributives before their head nouns using the Chinese "……的……" structure: " 传统下午茶是一种由手指三明治、夹有凝脂奶油和果酱的烤饼、甜点、蛋糕、当然，还有茶组成的小吃 ". To make it more concise and natural, we can omit the Chinese words " 是一种 " and " 的小吃 ". In doing so, we actually upshift an attributive clause to a main clause: " 传统下午茶由手指三明治、夹有凝脂奶油和果酱的烤饼、甜点、蛋糕、当然，还有茶组成 ".

④ These royal receptions could have as many as two hundred guests with an "at home" invitation to visit between 4 p.m. and 7 p.m., during which they could come and go as they pleased.

Now, let us move to the last sentence.

As we can see, this is a simple but long sentence. This is because the noun "guests" has two long attributives. "As many as two hundred" serves as the premodifier, and the long prepositional phrase initiated by "with" functions as the postmodifier. They work together to provide necessary information about the capacity of the receptions— what the guests need to take with to participate in the party, how long the party would last, and whether the guests would be free to come and go.

How do we translate this sentence? Well, as mentioned earlier, when the postpositive attributives are long and complex, it may not be a good idea to place all the postmodifiers before the head noun. Or we may have another awkward sentence like this: "这些皇室茶话会能容纳多达 200 位带着'家庭'邀请函在下午 4 点到 7 点间拜访并可以随意来去的客人". None of us would speak Chinese in that way.

To deal with this long sentence, the translation techniques "division" and "the adjustment of linguistic levels" are still helpful. We can first divide the whole sentence into smaller parts and upshift those parts into independent clauses. For better understanding, we can rewrite this sentence in this way: "These royal receptions could have as many as two hundred guests; those guests take with an "at home" invitation and visit between 4 p.m. and 7 p.m.; during this time, they could come and go as they pleased".

As long as we have clarified the logical relationships between the modified and the modifiers, we can translate this sentence into Chinese with ease: "这些皇室茶话会能容纳多达 200 位客人，客人们带着'家庭'邀请函在下午 4 点至 7 点间拜访。在此期间他们可以随意来去".

3. Parallel Texts

Here we can compare the source text and its Chinese translation.

What is Afternoon Tea?

Afternoon Tea is a tea-related ritual, introduced in Britain in the early 1840s. It evolved as a light meal to stem (阻止) the hunger and anticipation of a dinner at 8 p.m.

Afternoon Tea is a snack that is traditionally composed of finger sandwiches, scones with clotted cream and jam, sweet pastries, cakes, and of course, tea.

Afternoon Tea initially developed as a private social event for ladies of the affluent (富裕的) classes. It was only when Queen Victoria engaged in the Afternoon Tea ritual that it became a formal occasion on a larger scale, known as "tea receptions".

These royal receptions could have as many as two hundred guests with an "at home" invitation to visit between 4 p.m. and 7 p.m., during which they could come and go as they pleased; this was the genesis (起源) of the Afternoon Tea as we know it.

什么是下午茶?

下午茶是 19 世纪 40 年代初传入英国的一种与茶相关的仪式。它逐渐演变成一种简餐，用以消除饥饿，抑制对 8 点晚餐的期望。

传统的下午茶包括手指三明治、夹有凝脂奶油和果酱的烤饼、甜点、蛋糕，当然，还有茶。

下午茶最初只是富裕阶级名媛们的私人社交活动。直到维多利亚女王参与其中，下午茶才成为一个大型正式的仪式，也就是众所周知的"茶话会"。

这些皇室茶话会能容纳多达 200 位客人，客人们带着"家庭"邀请函在下午 4 点至 7 点间拜访。在此期间他们可以随意来去。这就是我们所知的下午茶的来历。

→ 4. Translation Skills Summarized

In today's lesson, we have learned translation techniques dealing with attributive elements in English sentences.

As the table shows, when the attributives are prepositive, we can translate them in their original sequence.

When the attributives are postpositive but short and simple, we can simply convert them into the Chinese "……的……" structure and place them before their head nouns.

When the attributives are postpositive and long and complex, we can consider dividing them into smaller and more manageable parts, converting their grammatical roles, adjusting their linguistic level or order when necessary.

Above all, the most important thing for every translator is to realize the differences between English and Chinese and to make a way out, accurately representing the meaning of the original sentence while at the same time conforming to Chinese syntax.

attributives	components	conditions	techniques
prepositive 前置定语	● nouns ● adjectives		● translating in the original sequence 保持原有语序
postpositive 后置定语	● participles (present and past) ● to-infinitives ● prepositional phrases ● attributive clauses	short & simple	● adjusting the order 调整语序
		long & complex	● adjusting the order 调整语序 ● dividing 拆分 ● adjusting linguistic levels 调整语言层级

⌐ 5. Cultural Expressions

The passage we read just now tells that Afternoon Tea was initially used to relieve (延缓) hunger. The reason is quite interesting. Back then, lunch for the upper class was generally a light meal, and dinner was served no earlier than 7:30 p.m., which left a long period of time in between.

According to the acceptable legend, one afternoon, Anna, the 7th Duchess of Bedford, felt hunger pangs (因饥饿产生疼痛) and ordered tea, bread, butter, and cakes to her bedroom. And this tea break soon became a habit of hers and gradually a habit of people in aristocratic (贵族的) circles.

Traditionally, Afternoon Tea is served in a three-tier tray stand (三层托盘架), with finger sandwiches on the bottom. And moving up, you have a scone tier, and on the top, pastries and cakes. This is also the sequence you enjoy your Afternoon Tea, starting from the bottom and eating your way up through the tiers.

Cultural Knowledge

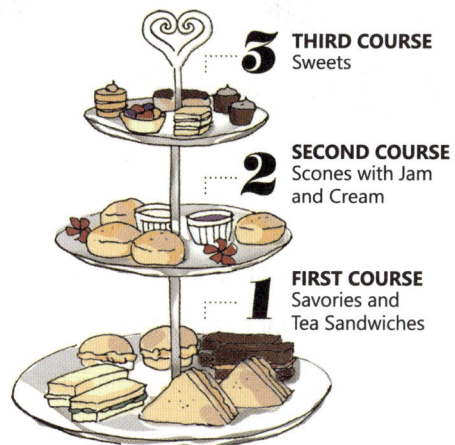

3 THIRD COURSE Sweets

2 SECOND COURSE Scones with Jam and Cream

1 FIRST COURSE Savories and Tea Sandwiches

What merits attention is that finger sandwiches are not sandwiches made of fingers. They are sandwiches usually cut into small pieces, easy to handle with fingers and capable of being eaten in two or three bites. Finger sandwiches may take different forms, and they are meant to be eaten at afternoon teatime to ease hunger. This is why they are also called "tea sandwiches."

Cultural knowledge

Finger Sandwich

Now, Afternoon Tea is not only to bridge the gap between lunch and dinner; it is an important occasion for friends and family to meet and eat. And tea, which used to be one of the essential components of the traditional afternoon repast (餐食), has also been off and on replaced by champagne or simply a cup of coffee. Even when people are drinking tea, they do not necessarily use a filter to catch the tea leaves, but a tea bag.

↳ 6. Questions for Discussion

1) What do people usually do during the afternoon tea?

2) How do you deal with attributive elements in English sentences in E-C translation?

III Table Manners in Britain and America

1. Cultural Background

Here are a few things to consider if you are invited to someone's home. For example, what time should you arrive at the host's home? It's impolite to arrive early if it's a social **gathering**[1] rather than business. The **hostess**[2] is getting ready and it will embarrass her to see you arrive before she is quite ready. Ten minutes late is best. Half an hour's delay is too late, and an **apology**[3] to the host is required. When should you leave? There's no rule, but it's rude to sit up late at your host's house. If it's just an invitation to dinner and chat, you'd better leave between 10 and 11 or say goodbye an hour after dinner. If you are invited to stay for a few days or a weekend, go out of your way to buy your hostess a bunch of flowers before you leave. It will make her very happy. Also, the day after you leave, send a note thanking your host with a small gift such as a box of chocolates or some flowers.

There are many kinds of **banquets**[4] in Britain, including tea parties and banquets. Tea parties include formal and informal tea parties. British people at the table do not serve food or encourage wine, all according to the interests of the **guests**[5]. Guests will take the food to eat up just polite. Do not drink when the waiter is pouring wine, and just hand the cup to the mouth. Guests may shake hands or nod their heads to say goodbye.

Words and Expressions:

1 gathering /ˈɡæðərɪŋ/ n. 聚会；集会

2 hostess /ˈhəʊstəs/ n. 女主人，女东道主

3 apology /əˈpɑːlədʒi/ n. 道歉；致歉

4 banquet /ˈbæŋkwɪt/ n. 宴会；筵席

5 guest /ɡest/ n. 客人，宾客

↳ 2. Translation Examples Explained

In this section, we are going to explore the method to deal with adverbial elements by translating a short passage about table manners. Here is the passage.

Table Manners in Anglo-America

①*The first thing to remember when attending a dinner at a Western home is that you are the guest and that you are foreign.* ②*As you do not come from the same country or culture as your host, they will be aware of this, and will be very forgiving if you unintentionally do or say something which would otherwise offend them.*

③*For more formal affairs, you will probably be told what to wear, such as "formal dress requested," etc.* A tie and jacket or tuxedo for the gents and an evening gown for the ladies would be in order here. If you are unsure what to wear, you can always ask the host. Your host in his home will usually motion you where to sit. At formal gatherings, name cards are sometimes provided, or you will be told where to sit. ④*Do not be alarmed by a great deal of cutlery: simply start from the outside and work your way in.* ⑤*Formal affairs often have several courses of food with the appropriate cutlery for each dish.* There is no harm in checking with your neighbor to see what implement he is using. After all, "When in Rome, do as the Romans do."

---

① The first thing to remember when attending a dinner at a Western home is that you are the guest and that you are foreign.

Let us look at the first example. We can find the main clause where the conjunction "when" is used as the time indicator. It indicates in what case the act often takes place, and thus the whole is used as the adverbial clause of time.

V1: 首先要记住的是：当你参加西方家庭的晚宴时，你是客人，而且是个外国人。

V2: 当参加西方家庭的晚宴时，首先要记住你是客人，而且是个外国人。

Here we may advance the adverbial clause of time to the beginning as in the Chinese translation Version 1, and thus the background information is emphasized first and then followed by the focus of message, which is what the Chinese readers prefer.

---

② As you do not come from the same country or culture as your host, they will be aware of this, and will be very forgiving if you unintentionally do or say something which would otherwise offend them.

We can see two subordinate clauses led by the typical conjunctions of "as" and "if". When we translate them into Chinese following their order in the original sentence, the

Chinese translation reads kinds of unnatural as in Version 1.

V1: 因为你来自和主人不同的国家和文化，他们会明白这点。他们会非常宽宏大量的，假使你无意间做了或说了某些冒犯他们的事。

V2: 因为你来自和主人不同的国家和文化，他们会明白这点。所以假使你无意间做了或说了某些冒犯他们的事时，他们会非常宽宏大量的。

In Version 2, however, the adverbial clause of conditions with the conjunction "if" is rearranged to the beginning in the translation, as the Chinese speakers prefer to state the conditions first before the result.

③ For more formal affairs, you will probably be told what to wear, such as "formal dress requested", etc.

As for the third example, we can easily identify the prepositional group with "for" used to indicate the purpose of the act. In translation, the prepositional group is converted from an adverbial of purpose to an adverbial of condition in: " 在较正式的情况下，你很可能会接到着装要求，例如'请着正式服装'等等 ".

④ Do not be alarmed by a great deal of cutlery: simply start from the outside and work your way in.

We can easily identify the main structural elements in the two imperative sentences. As for the elements that modify the predicates, we can be assured that they are adverbials of different kinds. The passive voice can be expressed with the indicator "被" in the Chinese translation, which usually comes before the predicate in Chinese.

不要被一大堆刀叉餐具吓着了：只要由外往内按顺序使用就行了。

As for the dining etiquette (用餐礼仪) in the latter part of the sentence, we can advance the adverbial of direction ahead of the predicates so that the translation sounds natural. While the English adverbial elements can occur more flexibly in different places in a sentence, the position of Chinese adverbs often appears before the predicate.

⑤ Formal affairs often have several courses of food with the appropriate cutlery for each dish.

Let us move on to the last instance. Shall we translate it into Version 1 or Version 2?

V1: 正式宴会常会有几道菜，伴随着每道菜有特定的刀叉。

V2: 正式宴会通常有几道菜须使用特定的刀叉。

In Version 1 the adverbial retains the literal meaning of the preposition "with", while in Version 2 the adverbial of manner in the form of "with+ n" is converted to the verbal phrase in Chinese, since "with" is a preposition indicative of motion and action. This follows the Chinese preference to use short verbal phrases in a sequence to organize a sentence. It is target language-oriented and reads fluent.

3. Parallel Texts

Here is the original and the translated texts in comparison. Please read them carefully and reflect on the skills used to translate English adverbials into Chinese.

Table Manners in Anglo-America

The first thing to remember when attending a dinner at a Western home is that you are the guest and that you are foreign. As you do not come from the same country or culture as your host, they will be aware of this, and will be very forgiving if you unintentionally do or say something which would otherwise offend them.

For more formal affairs, you will probably be told what to wear, such as "formal dress requested," etc. A tie and jacket or tuxedo for the gents and an evening gown for the ladies would be in order here. If you are unsure what to wear, you can always ask the host. Your host in his home will usually motion you where to sit. At formal gatherings, name cards are sometimes provided, or you will be told where to sit. Do not be alarmed by a great deal of cutlery: simply start from the outside and work your way in. Formal affairs often have several courses of food with the appropriate cutlery for each dish. There is no harm in checking with your neighbor to see what implement he is using. After all, "When in Rome, do as the Romans do.

英美餐桌礼仪

当参加西方家庭的晚宴时，首先要记住你是客人，而且是个外国人。因为你来自和主人不同的国家和文化，他们会明白这点，所以假使你无意间做了或说了某些冒犯他们的事时，他们会非常宽宏大量的。

在较正式的情况下，你很可能会接到着装要求，例如"请着正式服装"等等。此时，男士宜穿西装、打领带或穿燕尾服，女士则穿晚礼服。如果你拿不准该穿什么服装，问主人就好了。屋里的主人通常会招呼你就座。在正式的聚会中，有时会摆出写上名字的卡片，要不然人家会告诉你坐那儿。不要被一大堆刀叉餐具吓着了：只要由外往内按顺序使用就行了。正式宴会常会有几道菜须使用特定的刀叉餐具，这时不妨咨询一下邻座的人看他用什么餐具。毕竟，人总要"入乡随俗"嘛。

4. Translation Skills Summarized

What are the basic techniques to translate adverbial elements from English to Chinese? They are summarized in the following charts.

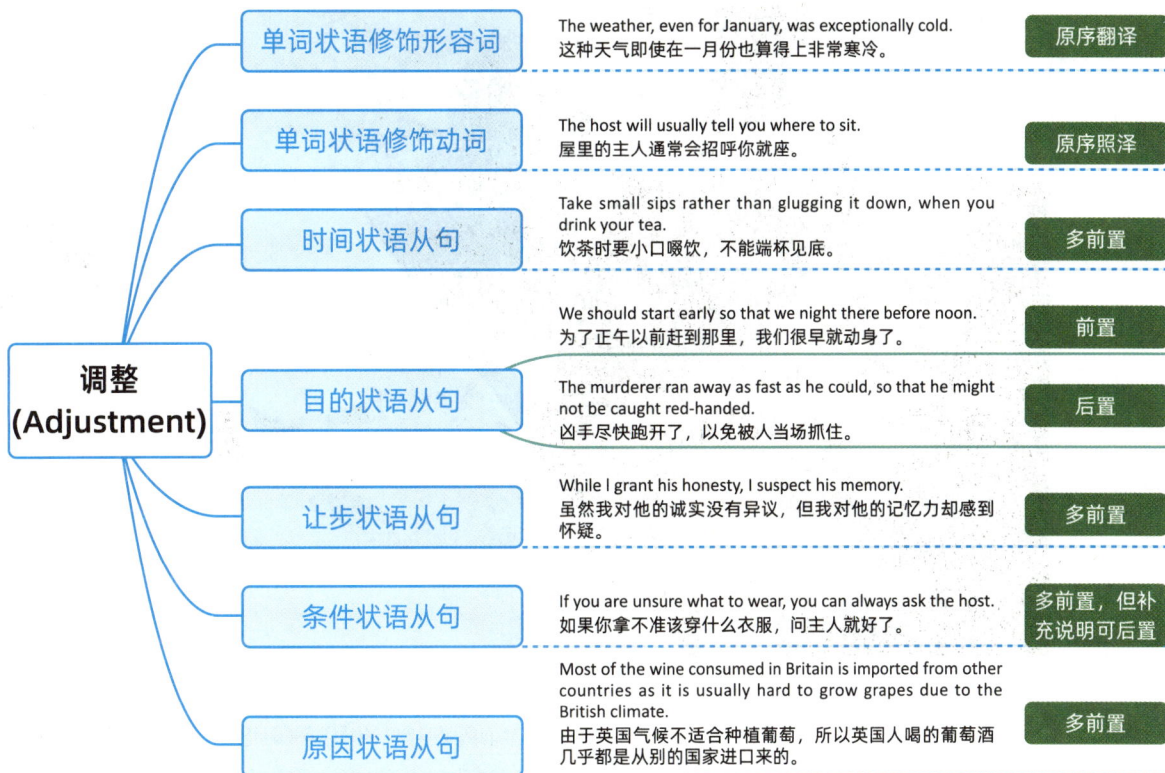

调整 (Adjustment)

- 单词状语修饰形容词
  The weather, even for January, was exceptionally cold.
  这种天气即使在一月份也算得上非常寒冷。 — 原序翻译

- 单词状语修饰动词
  The host will usually tell you where to sit.
  屋里的主人通常会招呼你就座。 — 原序照译

- 时间状语从句
  Take small sips rather than glugging it down, when you drink your tea.
  饮茶时要小口啜饮，不能端杯见底。 — 多前置

- 目的状语从句
  We should start early so that we might there before noon.
  为了正午以前赶到那里，我们很早就动身了。 — 前置
  The murderer ran away as fast as he could, so that he might not be caught red-handed.
  凶手尽快跑开了，以免被人当场抓住。 — 后置

- 让步状语从句
  While I grant his honesty, I suspect his memory.
  虽然我对他的诚实没有异议，但我对他的记忆力却感到怀疑。 — 多前置

- 条件状语从句
  If you are unsure what to wear, you can always ask the host.
  如果你拿不准该穿什么衣服，问主人就好了。 — 多前置，但补充说明可后置

- 原因状语从句
  Most of the wine consumed in Britain is imported from other countries as it is usually hard to grow grapes due to the British climate.
  由于英国气候不适合种植葡萄，所以英国人喝的葡萄酒几乎都是从别的国家进口来的。 — 多前置

转化 (Conversion)	副词转译为动词	She opened the window to let fresh air in. 她把窗户打开，让新鲜空气进来。
	副词转译为名词	He is physically weak, but mentally sound. 他身体虽弱，但思想健康。
	副词转译为形容词	In the past ten years, China's GDP has increased greatly. 在过去的十年里，中国的国内生产总值有了很大的增长。

拆分 (Division)	副词	They, not surprisingly, did not respond at all. 他们根本没有答复，这是不足为奇的。
	分词短语	Sunrays fitered in wherever they could, driving out darkness and choking the shadow. 阳光射入了它所能透过的所有地方，赶走了黑暗，驱散了幽影。
	介词词组	Their power increased with their number. 他们人数增加了，力量也随之增强。

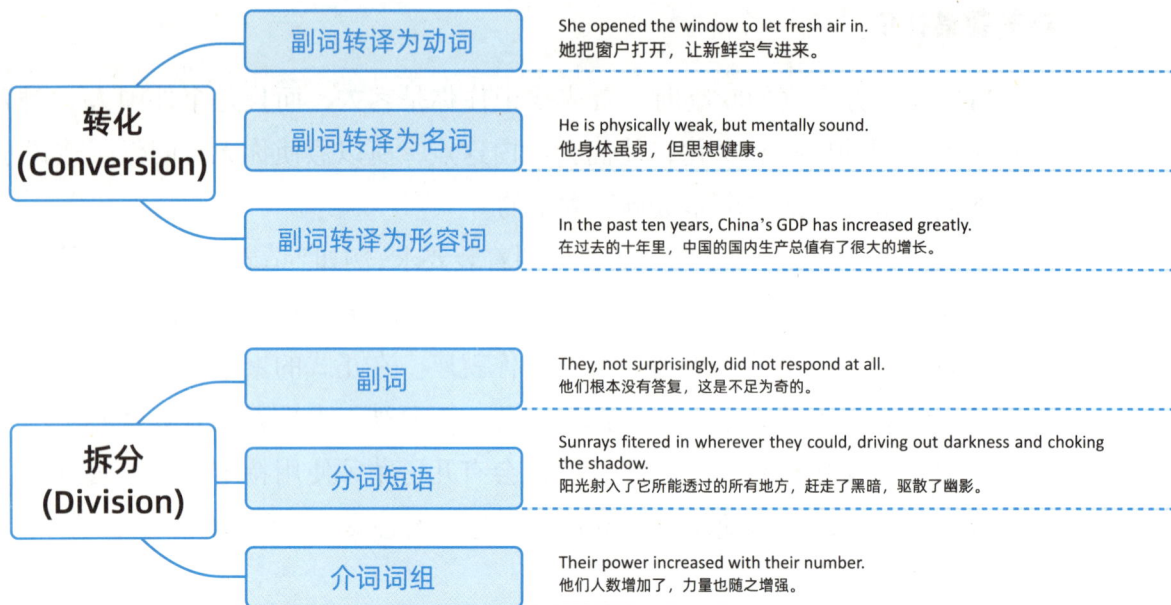

5. Cultural Expressions

If you are ever invited to dinner in Britain or America, I am sure that you will be confused at first about in what order to use the dining utensils.

Guests at very formal dinner parties are provided with a range of courses, each served separately and designed to balance the menu and complement the previous and following courses. A formal dinner will include at least seven courses, as what are presented here:

Courses

◆ Appetizer

◆ Soup

◆ Fish

◆ Intermezzo or other palate cleanser

◆ Main course with vegetables and other accompaniments

◆ Cold dish or salad

◆ Dessert

However, depending on the tastes of the host, traditions of an establishment, or other aspects of the formal dinner, the courses may vary. As the number of courses increases, the size of the portions decreases so that guests can enjoy each course without becoming too full.

For each of these courses, separate pieces of flatware will be placed on the table before the course is served. Because the flatware will be presented for each course, you will not have any extra forks, knives, and spoons. In that case, you have to know what to use.

Even if there are lots of utensils that may be new to you, there are two critical rules. First, watch what flatware the host or hostess is using and follow that pattern. Second, eat from the outside in, which means that if the course calls for a fork and a knife, use the fork on the furthest left and the knife at the furthest right. If it calls for a spoon, take the outside spoon.

(1) 餐巾	napkin	
(2) 鱼叉	fish fork	
(3) 主菜叉	dinner or main course fork	
(4) 沙拉叉	salad fork	
(5) 汤杯及汤底盘	soup bowl & plate	
(6) 主菜盘	dinner plate	
(7) 主菜刀	dinner knife	
(8) 鱼刀	fish knife	
(9) 汤匙	soup spoon	
(10) 面包及奶油盘	bread & butter plate	
(11) 奶油刀	butter knife	
(12) 点心匙及点心叉	dessert spoon and cake fork	
(13) 水杯	sterling water goblet	
(14) 红酒杯	red wine goblet	
(15) 白酒杯	white wine goblet	

To handle the flatware gracefully, please keep these tips in mind:

Flatware

◆ Use your fork or spoon in your right hand.

◆ Put only bite-sized morsels on your utensil.

◆ Pick up your fork in your right hand, pass it to your left hand, and then turn it over.

◆ Put the knife on the top edge of the plate, and transfer the fork to the right hand.

◆ Use your fork to pick up the food and transfer it to the mouth.

This is the American way of eating, but in Britain, the proper way to eat is to keep the fork in the left hand, both to hold the food when cutting it and then to move the food to the mouth.

When you are leaving the meal, how can we place the cutlery properly? It is one of the indications that you have finished eating even if you leave food on your plate. In America, people often place the fork and knife at four o'clock with the fork tines (叉尖) facing toward ten o'clock and the knife blade (刀刃) facing into the plate.

Why? Resting the knife and fork on the plate at four o'clock ensures that they will not slide when being carried to the kitchen, but the British often place the knife and fork at nine o'clock and three o'clock to indicate that they are finished with eating.

Some people may get scared being presented with several glasses. A simple rule can help you out, which involves the sequence and order. In a dinner party situation, where wine is being served along with food, the glass nearest you to the right of the dinner plate is typically used for the first wine course, and the rest of the wine glasses are placed in front of you and toward the center of the table according to the order of their service. If there is more than one wine glass, use the one closest to you first and then use them in order, moving away from you.

Glass and Stemware

When lifting a wine glass, lift it by the bowl and then hold it by the stem in case the heat of the hand warms the wine.

01

02

03

According to Mayo and Gold (2017), good table manners mean you should enjoy the meal if you are a guest, follow the cues provided by the host, refrain from drawing attention to yourself, and engage individuals, or the group, if appropriate, in interesting conversation.

Please look at the pictures, and do you think they are appropriate manners?

Here are some guidelines for an enjoyable dinner.

Dos and Don'ts

- Take your cues for what to do from the person in charge of the event.

- Keep your napkin in your lap.

- Serve others before yourself.

- Pass the salt and pepper together.

- Place your napkin on your seat when you leave the table.

- ◆ Do not season your food before tasting it.
- ◆ Do not ask for more food; wait for it to be offered.
- ◆ Do not point with flatware (especially with food on the fork, knife, or spoon).
- ◆ Do not blow your nose into your napkin.
- ◆ Do not talk with your mouth full.
- ◆ Don't place the elbows on the table.
- ◆ Don't slurp soup.
- ◆ Don't smoke or ask to smoke at the dinner table.
- ◆ Don't leave the flatware loose on the plate at the end of the meal.
- ◆ Don't place your napkin on your plate when leaving the table.

6. Questions for Discussion

1) Do you know the differences of the manner between China and Western countries when attending a dinner?

2) Can you conclude briefly the basic techniques to translate adverbial elements from English to Chinese?

IV McDonald's

1. Cultural Background

McDonald's is a global large-scale **transnational**[1] restaurant **chain**[2], founded in 1955 in the United States Chicago. It mainly sells hamburgers, as well as fast food such as French fries, fried chicken, soda, ice, salad, fruit and so on.

Most McDonald's restaurants offer counter and drive-through service, which means you can order a meal without getting out of the car. Customers can drive to the door and order, then bypass the restaurant and pick it up at the exit. Both options are available, as well as indoor and sometimes outdoor seating. A **drive-thru**[3] usually has several separate stops — the stop, the check out, and the pick-up point — but the latter two are usually combined.

What is the core product of McDonald's? It's just hamburgers, colas and fries. Do customers really like them? In the under-16s, 90 per cent said they liked, but in the over-16s, this rate gradually declined with age. This includes many personal business travelers, **fashionistas**[4], friends gathering, etc., who go to McDonald's not because they like it, but because they feel "**sanitary**[5] and convenient."

"Children's Paradise" has firmly caught the young customers, and "**hygiene**[6] and convenience" have attracted many temporary customers. McDonald's is not selling products, but an environment and an experience.

Words and Expressions:

1 transnational /ˌtrænzˈnæʃnəl/ *adj.* 跨国的；多国的

2 chain /tʃeɪn/ *n.* 连锁商店（或旅馆）

3 drive-thru 即 drive-through，不必下车即可得到服务的餐馆（或银行等）

4 fashionista /ˌfæʃnˈiːstə/ *n.* 时装设计师；穿着入时的人

5 sanitary /ˈsænəteri/ *adj.* 卫生的；清洁的

6 hygiene /ˈhaɪdʒiːn/ *n.* 卫生

↳ 2. Translation Examples Explained

In this section, we are going to talk about McDonald's and at the same time to explore the methods of translating appositive (同位语) and complement (补语) elements.

The Success of McDonald's

①*Let our memory roll back to 1954, when Raymond Kroc, a multimixer salesman, came across the McDonald brothers' (Richard and Maurice) small hamburger shop in Southern California.* ②*So impressed was Ray Kroc with the brothers' approach that he became their national franchise agent, relying on the shop's proven operating system—the Speedee Service System, to maintain quality.*

Kroc opened his first McDonald's in 1955 in Des Plaines, Illinois. ③*He never changed the fundamental rules devised by the brothers, namely low prices, simple menu, prompt service and consistent products.* ④*He also believed in a high level of cleanliness that everything should be spotless from the parking lot to the kitchen floor and the staff uniforms.* ⑤*Another key point of McDonald's success was Kroc's belief in advertising.* ⑥*From the original mascot "Speedee" to the creation of Ronald McDonald, the company has always made sure to invest heavily in advertising.*

With consistency and cleanliness, and carefully-chosen marketing campaigns, McDonald's turned out to be a successful venture.

① Let our memory roll back to 1954, when **Raymond Kroc**, a multimixer salesman, came across the McDonald brothers' (Richard and Maurice) small hamburger shop in Southern California.

Please pay attention to the bold words. "Raymond Kroc" is the subject in the adverbial clause of time (时间状语从句), and "a multimixer salesman" is the appositive of Raymond Kroc. Below are two versions of translation to it.

Version 1 follows the order of the sentence elements as in the English original. Therefore, we can translate it as "雷蒙·克罗克，一个多功能搅拌机的推销员". On the contrary, Version 2 puts the appositive in front of the subject to modify Raymond Kroc, i.e., "推销多功能搅拌机的雷蒙·克罗克". These two versions are both acceptable by the Chinese readers.

V1: 让我们的记忆之轮转回到 1954 年。那一年，雷蒙·克罗克，一个多功能搅拌机的推销员，偶然来到加利福尼亚南部麦当劳兄弟（理查德和莫瑞斯）经营的小汉堡包店。（顺译）

V2: 让我们的记忆之轮转回到 1954 年。那一年，推销多功能搅拌机的雷蒙克罗克，偶然来到加利福尼亚南部麦当劳兄弟（理查德和莫瑞斯）经营的小汉堡包店。（逆译）

② So impressed was Ray Kroc with the brothers' approach that he became their national franchise agent, relying on the shop's proven operating system — the Speedee Service System, to maintain quality.

We can see "their national franchise agent" are the subjective complement (主语补足语), also called the predicative (表语) as we usually call it. From the previous section we learned that, we generally translate the "主系表" structure in the order of the English original.

"The Speedee Service System" is the appositive of "the shop's proven operating system", which was connected by the dash (破折号). The function of "Speed Service System" is to name the shop's proven operating system. When we translate the sentence, we can always follow the English original. The translation can be: "麦当劳兄弟的经营方法令他极为触动，于是他成为了他们的全国特许经营代理。当然，每家特许经营店都采纳小店行之有效的运行机制——快速服务，来保证服务质量"（顺译）.

③ He never changed the fundamental rules devised by the brothers, namely low prices, simple menu, prompt service and consistent products.

As we can see, "devised by the brothers" is the complement of the object. There is a passive relationship between the object and the object complement. When we translate this sentence into Chinese, we can turn the object complement to a pre-modifying element (前置修饰语) and place it in front of the object.

"The fundamental rules" is the object in the main clause. The appositive of "the fundamental rules" is induced by "namely". Generally speaking, if the appositive is induced by words like "namely" and "such as", we can follow the sentence order of the English original. So the sentence can be translated as: "他从未改变麦当劳兄弟俩制定的（定语前置）基本原则，那就是低廉的价格、简单的菜单、迅捷的服务和一致的产品"（顺译）.

④ He also believed in a high level of cleanliness that everything should be spotless from the parking lot to the kitchen floor and the staff uniforms.

In this sentence, "cleanliness" is the object in the main clause and the appositive clause is induced by that-clause. When we translate this sentence, we can translate the main clause first and then translate the appositive clause, as in Version 1. The main clause and the appositive clause can be connected with "即""逗号""冒号" and "破折号".

V1: 他还高度认可清洁，即从停车场，到厨房的地板以及制服，一切都要一尘不染。

Alternatively, if the noun is the subject in the main clause, we will translate the appositive clause first and then the main clause, just like the following sentence.

A high level of cleanliness that everything should be spotless from the parking lot to the kitchen floor and the staff uniforms was believed by him.

V2. 从停车场，到厨房的地板以及制服，一切都要一尘不染，这一条是他高度认可的。

⑤Another key point of McDonald's success was Kroc's belief in advertising.

The subject in the sentence is "Another key point", and "of McDonald's success" is its appositive. When we translate "Another key point of McDonald's success", we would better put the appositive in front of the subject as a pre-modifier (前置修饰语), because it is short. So the translation can be: " 麦当劳取得成功的另一关键点是克罗克非常相信广告的力量 "（逆译）.

⑥ From the original mascot "Speedee" to the creation of Ronald McDonald, the company has always made sure to invest heavily in advertising.

It is easy for us to find out the appositive in this sentence. "Speedee" is the appositive of "the original mascot". We can follow the English original when we translate this sentence. Here comes the translation: " 从最初的吉祥物 'Speedee' 到罗纳德·麦当劳叔叔形象的问世，麦当劳公司无疑在广告方面下了大手笔 "（顺译）.

↳ 3. Parallel Texts

The following is the comparison of the source and target texts. Read them carefully and reflect on how appositive (clause) and complement elements in English sentences were translated.

The Success of McDonald's

Let our memory roll back to 1954, when Raymond Kroc, a multimixer salesman, came across the McDonald brothers' (Richard and Maurice) small hamburger shop in Southern California. ① So impressed was Ray Kroc with the brothers' approach that he became their national franchise agent, relying on the shop's proven operating system – the Speedee Service System, to maintain quality.

Kroc opened his first McDonald's in 1955 in Des Plaines, Illinois. ② He never changed the fundamental rules devised by the brothers, namely low prices, simple menu, prompt service and consistent products. ③ He also believed in a high level of cleanliness that everything should be spotless from the parking lot to the kitchen floor and the staff uniforms. ④ Another key point of McDonald's success was Kroc's belief in advertising. ⑤ From the original mascot "Speedee" to the creation of Ronald McDonald, the company has always made sure to invest heavily in advertising.

With consistency and cleanliness, and carefully-chosen marketing campaigns, McDonald's turned out to be a successful venture.

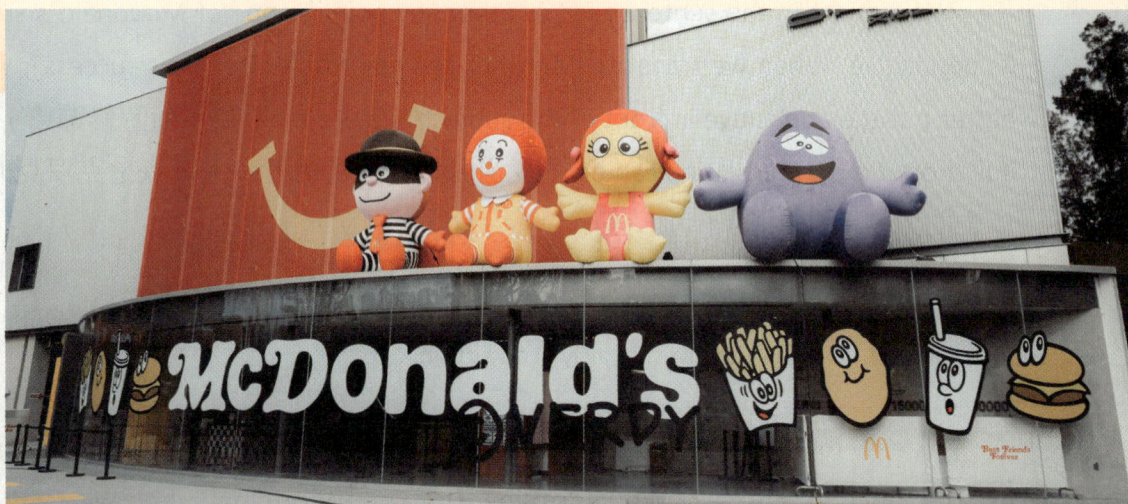

麦当劳的成功之道

让我们的记忆之轮转回到 1954 年。那一年，推销搅拌机的雷蒙·克罗克，偶然来到加利福尼亚南部麦当劳兄弟（理查德和莫瑞斯）经营的小汉堡包店。① **麦当劳兄弟的经营方法令他极为触动，于是他成为了他们的全国特许经营代理。**当然，每家特许经营店都采纳小店行之有效的运行机制——快速服务，来保证服务质量。

1955 年，克罗克的第一家麦当劳在伊利诺斯州的德斯普兰斯开始营业。② **他从未改变麦当劳兄弟俩制定的基本原则，那就是低廉的价格、简单的菜单、迅捷的服务和一致的产品。③ 他还高度认可清洁，即从停车场到厨房的地板以及制服，一切都要一尘不染。④ 麦当劳取得成功的另一关键点是克罗克非常相信广告的力量。⑤ 从最初的吉祥物 "Speede" 到罗纳德·麦当劳叔叔形象的问世，麦当劳公司无疑在广告方面下了大手笔。**

正是由于坚持始终如一的服务、秉持清洁至上的原则，以及精心选择每一个市场营销活动，麦当劳才有今日的成就。

4. Translation Skills Summarized

When the appositive (clause) and the complement are short, we usually have two options: to translate them in the original order (顺译), or in the reverse order (逆译), that is, to translate them as premodifiers (前置修饰语). When making choices between the two options, we should consider in what way the translation is more concise, natural and compliant with the Chinese linguistic habit.

For long appositives, or appositive clauses, we can split them off and translate them as independent clauses with the use of "即", comma, colon and dash, or the use of " 这 " and "那".

As well as the above translation techniques dealing with the appositive, there is another translation technique called conversion (转换), which has not been used in translating this text.

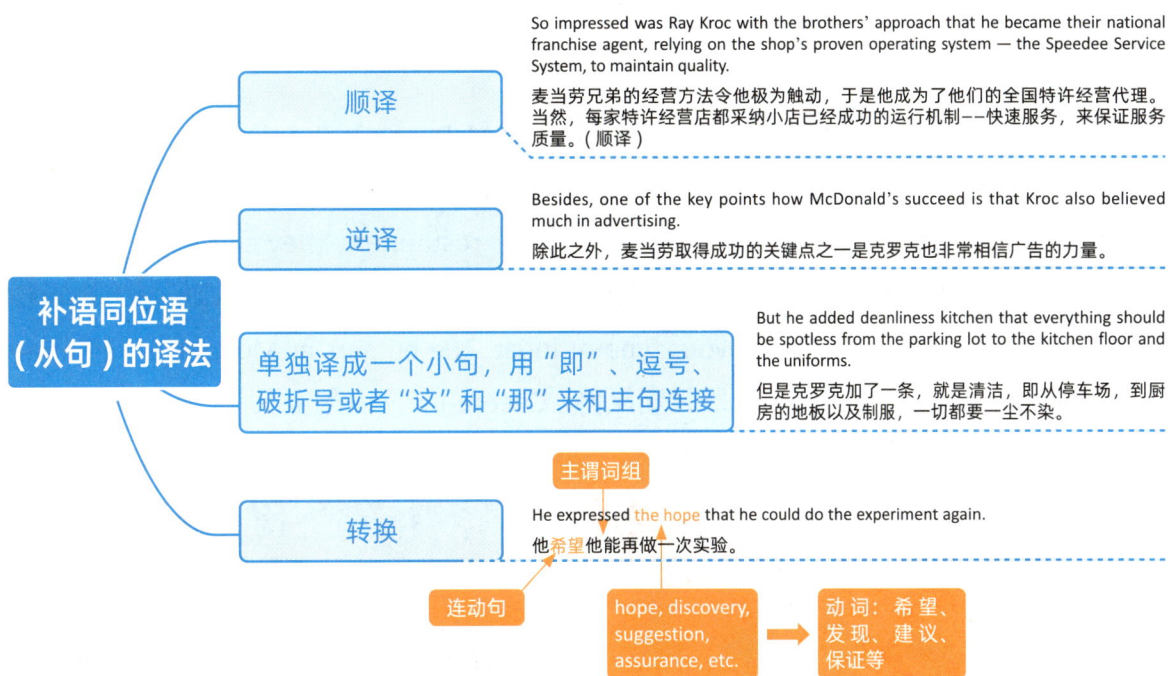

补语同位语（从句）的译法

顺译
So impressed was Ray Kroc with the brothers' approach that he became their national franchise agent, relying on the shop's proven operating system — the Speedee Service System, to maintain quality.
麦当劳兄弟的经营方法令他极为触动，于是他成为了他们的全国特许经营代理。当然，每家特许经营店都采纳小店已经成功的运行机制--快速服务，来保证服务质量。(顺译)

逆译
Besides, one of the key points how McDonald's succeed is that Kroc also believed much in advertising.
除此之外，麦当劳取得成功的关键点之一是克罗克也非常相信广告的力量。

单独译成一个小句，用"即"、逗号、破折号或者"这"和"那"来和主句连接
But he added deanliness kitchen that everything should be spotless from the parking lot to the kitchen floor and the uniforms.
但是克罗克加了一条，就是清洁，即从停车场，到厨房的地板以及制服，一切都要一尘不染。

转换
主谓词组
He expressed the hope that he could do the experiment again.
他希望他能再做一次实验。

连动句　　hope, discovery, suggestion, assurance, etc. → 动词: 希望、发现、建议、保证等

Please look at this sentence: He expressed the hope that he could do the experiment again. When we translate this sentence into Chinese, we can translate the noun "hope" into a verb "希望": "他希望他能再做一次实验". So, if the noun explained by an appositive clause has a strong action meaning, such as hope, discovery, suggestion, assurance, etc., such a word generally can be translated into verbs, and the appositive clause can be translated into Chinese subject-predicate groups (主谓词组) to act as the object of the verb. In this way, we make use of the special Chinese sentence structure called "连动句".

He expressed <u>the hope</u> that he could do the experiment again.

↓ Noun

他**希望**（**动词**）他能再做（动词）一次实验。 连动句

Tips: Hope, discovery, suggestion, assurance (Nouns)

↓

希望，发现，建议，保证（动词）

5. Cultural Expressions

From the text we learned the history of McDonald's and the reasons for its success. If you go abroad, can you order food in English at a McDonald's restaurant?

Although McDonald's is a hamburger restaurant, they sell many other products besides hamburgers. Let's see what's on the menu. We can start with the burgers. For the burgers, you can choose your type of meat. The burgers at McDonald's all have special names, such as Big Mac (巨无霸汉堡), Cheese Burger (芝士汉堡), Double Cheeseburger (双层芝士汉堡), and Quarter Pounder (足三两汉堡).

Big Mac   Cheese Burger   Quarter Pounder

Double Cheeseburger

Salads
沙拉

Chicken McNuggets
麦乐鸡

McFlurry
麦旋风

Sundae
圣代

Vanilla ice cream cone
香草冰淇淋甜筒

Baked Apple Pie
苹果派

Chocolate Chip Cookie
巧克力饼干

Combo套餐

Drink

French fries

Burger

Happy meal开心乐园套餐

Apart from ordering from the menu, you can order a combo (套餐). You can say "I'd like a number 1, please". Number 1, 2, and 3 are the meal numbers. It is the easiest way for you to order food. In a combo, you can get three products. You get French fries, a drink and a burger. Compared with individual menu items, combo meals are cheaper. The Happy Meal (开心乐园套餐) is a combo for kids, but they are also sold to adults. They could reduce the calorie intake (卡路里摄入量) a bit. If you crave the classic McDonald's taste but do want to eat at least a little healthier, you could consider ordering a Happy Meal. The small pouch (小袋) of fries, kid-size drink and fresh fruit will be slightly better for your waistline (腰围).

可口可乐 Coca-Cola®　雪碧 Sprite®　芬达 Fanta®

草莓奶昔 Strawberry Shake　卡布奇诺咖啡 Cappuccino

The famous culture of McDonald's is QSCV and the "three-legged stool" (官方用词), which helps this company spread so fast.

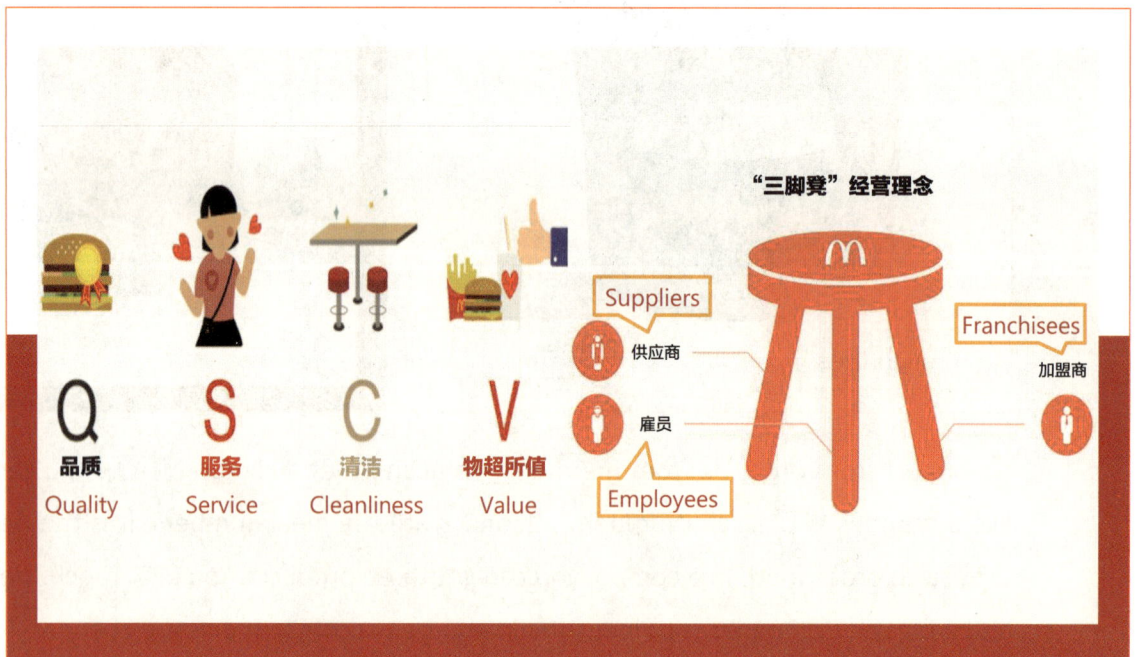

Q 品质 Quality　S 服务 Service　C 清洁 Cleanliness　V 物超所值 Value

"三脚凳"经营理念

Suppliers 供应商　Employees 雇员　Franchisees 加盟商

QSCV, that is "Quality, Service, Cleanliness and Value," is the business philosophy that McDonald's has always adhered to. At any McDonald's around the world, customers can enjoy a good taste with consistent standards.

Q refers to quality. McDonald's commitment to customers is to always allow customers to enjoy the freshest and purest food, thereby establishing a high degree of credit.

S refers to service. Smile is a feature of McDonald's. All the shop assistants are smiling, talking and doing things with customers cheerfully to make customers feel satisfied.

C refers to cleanliness. One of the provisions (规定) of McDonald's employee code is "It is better to get up and sweep the floor rather than resting against a wall." All employees in more than 10,000 chain stores around the world must comply with this provision.

V refers to value. Every chain store will provide customers with original, valuable, and high-quality food.

Kroc has a famous "three-legged stool" theory and expressed it as: McDonald's development depends on the joint efforts of suppliers, franchisees, and employees. The three parties unite as a whole of common interests, and work together to promote the progress of each restaurant.

6. Questions for Discussion

1) Do you like eating food in McDonald's? What is the secret of McDonald's success?
2) How can we deal with the appositive (clause) and complement that are short in E-C translation?

Ⅳ Exercises

Section A. True or false (5 items)

_____ 1) Afternoon Tea initially developed as a private social event for ladies of the affluent classes in the UK.

_____ 2) Even if there are lots of utensils that may be new to you, one critical rule is to eat from the outside in. That is, if the course calls for a fork and a knife, use the fork on the furthest left and the knife at the furthest right.

_____ 3) In English, long attributive elements, such as the attributive clause, are often placed after the modified element; but in Chinese, attributive elements usually are placed before the modified element.

_____ 4) Adverbial elements may appear in different places in English and Chinese sentences. Therefore, we sometimes need to change their sentence order to comply with the usage in the target language in translation.

_____ 5) When the attributives are prepositive, we can translate them in their original sequence. When the attributives are postpositive but short and simple, we can simply convert them into the Chinese "……的……" structure and place them before their head nouns.

Section B. Multiple choice (5 items)

_____ 1) Pub culture is designed to promote sociability in the British society known for its reserve.

A. 在以冷漠著称的英国，酒吧文化是被设计来促进社会性。

B. 在以冷漠著称的英国，酒吧文化的形成是为了促进社会交往。

C. 酒吧文化的形成是为了促进社会交往，在以冷漠著称的英国。

_____ 2) Standing at the bar for service allows you to chat with others waiting to be served.

A. 站在吧台等候的时候，你可以和其他人交谈，这些人也等着被服务。

B. 站在吧台等着服务时，你可以和其他人交谈，这些人也等着服务。

C. 站在吧台等候的时候，你可以和其他排队的人交谈。

_____ 3) Visitors to Britain may find the best place to sample local culture is in a traditional pub.

A. 到访英国的人会发现，最能领略当地文化的地方是在传统英国酒吧。

B. 到访英国的人会发现，最能领略当地文化的地方是传统英国酒吧。

C. 到访英国的人会发现，传统英国酒吧是最能取样当地文化的地方。

_____ 4) Most of wine consumed in Britain is imported from other countries as it is usually hard to grow grapes due to the British climate.

A. 由于气候不适合种植葡萄，英国消费的大多数葡萄酒都是从他国进口的。

B. 在英国被消费的大多数葡萄酒都是从别国进口的，因为英国的气候不适合种植葡萄。

C. 英国消费的大多数葡萄酒都是从别国进口的，因为葡萄很难种植，由于英国的气候。

_____ 5) Taking small sips rather than glugging it down when you drink your tea.

A. 饮茶时要小口啜饮，不能端杯见底。

B. 要小口抿茶而不是大口喝茶，在饮茶时。

C. 饮茶时要小口小口地喝，不能大口喝茶。

Ⅴ Test

Section A. Multiple choice (5 items*4 points=20 points)

_____ 1) Wine is increasingly drunk, both in pubs and in the home.

A. 葡萄酒的饮用量都在增大，无论是在家中还是在酒吧。

B. 无论是在家中还是在酒吧，葡萄酒的饮用量都在增大。

C. 无论是在家中还是在酒吧，葡萄酒都被喝得越来越多。

_____ 2) Many businessmen habitually have lunch in a pub near their office.

A. 许多商人习惯性地就餐于办公室附近的酒吧。

B. 许多商人习惯性地在办公室附近的酒吧吃午餐。

C. 许多商人在办公室附近的酒吧吃午餐，这已成为一种习惯。

_____ 3) There are many hotels offering the quintessential afternoon tea experience in London.

A. 伦敦有许多酒店能为你提供精致的下午茶体验。

B. 许多酒店能为你提供精致的下午茶体验，在伦敦。

C. 在伦敦有许多酒店能为你提供精致的下午茶经历。

_____ 4) Traditional afternoon tea is typically served between 4 p.m. and 6 p.m.

    A. 传统下午茶一般会被提供于下午，时间是四点到六点。

    B. 传统下午茶一般提供于下午四至六点。

    C. 传统下午茶一般在下午四至六点供应。

_____ 5) English beer is different from Continental beer. The latter should be served well chilled whereas English beer is at its best when it is little cool.

    A. 英国啤酒不同于欧洲大陆的啤酒。后者应该冰镇后饮用，而英国啤酒却是在略微冰凉的时候最适合饮用。

    B. 英国啤酒不同于欧洲大陆的啤酒。后者在足够冷却时适合饮用，而英国啤酒却在略微冰凉的时候最适宜饮用。

    C. 英国啤酒不同于欧洲大陆的啤酒。后者应该被饮用于冰镇后，而英国啤酒却最适宜饮用于略微冰凉的时候。

Section B. Sentence translation (5 items*6 points=30 points)

1) Their place of public entertainment is partly filled by what are colloquially known as "pubs", public houses.

2) Standing at the bar for service gives you a chance to chat with others waiting to be served.

3) Afternoon Tea is a snack that is traditionally composed of finger sandwiches, scones with clotted cream and jam, sweet pastries, cakes, and of course, tea.

4) As you do not come from the same country or culture as your host, they will be aware of this, and will be very forgiving if you unintentionally do or say something which would otherwise offend them.

5) He also believed in a high level of cleanliness that everything should be spotless from the parking lot to the kitchen floor and the staff uniforms.

Section C. Paragraph translation (50 points)

By definition, afternoon tea is a dainty meal. So, taking small sips rather than glugging it down when you drink your tea. There is a definite order to take tea, but the actual drinking of tea can take place throughout the "meal".

Unit 5
MUSIC AND MOVIE

I The Oscars

↳ 1. Cultural Background

The Oscars, also known as the Academy Awards, are a group of American film Awards **sponsored**[1] by the Academy of Motion Picture Arts and Sciences①, founded in 1929. It is the oldest, most **authoritative**[2] and professional film award in the United States, and the most influential film award in the world. The Academy Award is the highest award in the American film industry, together with the Emmy Awards (television awards)②, Grammy Awards (music awards)③, Tony Awards (drama awards)④, known as the American show business four awards (EGOT).

The Academy of Motion Picture Arts and Sciences presents a series of competitive awards annually, covering various categories such as Best Picture, Best Director, and Best Actor. In addition to these, the Academy also presents several honorary awards, including the Jean Hersholt Humanitarian Award and the Honorary Award, which are given to recognize lifetime achievement or other special contributions. All these awards are **collectively**[3] known as the Academy Awards. The Academy Awards are held once a year, generally in February or March at the Dolby Theatre in Hollywood, Los Angeles, ..., and more than 200 countries and regions around the world **broadcast**[4] it on television or live network.

◇◇◇◇◇◇◇◇

① Academy of Motion Picture Arts and Sciences 美国电影艺术与科学学院
中文简称"美国影艺学院",英文缩写为"AMPAS",致力于研究、提高电影的艺术和技术质量,加强电影界内部各个专业之间的团结和协作,以促进电影事业的发展。学院从成立起主要以颁发一年一度的"学院奖"(后又称"奥斯卡奖")来检阅和促进影片的质量。

② Emmy Awards 艾美奖
艾美奖是美国电视界关于电视节目和制作人员的奖项。"艾美奖"不是一个单独的奖项,而是一个电视奖系列,每年9~11月举办,美国国内或国外上年度出品的电视节目均可参评,评奖项目众多,主要包括最佳节目、最佳男女主角、最佳男女配角、最佳导演、最佳编剧、最佳摄影、最佳美工、最佳音乐、最佳剪辑、最佳音响等。

③ Grammy Awards 格莱美奖
格莱美奖是美国国家录音与科学学会(The National Academy of Recording Arts & Science)举行的一个年度大型音乐评奖活动,被誉为"音乐界奥斯卡"。"格莱美"(GRAMMY)是英文Gramophone(留声机)的变异谐音,其奖杯形状如一架老式的留声机。

④ Tony Awards 托尼奖
"托尼奖"设立于1947年,是百老汇联盟以及美国戏剧委员会共同设立的国际戏剧行业最高奖项,与电影"奥斯卡奖"、音乐"格莱美奖"以及电视"艾美奖"并称为美国艺术界四大顶级奖项。

1 sponsor /ˈspɑːnsər/ v. 赞助（活动、节目等）

2 authoritative /əˈθɔːrəteɪtɪv/ adj. 权威性的

3 collectively /kəˈlektɪvli/ adv. 全体地；共同地

4 broadcast /ˈbrɔːdkæst/ v. 播送（电视或无线电节目）；广播

↳ 2. Translation Examples Explained

Please read the following passage. It is a brief introduction to the Academy Awards. Do take note of the translation techniques used when translating the bold sentences.

> ### *The Academy Awards*
>
> ①*As one of the most prominent and glittering award ceremonies in the world, the Academy Awards ceremony, more popularly known as the Oscars, is televised live to more than one billion viewers in about 200 countries each spring. The Oscars is the oldest award ceremony in the media. Other equivalent awards like the Grammy Awards for music, the Emmy Awards for television, and the Tony Awards for theater are modeled after it.* ②*Every year since 1929, the big names and shining stars have gathered annually in Hollywood for a lavish evening of celebration and recognition of excellence in cinematic achievements. Statuettes nicknamed Oscars are given to winners in over 20 categories, including Best Picture, Best Actor, Best Actress, etc.* ③*Award winners are chosen by members of the Academy of Motion Picture Arts and Sciences (AMPAS) before the ceremony, but the winners' names are kept secret in sealed envelopes until the presentation night when celebrities in the film industry announce the results.* The suspense is a huge reason why the Oscars draws so many viewers from afar.

> ① As one of the most prominent and glittering award ceremonies in the world, the Academy Awards ceremony, more popularly known as the Oscars, is televised live to more than one billion viewers in about 200 countries each spring.

To understand the main idea of this long sentence, we first need to figure out its core parts (主干) "ceremony is televised to viewers". The additional elements (枝叶) include two adverbials (状语), and a couple of attributes (定语). Then, we can translate this sentence by following its original order as in Version 1:

> **V1:** 作为世界上最引人注目和最盛大的颁奖典礼之一，被我们所熟知为"奥斯卡金像奖"的学院奖颁奖典礼在每年春季会向约 200 个国家的 10 亿多观众进行电视直播。

But don't you think it sounds awkward and wordy? Here we have a different translation as in Version 2:

> **V2:** 作为世界上最引人注目的颁奖盛典之一，学院奖颁奖典礼每年春季会向约 200 个国家的 10 亿多观众进行电视直播。这也是我们所熟知的"奥斯卡金像奖"。

For one thing, the post-modifier (后置定语) "more popularly known as the Oscars" was separated from the original structure and translated as an independent sentence as: "这也是我们所熟知的'奥斯卡金像奖'". The separation of this part, what we call division, does not only make what goes before short and compact (紧凑的), but also coheres (衔接) well with what follows it. It is because from here on the Academy Awards in this passage is called "the Oscars" in the following statements.

For another, the adjective "glittering" is combined with the following phrase "award ceremonies" in the Chinese translation: "颁奖盛典", a frequently used Chinese phrase.

With the use of both division and combination, Version 2 appears to be shorter, clearer and more colloquial (通俗易懂的).

> ② Every year since 1929, the big names and shining stars have gathered annually in Hollywood for a lavish evening of celebration and recognition of excellence in cinematic achievements.

As usual, we need to identify the sentence core parts to correctly understand the main idea — "the big names and shining stars have gathered". All the remaining parts are adverbial modifiers (状语). They are adverbials of time, place, or purpose.

For this sentence we also have two options. We can follow the original order and translate it as Version 1.

> **V1:** 自 1929 年以来，每年知名人士和耀眼明星们都在好莱坞齐聚来渡过一个庆祝与嘉奖他们在电影事业上斩获佳绩的奢华绚烂之夜。

But don't you think there is a problem in Version 1? It has a long and very complex structure and it is difficult to read over with one breath even for a native Chinese speaker.

We can see that the long and complex structure in Version 1 was cut and divided into three shorter clauses in the form of verb phrases (动词短语) without connectives (连接词) to combine them. These short verb phrases are called run-on sentences (流水句), which are considered a typical feature in Chinese but grammatical errors in English. By using the division method, the translation in Version 2 better complies (遵从) with Chinese sentence structure, hence easier to pronounce and understand.

In addition to the use of division, we also employed the method of combination in Version 2. The compound subject (复合主语) "the big names and shining stars" was condensed (浓缩) by using an idiomatic Chinese expression "明星大腕".

V2: 自 1929 年以来，每年明星大腕们都在好莱坞齐聚一堂，共庆这奢华绚烂的一晚，嘉奖他们在电影事业上斩获的佳绩。

③ Award winners are chosen by members of the Academy of Motion Picture Arts and Sciences (AMPAS) before the ceremony, but the winners' names are kept secret in sealed envelopes until presentation night when celebrities in the film industry announce the results.

In this sentence, the word "but" connects two main parts, and each of them has adverbial (状语的) phrases or clauses. In particular, the adverbial clause "when" makes this sentence long and complex. To translate this sentence, we offer two options. We can follow its original order as in Version 1.

V1: 获奖者由美国电影艺术与科学学院的成员在典礼之前评选产生，但获奖人的名字却当作秘密封存于信封一直到颁奖夜当电影业知名人士公布结果时才知道。

Or we use the method of division to cut this compound sentence (并列复合句) as in Version 2. The second version is preferable. In this version, the long compound English sentence is divided into two shorter Chinese sentences, and with their adverbials (状语) divided even shorter by using two commas (逗号). It reads clearer than the first version. First, the long sentence was cut into shorter ones, segments (分段) or pieces with clearer meanings. Moreover, in Version 2, two adverbial phrases " 在典礼之前 " and "直到颁奖夜" were placed at the beginning of each sentence. Then the two new Chinese sentences are in a similar structure and share a pleasing rhythm (韵律) as we read. The third reason of making division is closely related to how we tackle the sentecnce that follows.

V2: 在典礼之前，获奖者由美国电影艺术与科学学院的成员评选产生。直到颁奖夜当晚，被秘密封存于信封中的获奖人名字才由电影业知名人士当众公布。

The following table presents the original text and its Chinese translation. Compare them carefully and see how the methods of division and combination were used together.

The Academy Award

As one of the most prominent and glittering award ceremonies in the world, the Academy Awards ceremony, more popularly known as the Oscars, is televised live to more than one billion viewers in about 200 countries each spring. The Oscars is the oldest award ceremony in the media. Other equivalent awards like the Grammy Awards for music, the Emmy Awards for television, and the Tony Awards for theater are modeled after it. Every year since 1929, the big names and shining stars have gathered annually in Hollywood for a lavish evening of celebration and recognition of excellence in cinematic achievements. Statuettes nicknamed Oscars are given to winners in over 20 categories, including Best Picture, Best Actor, Best Actress, etc. Award winners are chosen by members of the Academy of Motion Picture Arts and Sciences (AMPAS) before the ceremony, but the winners' names are kept secret in sealed envelopes until presentation night when celebrities in film industry announce the results. The suspense is a huge reason why the Oscars draws so many viewers from afar.

奥斯卡金像奖

作为世界上最引人注目的颁奖盛典之一，学院奖颁奖典礼每年春季会向约200个国家、10亿多观众进行电视直播。这也是我们所熟知的"奥斯卡金像奖"，它是媒体行业里历史最为悠久的颁奖典礼。同类的其它奖项如音乐类格莱美奖、电视类艾美奖、戏剧类托尼奖都是参照它的模式所设置。从1929年起，每年明星大腕们在好莱坞齐聚一堂，共庆这奢华绚烂的一晚，嘉奖他们在电影事业上所斩获的佳绩。奥斯卡小金人被授予给二十多个奖项的获胜者，包括最佳影片、最佳男主角、最佳女主角等。在典礼之前，获奖者由美国电影艺术与科学学院的成员评选产生。直到颁奖夜当晚，被秘密封存于信封中的获奖人名字才由电影业知名人士当众公布，这份悬念也是奥斯卡奖能吸引世界各地观众的重要原因。

4. Translation Skills Summarized

As we have learned in the practice above, both division and combination are commonly used, either alone or together, for better reproducing the original text in the target language. But division is used more frequently since English sentences tend to be longer than Chinese sentences. In brief, the purposes of using them are:

to present ideas clearly across languages;

to build a cohesion in the target language;

and to comply with the sentence patterns in Chinese.

Using Division and Combination Strategically

分译

Division

合译

Combination

- To present ideas clearly across languages;
- To build a cohesion in the target language;
- To comply with the sentence patterns in Chinese.

5. Cultural Expressions

The word "Oscar" represents both the Academy Awards ceremony and the small gold-plated (镀金的) statuette (雕像).

What does "Oscar" stand for?

The Academy Awards ceremony is more popularly known as the Oscars.

学院颁奖典礼

Statuettes nicknamed Oscars are given to winners in over 20 categories.

小雕像

"Oscar" was originally the nickname of the statuette. It is said that the academy (AMPAS) librarian Margaret Herrick claimed that the statuette looked like her Uncle Oscar. Then that became the most believed story. Every spring, dozens of Oscars are presented to recognize the highest honor in film-making. So, the officially called "Academy Awards" is more commonly known as "the Oscars".

What does "Oscar" stand for?

MARGARET HERRICK, FILM HISTORY TRAILBLAZER(开拓者)

As one of the most-watched award ceremonies in the world, the "Oscars" has a history of almost 100 years. Here are some remarkable moments from its long history.

In 1927, the academy was established to promote the film industry.

Two years later, the first ceremony was held at a hotel with 270 attendees (参加者).

The Oscars was first televised in the US in 1953 and telecasted in color over a decade later.

Since 1969, they have been broadcasted and televised internationally.

By the late 20th century, the Oscars viewership hit high records. As in 1998, 55 million international viewers watched the presentation night.

In the 92nd ceremony, *Parasite* (《寄生虫》), a South Korean film, made Oscars history by becoming the first foreign film to win Best Picture.

At the end of 2020, the first officially built museum, Academy's Museum of Motion Pictures, opened to the world.

Remarkable moments in the history of Oscars

1966
Telecasted in color

1953
1st televised Oscars

1929
1st Academy Award ceremony

1966
Televised internationally

1927
Birth of the academy

By the late 20th century
Oscars viewership hit new high.

2020
"Parasite" made Oscars history.

2020
The Academy's Museum of Motion pictures opened to the world.

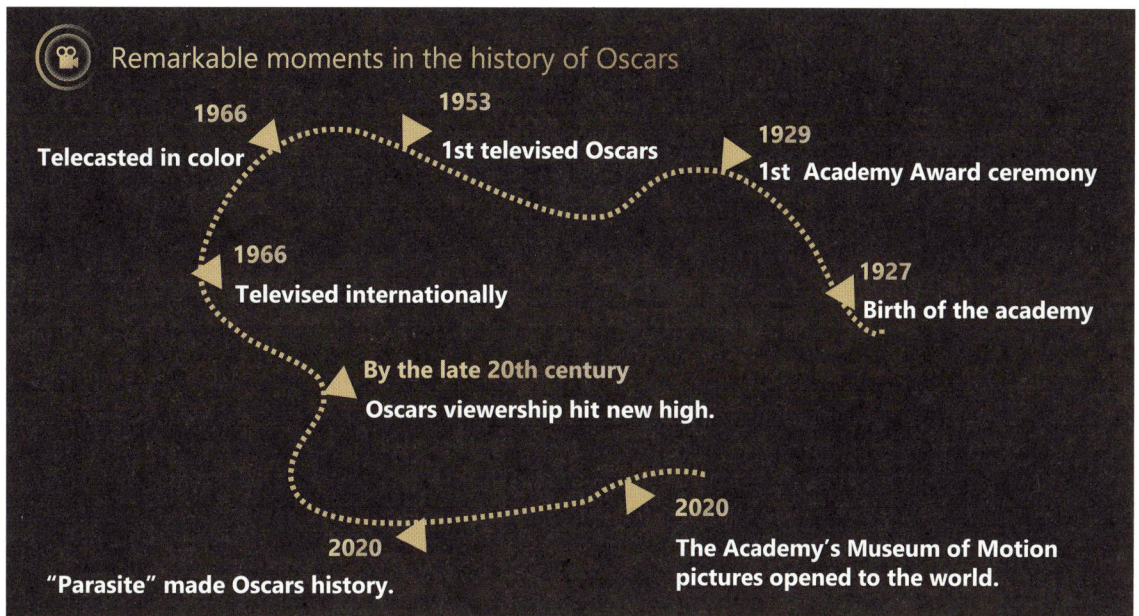

As we are told in the passage, the academy (AMPAS) with about 8,000 members is responsible to vote for the Oscars winners. But how?

Frist, vote for the nominations (提名)! Members of the Academy, in 17 branches, vote for candidates in 24 categories. The nominees (被提名者) in each category are chosen by the members of a corresponding branch, but the nominees for *best picture* are voted by the entire membership.

Second, vote for the winners! The second stage of voting calls for all active or lifetime academy members to cast ballots (投票). The voting process involves several complicated

Before the ceremony

Vote for the Winners!
All active or lifetime members will cast ballots.

Vote for the Nominations!
AMPAS
8,000 members
17 branches
24 awards categories

Keep them Secret!
Two PWC accountants
Memorize the names
Stuff two sets of envelopes
Store in two briefcases

rounds (几轮) called the preferential voting system (优先级投票制).

Third, keep them secret! The winners are finally determined, but the results are only known by two accountants from PWC (普华永道). They memorize the names of the winners, write them down on two sets of envelopes, and store in two briefcases until the night when the presenters (颁奖人) open an envelope and say : "And the Oscar goes to..."

Eventually, we turn our attention to the exciting night.

Our favorite A-list (一线的、最重要的) nominees will be in attendance, in the hope of taking home one of the golden statuettes. The star-studded (明星荟萃) Red Carpet show, humorous openings given by notable hosts, impressive encouragements from presenters (颁奖人), powerful or touching acceptance speeches (获奖感言) from winners are all the highlights of the amazing night.

During the ceremony

The star-studded Red Carpet show

Humorous openings giving by hosts

Impressive encouragements from presenters

Powerful or touching acceptance speeches from winners

After the ceremony, winners' fame is booming. The awards can significantly increase the box office earnings of the winning film. For actors, directors or producers, the awards often result in higher salaries, increased media attention, and better film offers.

After the ceremony

BEST PICTURE OSCAR WINNERS
BOX OFFICE REACTION

YEAR	OSCAR WINNER	% GROSS AFTER WIN	% OF GROSS AFTER NOMINATION
2019	Green Book	18.1%	50%
2018	The Shape of Water	9.8%	52%
2017	Moonlight	20.6%	43%
2016	Spotlight	13.2%	36%
2015	Birdman	10.8%	37%
2014	12 Years A Slave	11.2%	27%
2013	Argo	4.7%	19%

Increased box office (earnings)

Higher salaries

Increased media attention

Better film offers

↳ 6. Questions for Discussion

1) Do you know the history of the Oscars? Can you briefly introduce it?

2) Division and combination are two frequently used translation methods. While translating from English to Chinese, which method is likely to be used more? And why?

II The Grammy Awards

1. Cultural Background

The Grammy Awards, or Grammy Awards, are organized by the Academy of Recording Arts and Sciences of the National Academy of Sciences in the United States. The Grammy Awards, along with the Academy Awards, the Emmy Awards and the Tony Awards, are the top four **entertainment**[1] awards in the United States.

The Grammys cover pop, rock, R&B, rap, country, Gospel, jazz, Latin, classical and other music **genres**[2], and are voted on by professionals to **determine**[3] winners. The most important Grammys go to the four broad **categories**[4]: Album of the Year, Record of the Year, Song of the Year and Best New Artist.

The **trophy**[5] for the Grammy is a small gold-plated figure of a **phonograph**[6] designed by Billings Crafts, a company based in Colorado, US. In 1990, to strengthen the trophy and make it more **resistant**[7] to damage, the organizers increased the size of the trophy and changed the gold-plated material to an **alloy**[8]. In order to ensure fairness, the organizers also **stipulated**[9] that the award and name of the winner should be **engraved**[10] on the trophy only after the name of the winner has been announced.

Words and Expressions:

1 entertainment /ˌentərˈteɪnmənt/ n. 娱乐；娱乐活动；文娱节目

2 genre /ˈʒɑːnrə/ n.（文学、艺术、电影或音乐的）体裁；类型

3 determine /dɪˈtɜːrmɪn/ v. 决定；确定

4 category /ˈkætəgɔːri/ n.（人或事物的）类别；种类

5 trophy /ˈtroʊfi/ n.（颁发给竞赛获胜者的）奖品；奖杯；奖座

6 phonograph /ˈfoʊnəˌgræf/ n. 留声机；唱机

7 resistant /rɪˈzɪstənt/ adj. 抗……的；耐……的；抵抗的

8 alloy /ˈælɔɪ/ n. 合金

9 stipulate /ˈstɪpjuleɪt/ v. 规定；明确要求

10 engrave /ɪnˈɡreɪv/ v. 在……上雕刻（字或图案）

2. Translation Examples Explained

The following passage briefly introduces the history of the Grammys. Please pay attention to the three bold sentences for translation practice.

> ### A Short History of the Grammys
>
> ① *The Grammys, or the Grammy Awards, presented annually by the National Academy of Recording Arts and Sciences (美国国家录音科学艺术协会), are considered the most prestigious awards in the music industry.*
>
> The awards had their origin in the Hollywood Walk of Fame project (好莱坞星光大道项目) in the 1950s. ② *When the recording executives chosen for the Walk of Fame committee were compiling (汇 编) a list of important recording industry people who might qualify for a Walk of Fame star, they realized there were many more people who were leaders in their business who would never earn a star on Hollywood Boulevard (好莱坞大道).* ③ *The music executives decided to rectify (改正) this by creating an award given by their industry similar to the Oscars and the Emmys to acknowledge the most talented music professionals.* This marked the beginning of the Grammys.
>
> The Grammy Awards were originally known as the Gramophone awards, which was shortened over time to "the Grammys".

① The Grammys, or the Grammy Awards, presented annually by the National Academy of Recording Arts and Sciences, are considered the most prestigious awards in the music industry.

There are two translations for the first sentence. Which one do you think is better?

V1: 每年由美国国家录音科学艺术协会颁发的格莱美或格莱美奖被认为是音乐界最负盛誉的奖项。

V2: 格莱美又叫格莱美奖，每年由美国国家录音科学艺术协会颁发，被认为是音乐界最负盛誉的奖项。

Version 2 consists of three short verbal phrases, reading clearly and rhythmically in Chinese. In translating this sentence into Chinese, this translator separated the appositive (同位语的) and the participial (分词的) attributive phrases and turned them into several loosely-connected clauses, parallel to the main clause of this sentence:

This sample division illustrates that punctuation marks such as commas (逗号), colons (冒号), semicolons (分号), and dashes (破折号) that indicate a pause in a sentence are natural points for sentence division.

①　名词短语作同位语　　　　　　分词短语作定语

The Grammys, or the Grammy Awards, presented annually by the National Academy of Recording Arts and Sciences, are considered the most prestigious awards in the music industry.

The Grammys are also called the Grammy Awards. | They are presented annually by the National Academy of Recording Arts and Sciences. | They are considered the most prestigious awards in the music industry.

♪ 格莱美又叫格莱美奖，每年由美国国家录音科学艺术协会颁发，被认为是音乐界最负盛誉的奖项。

For example, in this sentence, the three commas, which set off the two parenthetic elements (插入成分) — the appositive and the participial phrases — suggest three possible dividing points.

In translating this sentence, an important method in E-C translation was involved, which was "division." And this method is especially useful when we cope with long English sentences.

② When the recording executives chosen for the Walk of Fame committee were compiling a list of important recording industry people who might qualify for a Walk of Fame star, they realized there were many more people who were leaders in their business who would never earn a star on Hollywood Boulevard.

Take the second sentence as an example. This sentence is very long, consisting of 52 words. A thorough analysis of and sentence structure tells that it is a complex sentence (复杂句), with a main clause and an adverbial clause of time separated by a comma. Although it is a long sentence, the main sentence structure is quite simple, i.e. "They realized something."

② When the recording executives chosen for the Walk of Fame committee were compiling a list of important recording industry people who might qualify for

宾语从句　　　　　　　　　　　定语从句
a Walk of Fame star, they realized there were many more people who were

定语从句
leaders in their business who would never earn a star on Hollywood Boulevard.

△

The object is made up of three clauses: the object clause (宾语从句) includes two who-clauses that respectively modifies "people" and "leaders".

As to the time clause led by "when", its core parts are "Executives were compiling list".

分词短语作定语

2. When the recording executives chosen for the Walk of Fame committee were

介词短语作定语　　　　　　　定语从句

compiling a list of important recording industry people who might qualify for

a Walk of Fame star, they realized there were many more people who were

leaders in their business who would never earn a star on Hollywood Boulevard.

Among other additional elements, the past-participial phrase (过去分词短语) modifies "executives", and the long prepositional phrase modifies "list", in which the who-clause modifies "people".

To translate this long sentence, we can use the method of division, dividing the English original into smaller segments (分段) and then upshifting those segments into several running clauses:

② When the recording executives chosen for the Walk of Fame committee were compiling a list‖of important recording industry people who might qualify for a Walk of Fame star,‖they realized there were many more people ‖who were leaders in their business‖who would never earn a star on Hollywood Boulevard.

♪ At that time, the recoding executive chosen for the Walk of Fame committee were compiling a list. | This list included important recording industry people who might qualify for a Walk of Fame star. | When doing so, the executives realized there were many more people. | Those people were leaders in their business. | They hose leaders would never earn a star on Hollywood Boulevard.

Then, the translation can be as follows:

当时，入选星光大道组委会的唱片公司主管正在汇编名单，列出唱片行业可能有资格获得星光大道之星的重量级人物。汇编时，这些主管意识到还有更多人虽是自己行业的领军人物，却可能永远无法在好莱坞大道上留下星星。

This translation reads natural. It clearly reproduces the meaning of the original sentence. This sample division also suggests that subordinate clauses (从句) can be the first consideration when we divide a sentence. Accordingly, words such as conjunctions and relative pronouns always merit our attention. In this sentence, the conjunction (连词) "when" and the pronoun (代词) "who" are good examples.

Apart from that, phrases, especially when used as postpositive attributes, can also be separated from the elements they modify. For example, the prepositional phrase introduced by "of" was translated as an independent clause.

However, if you are a careful reader, you may find that the attributive clause "who might qualify for a Walk of Fame star" and the participial phrase "chosen for the Walk of Fame Committee" were not set off in translation. Why? Because there is always more than one way to divide and translate a single sentence. Where to separate should always depend on the specific situation.

③ The music executives decided to rectify this by creating an award given by their industry similar to the Oscars and the Emmys to acknowledge the most talented music professionals.

Now, try to use what we have just learned to divide this sentence into parts, translate each part one by one, and combine them into a fluent Chinese translation.With the knowledge of sentence division, we can split the original sentence into three segments:

③ The music executives decided to rectify this | by creating an award | **介词短语** given by **分词短语** their industry | similar to the Oscars and the Emmys | **形容词短语** to acknowledge the **不定式短语** most talented music professionals.

The music executives decided to rectify this. | They decided to create an award similar to the Oscars and the Emmys. |The award would be given by their industry. | This award would be presented to acknowledge the most talented music professionals.

Then, those segments were translated one by one into Chinese: "这些音乐主管决定弥补这一缺憾，成立一个类似于奥斯卡和艾米奖的奖项，由各自己的行业颁发，用以褒奖最具天赋的音乐从业人员".

Likewise, this sample division seems to reinforce phrases that can be separated and upshifted as independent clauses, especially when acting as postpositive attributes or adverbials.

↳ 3. Parallel Texts

The following are the original and the translated texts in comparison. Please read them carefully and think about the use of division method in translation.

A Short History of the Grammys

The Grammys, or the Grammy Awards, presented annually by the National Academy of Recording Arts and Sciences (美国国家录音科学艺术协会), are considered the most prestigious awards in the music industry.

The awards had their origin in the Hollywood Walk of Fame project (好莱坞星光大道项目) in the 1950s. When the recording executives chosen for the Walk of Fame committee were compiling (汇编) a list of important recording industry people who might qualify for a Walk of Fame star, they realized there were many more people who were leaders in their business who would never earn a star on Hollywood Boulevard (好莱坞大道). The music executives decided to rectify (改正) this by creating an award given by their industry similar to the Oscars and the Emmys to acknowledge the most talented music professionals. This marked the beginning of the Grammys.

The Grammy Awards were originally known as the Gramophone Awards, which was shortened over time to "the Grammys".

格莱美简史

格莱美又称格莱美奖，每年由美国国家录音科学艺术协会颁发，被认为是音乐界最负盛誉的奖项。

当时，入选星光大道组委会的唱片公司主管正在汇编名单，列出唱片行业可能有资格获得星光大道之星的重量级人物。汇编时，这些主管意识到还有更多人虽是自己行业的领军人物，却可能永远无法在好莱坞大道上获得一颗星星。这些主管决定弥补这一缺憾，成立一个类似于奥斯卡和艾米奖的奖项，由各自的行业颁发，用以褒奖最具天赋的音乐从业人员。格莱美就这样诞生了。

格莱美奖最初叫留声机奖，随着时间的推移，其名简化为如今的"格莱美"。

4. Translation Skills Summarized

In this section, we have learned the translation method of "division". This method often involves separating parts of a sentence, such as words, phrases, or clauses and translating as if those separated parts are independent clauses or sentences.

Accordingly, "division" is often used with another translation method "adjusting linguistic ranks" to upshift linguistic elements of lower levels to higher levels. This method will be explained in the next unit.

As the examples illustrated earlier, "division" is such an important method that every translator must acquire it. The reason can be traced back to the differences in sentence structures between English and Chinese.

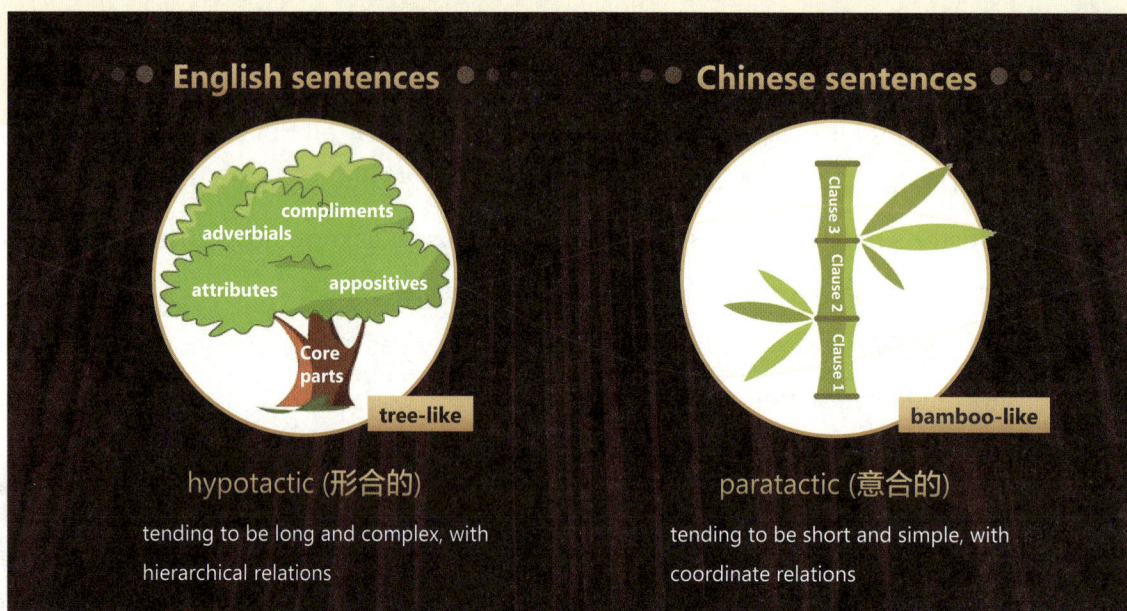

English is a tree-like, hypotactic (形合的) language. English sentences are often joined by connectives (连接词). Through those connectives, new elements can be added onto the core parts of a sentence layer by layer (一层一层地). This enables a sentence to expand, but it often creates long and complex sentences that are difficult to translate.

In contrast, Chinese is a bamboo-like, paratactic (意合的) language. Chinese sentences are often made up of phrases and short verbal clauses, usually placed one after another in a running sequence, without connecting words.

Therefore, when translating an English sentence, especially a long and complex one, we often need to convert its hypotactic structures into paratactic ones, following the Chinese sentence structure.

To use this method efficiently, we can take the following steps:

Tips for Efficient Sentence Division

- Identify the core sentence parts and the additional sentence elements;

- Clarify the relation between different sentence elements;

- Divide the sentence into smaller parts;

- Reconstruct the separated parts and translate them into Chinese one by one.

5. Cultural Expressions

The Grammy Awards is considered one of the four major annual American entertainment awards along with the Academy Awards, the Emmy Awards, and the Tony Awards.

The four major annual American entertainment awards

The Grammy Awards
格莱美奖
(music)

The Academy Awards
学院奖(奥斯卡金像奖)
(film)

The Emmy Awards
艾美奖
(television)

The Tony Awards
托尼奖
(theater and broadway)

The Grammy Awards are awarded in a series of categories. Each category recognizes a specific contribution to the recording industry.

The Grammy Categories

Pop 流行音乐

Rock 摇滚乐

Alternative 另类音乐

R&B 节奏布鲁斯

Dance/Electronic 舞曲/电子乐

Rap 说唱音乐

Traditional 传统音乐

Jazz 爵士音乐

Country 乡村音乐

Latin 拉丁音乐

Contemporary 现代音乐

New Age 新世纪

...

The "Big Four (四大)" in the General Field

Album of the Year
年度专辑奖

Record of the Year
年度制作奖

Song of the Year
年度歌曲奖

Best New Artist
最佳新人奖

Among those categories, the unchanged and the most coveted are the "Big Four," the four categories that make the General Field: "Record of the Year", "Song of the Year", "Album of the Year" and "Best New Artist". The four categories do not restrict nominees by genre or some other standards.

"Album of the Year (年度专辑奖)" is awarded to the performer, the songwriter(s), and the production team of a whole album.

"Record of the Year (年度制作奖)" is awarded to the performer and the production team of a single song.

"Song of the Year (年度歌曲奖)" is awarded to the songwriter(s) of a single song.

"Best New Artist (年度新人奖)" is awarded to an artist, who, according to the website of the Grammys, "during the eligibility year, releases the recording that first establishes the public identity of that artist," although this recording may not be the first album of that artist.

The winners of the Big Four will be announced in February during the television broadcast.

For many a musician, to win a Grammy award is the highest honor for their achievements in the music industry. If you were an artist and you wanted to bring a Grammy Trophy back home next year, what should you do?

First, submission. To qualify for the submission, make sure that you have commercially released albums on physical or online stores between the eligible time period. Then you need to ask the Academy members or your record company to submit your music or music videos to the Recording Academy for consideration.

After the submission, you will have to go through several stages similar to those of the Oscars: screening, a stage to make sure your submission is eligible, meets the qualifications, and has been placed in the proper nomination category, the first-round voting for nominations, the final voting.

The final results remain unknown until the Grammy Awards presentation. If you have survived all the previous stages, it is very likely that your name will be in one of the sealed envelopes and will be announced in the live show.

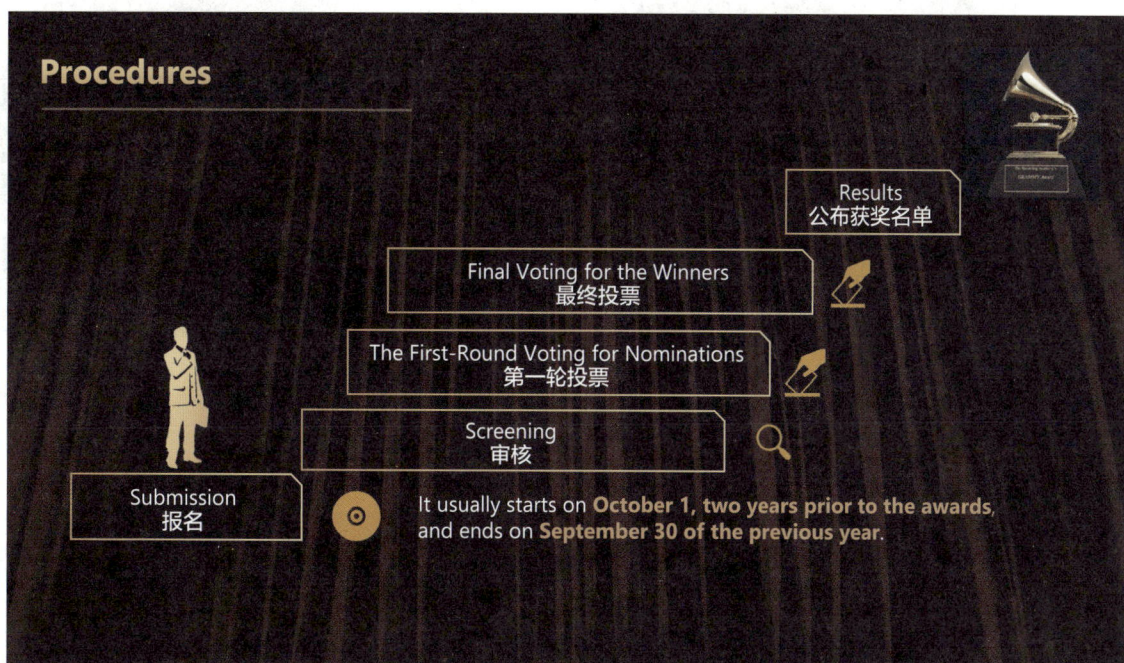

Procedures

Results
公布获奖名单

Final Voting for the Winners
最终投票

The First-Round Voting for Nominations
第一轮投票

Screening
审核

Submission
报名

It usually starts on **October 1, two years prior to the awards**, and ends on **September 30 of the previous year.**

There are also some facts you may not know about the Grammys.

Fact 1. Since the Grammy Awards include too many categories, only 30 percent of the awards are presented during the live show. The remaining 70 percent are awarded in the afternoon before the televised presentation.

Fun Facts about the Grammys

30 / 70 ■ televised

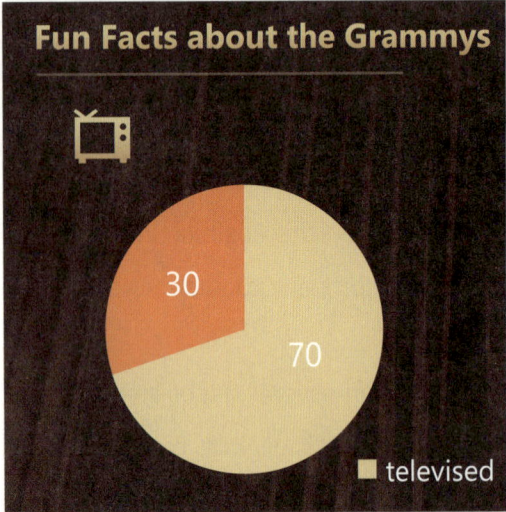

Fact 2. The Gramophone Awards was not actually the first name considered for the awards. One working name was the Eddie, to honor the inventor of the phonograph (蜡筒式留声机), Thomas Edison. But later, the National Academy of Recording Arts and Sciences decided to use the name of the invention of Emile Berliner, the gramophone (唱盘式留声机), and the Grammy Awards Trophy is also fashioned after (依照) the gramophone.

Fact 2: The Gramophone Awards was not actually the first name considered for the awards.

Thomas Edison and his phonography
(蜡筒式留声机)

Emile Berliner and his gramophone
(唱片式留声机)

Fact 3. As of 2024, Billie Eilish and Christopher Cross are among the few artists who have won all four of the General Field awards in a single ceremony.

Fact 3: As of 2024, Billie Eilish and Christopher Cross are among the few artists who have won all four of the General Field awards in a single ceremony.

Billie Eilish (2020)   Christopher Cross (1981)

Given its prestigious status in the entertainment industry, the Grammys, like the Oscars, have received criticism from artists and journalists. They have been constantly accused of paying too much attention to mainstream music and artists who are commercially successful. They are also criticized for setting up more awards than needed, which makes the ceremony merely a self-celebrating event to the industry.

Despite all those criticisms, the Grammys are still one of the most attractive music events. After all, the ever-changing nature of their categories is a proof of their efforts to adjust to the change of music trend and their respect for each music genre.

6. Questions for Discussion

1) Do you know any Chinese who have won Grammy Awards?
2) In the process of translating English into Chinese, why do we use "division" frequently? Can you give some examples?

III The Beatles

1. Cultural Background

The Beatles were a British rock band, formed by John Lennon, Ringo Starr, Paul McCartney and George Harrison. They were a group of musicians and songwriters. Formed in 1960 in Liverpool, England, the band's musical style is derived from 1950s rock music, and pioneered **psychedelic**[1] rock, pop rock and other styles.

The Beatles are a **legendary**[2] band. From its founding to its **disbanding**[3], they only **existed**[4] for a **decade**[5], but as revolutionaries of music culture, their cultural influence has already **exceeded**[6] their art itself. Their songs have influenced a generation's artistic taste, clothing and hairstyle, lifestyle and attitude towards life. In the 1960s, they not only set off the worldwide "**Beatlemania**[7]", but also influenced the music and ideas of rock bands from the 1960s onwards, and directly influenced the revolution of rock and roll.

The Beatles are more than just a band. They are a cultural heritage of a city, a global cultural phenomenon, and a pop music business model. As a global idol, The Beatles' influence is not limited to their music works. Their **personality**[8] **charm**[9] and behavior can affect the **nerves**[10] of the public. The Beatles not only shaped the world view of rock, they also defined what **mainstream**[11] rock would look like and what rock stars would look like.

Words and Expressions:

1 psychedelic /ˌsaɪkəˈdelɪk/ *adj.* 产生迷幻效果的

2 legendary /ˈledʒənderi/ *adj.* 传奇的；非常著名的；享有盛名的

3 disband /dɪsˈbænd/ *v.* 解散；解体

4 exist /ɪgˈzɪst/ *v.* 存在

5 decade /ˈdekeɪd/ *n.* 十年

6 exceed /ɪkˈsiːd/ *v.* 超越（法律、命令等）的限制；超过

7 Beatlemania /ˌbiːtlˈmeɪniə/ *n.* 披头士狂热

8 personality /ˌpɜːrsəˈnæləti/ *n.* 性格；个性；人格

9 charm /tʃɑːrm/ *n.* 魅力；吸引力

10 nerve /nɜːrv/ *n.* 神经

11 mainstream /ˈmeɪnstriːm/ *adj.* 主流的；主要倾向的

2. Translation Examples Explained

Here is a short passage about the Beatles. Read it and pay attention to the five examples in bold.

The Beatles, the most famous English rock band of the 20th century, are widely recognized as the most commercially successful band in the history of pop music.

①The Beatles in the 60's expressed their opinions of this world through their unique way of rock and roll. They created a miracle in pop music and influenced music appreciation tastes of a generation in Europe and America. ②The Beatles—with their buoyant spirits, their bottomless charm, their irrepressible wit and talent—could probably have boosted the mirth quotient at a clown convention.

Being the cultural revolutionaries of music that they were, the Beatles still hold the record for the best-selling album around the world. ③According to the RIAA (美国唱片工业协会), the Beatles have sold more albums in the United States than any other artist, selling over 170 million copies. It is believed that their global sales have exceed 1 billion. ④As far as their music influence is concerned, we can say the Beatles are unparalleled. ⑤They have changed the aesthetics of rock and pop music in the world. And they also changed almost all other music styles as well.

> ① The Beatles in the 60's expressed their opinions of this world through their unique way of rock and roll. They created a miracle in pop music and influenced music appreciation tastes of a generation in Europe and America.

Let us look at the first one. There are two sentences in this example.

Take a close look at the second sentence, and we will find the pronoun "they" refers back to "the Beatles" in the first sentence. That is, these two sentences have the same subject. The same subject is followed by three verbal phrases or clauses in the two sentences. If we translate them as they are in the English structure, the Chinese translation would consist of three loosely connected clauses in two sentences as follows. It reads choppy (支离破碎的). Each of the clauses is too short in Chinese.

T1: 20 世纪 60 年代的披头士就以他们独特的摇滚乐表达了对世界的看法。他们创造了流行乐坛的摇滚奇迹，左右了整整一代欧美青年的欣赏品味。

Instead, if we combine them into one Chinese sentence with three running clauses in sequence, the whole translation is more unified with three closely connected clauses. At the same time, there is no need to repeat the subject.The translation can go as follows:

T2: 20 世纪 60 年代的披头士就以他们独特的摇滚乐表达了对世界的看法，创造了流行乐坛的摇滚奇迹，左右了整整一代欧美青年的欣赏品味。

Compared with the first translation, the second translation expresses a more unified idea with three paralleling verbal phrases, reading concisely, forcefully and rhythmically. We can say that, with the use of the "combination" method, the second translation sounds better in Chinese.

This example tells us that if we have two short sentences that share the same subject, it may be a good option to combine them into one sentence, getting a compact and concise translation that expresses a more unified idea.

② The Beatles — with their buoyant spirits, their bottomless charm, their irrepressible wit and talent — could probably have boosted the mirth quotient at a clown convention.

When you read it, please focus your attention on the three juxtaposed phrases "their buoyant spirits", "their bottomless charm", "their irrepressible wit and talent". If we follow the original structure and translate them into Chinese, the three phrases do not make a perfect parallel structure as in Translation 1.

T1: 甲壳虫乐队似乎用他们快乐的精神、无穷的魅力、不可抗拒的才能和天赋，以类似滑稽演员的方式大大提高了人们的欣赏力。

What exactly causes this problem? On a close examination, we may find that among the three phrases the third one is more complex in that it has two nouns connected by the word "and". The word "wit" means "智慧" and the word "talent" means "才能". Instead of translating them into two separate Chinese words, we can easily combine them and translate them into one short Chinese word "才智" as in the second translation:

T2: 现在回想起来，披头士乐队用他们快乐的精神、无穷的魅力和非凡的才智，使人们的快乐指数像参加小丑大会一样高涨。

③ According to the RIAA (美国唱片工业协会), the Beatles have sold more albums in the United States than any other artist, selling over 170 million copies. It is believed that their global sales have exceed 1 billion.

Here is the third example, which contains two sentences. To translate it, you can remain the syntactic feature of the original text, with the second sentences loosely tagging along after the first one:

T1: 据美国唱片工业协会统计，披头士是在美国国内销量最高的音乐人，总销量 1.7 亿。据信他们的全球销量已超过 10 亿。

However, as we can see, the two figures 170 million and 1 billion in each sentence are related to the same issue, that is, the sales volume of the Beatles, one in the US and the other in the world. Because the second sentence is very short, we can merge it into the first one.

After combining them, we can get one compact sentence, talking about sales volumes with two contrasting figures:

T2: 据美国唱片工业协会统计，披头士是美国国内专辑销量最高的音乐人，总销量达 1.7 亿张，全球销量超过 10 亿张。

This translation is more concise and natural, conforming to Chinese syntax in which a sentence often contains loose clauses about a single topic.

④ As far as their music influence is concerned, we can say the Beatles are unparalleled.

This is a complex sentence, with one adverbial clause (状语从句) and one main clause. We can condense the two clauses into a single one by turning the adverbial clause into a noun phrase to act as the subject. After doing that, we get a simpler and shorter sentence to express the same idea briefly and clearly. The translation could be: 可以说，披头士的音乐影响力无人可及 .

⑤ They have changed the aesthetics of rock and pop music in the world. And they also changed almost all other music styles as well.

To translate the fifth example, we can still consider using the combination method, since the two sentences share the same subject "they." When translating, we only need to use the same subject once with the conjunctive pair " 不但……而且…… " to indicate the coordinating relationship between the two sentences in the original text. Then, we get the translation:

他们不但改变了全世界对摇滚乐和流行乐的审美品味，而且几乎改变了所有其他音乐风格。

This translation expresses the ideas and the syntactic relationship between them in a tighter, more unified and concise way.

Let us make a brief conclusion here. When there are two coordinating clauses with the same subject, we can combine them to get a more compact and concise version of translation.

Here is the original and the translated texts in comparison. Read them closely and reflect on the translation method of combination used.

The Beatles

The Beatles, the most famous English rock band of the 20th century, are widely recognized as the most commercially successful band in the history of pop music. ① **The Beatles in the 60's expressed their opinions of this world through their unique way of rock and roll. They created a miracle in pop music and influenced music appreciation tastes of a generation in Europe and America.** ② **The Beatles — with their buoyant spirits, their bottomless charm, their irrepressible wit and talent — could probably have boosted the mirth quotient at a clown convention.**

Still hold the record for the best-selling album around the world. ③ **According to the RIAA** (美国唱片工业协会), **the Beatles have sold more albums in the United States than any other artist, selling over 170 million copies. It is believed that their global sales have exceed 1 billion.** ④ **As far as their music influence is concerned, we can say the Beatles are unparalleled.** ⑤ **They have changed the aesthetics of rock and pop music in the world. And they also changed almost all other music styles as well.**

披头士

披头士是英国 20 世纪最著名的摇滚乐队，也被公认为是全球商业上最成功的乐队。①**在 20 世纪 60 年代，披头士就以他们独特的摇滚音乐表达了对世界的看法，创造了流行乐坛的摇滚奇迹，影响了整整一代欧美青年的欣赏趣味。**②**披头士用他们快乐的精神、无穷的魅力和非凡的才智，使人们的快乐指数像参加小丑大会一样高涨。**

作为一个音乐文化的革命者，披头士乐队拥有最高的唱片销售记录。③**据美国唱片工业协会统计，披头士是美国国内专辑销量最高的音乐人，总销量达 1.7 亿张，全球销量超过 10 亿张。**④**可以说，披头士的音乐影响力无人可及。**⑤**他们不但改变了全世界范围对摇滚乐和流行乐的审美品味，而且几乎改变了所有其他音乐风格。**

4. Translation Skills Summarized

To sum up, the method of combination is considered usually in the following three situations.

Firstly, we combine the neighboring words and phrases into one in order to achieve expressive conciseness, structural balance and neat antithesis (工整对仗).

Secondly, we combine the main clause and the subordinate clause from one complex sentence to make the translation version clearly and briefly.

Finally, we combine two independent sentences when necessary. The method of combination can be used not only in the process of translating two simple sentences with the same subject but the neighboring simple sentences with close meanings as well.

合译		
合译词组	合译小句	合译句子
合译相邻词组和短语以使译文凝炼隽永、工整对仗、结构平衡	复合句中主句和从句根据逻辑关系可采用合译	具有相同的主语的两个简单句，可以考虑采用合译 两个相邻简短句，语义较紧密时可考虑合译

5. Cultural Expressions

The Beatles were an English rock band formed by John Lennon, Ringo Starr, Paul McCartney and George Harrison.

John Lennon   Paul McCartney   Ringo Starr   George Harrison

The Beatles were the first band to become a symbol of an era in the name of rock music. Their music embodies the true essence of rock and roll and defined a generation. As one of the most influential bands in the history of popular music, they have made great contributions to the development of rock and roll around the world. The band was only active for ten years, but their cultural influence has already exceeded their art itself. Their songs influenced the artistic taste, fashion, lifestyle and attitude of a generation. They enriched and developed rock music with the spirit of innovation, bringing rock music to another historical stage. Since then, rock music has been more than just entertainment.

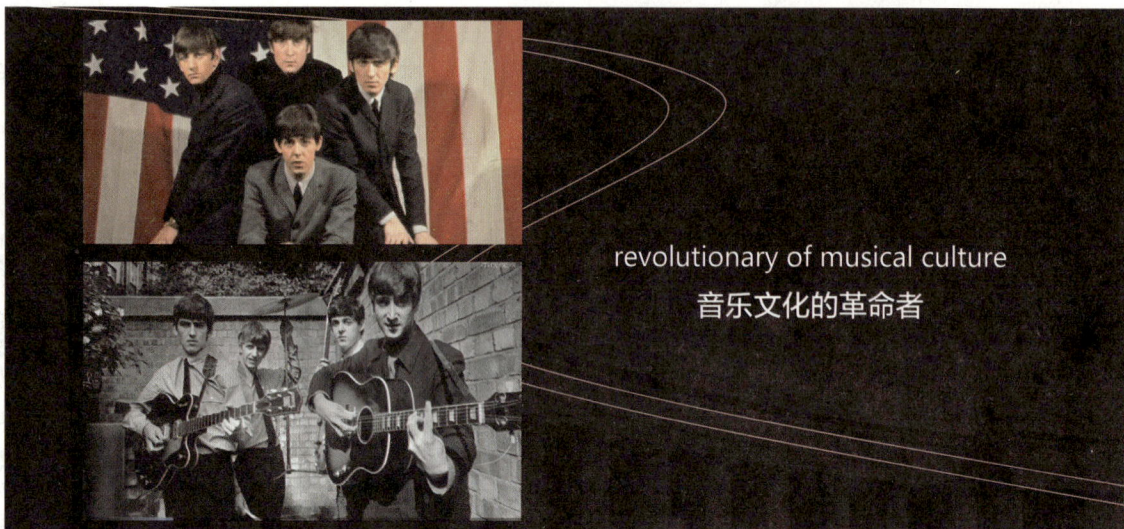

revolutionary of musical culture
音乐文化的革命者

The Beatles were more than just a band. They were the cultural heritage of a city, a global cultural phenomenon, and a business model for popular music. As a global icon, the Beatles' influence is not limited to their musical works, but their personalities and charm also won the public's hearts. The four members of the band had instinct personalities, clear division of labor and outstanding personality charm. The band's central figures, John Lennon and Paul McCartney, embraced the doctrine "with great power comes great responsibility". At their highest level, the Beatles not only shaped the world view of the rock scene, they also defined what mainstream rock would look like and what rock stars would do.

⌐→ 6. Questions for Discussion

1) Do you know the Beatles' music? Can you briefly introduce them?

2) In the process of translating English into Chinese, why do we need to use combination, and can you give some examples?

Ⅳ Exercises

Section A. True or false (5 items)

_____ 1) The Academy Awards ceremony is known as the Oscars, which is the oldest major award ceremony in the film industry in America.

_____ 2) The Beatles, the most famous English rock band of the 20th century, still holds the record for the best-selling album around the world.

_____ 3) English is a hypotactic (形合的) language, so there is no need for conjunctions between sentences.

_____ 4) The division method requires parts of a sentence such as words, phrases, clauses or sentences to be separated and translated respectively.

_____ 5) The Grammys, or the Grammy Awards, presented annually by the National Academy of Recording Arts and Sciences (美国国家录音科学艺术协会), are considered the most prestigious awards in the music industry.

Section B. Multiple choice (5 items)

_____ 1) But now it makes much more sense how she snagged a Grammy.

A. 不过现在更有意义，她如何获得格莱美奖。

B. 不过现在看来，她获得格莱美奖是情理之中的事。

C. 不过现在看来，她如何抓住格莱美奖更有意义。

_____ 2) As far as their music influence is concerned, we can say the Beatles are unparalleled.

A. 披头士乐队的音乐影响力可以说是无人可及。

B. 就他们的音乐影响力而言，我们可以说披头士是无人可及的。

C. 就他们的音乐影响力而言，我们可以说披头士无人可及。

_____ 3) The Emmy Awards ceremony marks the opening of the new broadcasting season from September to April of the following year.

A. 艾美奖颁奖典礼为新一季电视剧的播放拉开序幕，播出季从每年9月持续到次年4月。

B. 艾美奖颁奖典礼为新一季电视剧播放拉开序幕，从每年9月到次年4月。

C. 艾美奖颁奖典礼为新一季从每年9月持续到次年4月的电视播出季拉开序幕。

_____ 4) The sitcom *Friends*, which has ended its 10-year run on TV, will be remembered as one of those rare shows that marked a change in American culture.

A. 已经在电视上结束了为期 10 年播放的情景喜剧《老友记》必将作为为数不多的标志着美国文化变迁的电视剧之一为人们所铭记。

B. 情景喜剧《老友记》已经结束了在电视上为期 10 年的播出，作为为数不多的标志着美国文化变迁的电视剧之一，必将为人们所铭记。

C. 情景喜剧《老友记》，在电视上为期 10 年播放已经被结束了，必将作为为数不多的标志着美国文化变迁的电视剧之一为人们所铭记。

_____ 5) *Downton Abbey* is a British period drama television series created by Julian Fellowes and coproduced by Carnival Films and Masterpiece.

A. 英国历史连续剧《唐顿庄园》由朱利安·费罗斯主创，嘉年华电影公司与精英娱乐公司共同出品。

B. 《唐顿庄园》是朱利安·费罗斯主创、嘉年华电影公司与精英娱乐公司共同出品的英国时期戏剧电视连续剧。

C. 《唐顿庄园》是朱利安·费罗斯主创、嘉年华电影公司与精英娱乐公司共同出品的英国历史戏剧电视连续剧。

Ⅴ Test

↳ Section A. Multiple choice (5 items*4 points=20 points)

_____ 1) They sat down in the waiting-room to do some reading. People came to and from there.

A. 他们在候车室坐下来看点书。人来人往，那里。

B. 他们在人来人往的候车室里坐下来看点书。

C. 他们在候车室坐下来看点书。人们从那儿来又到那里去。

_____ 2) The Grammy Awards are named for the trophy, which is a small and gilded gramophone statuette.

A. 格莱美奖是以纪念品命名的，一个小且镀金的留声机小雕像。

B. 格莱美奖是以奖杯命名的，这是一个小且镀金的留声机小雕像。

C. 格莱美奖是以一个镀金的留声机小雕像来命名的。

_____ 3) The formal ceremony, where the awards are presented, is one of the most prominent award ceremonies in the world.

A. 正式颁奖仪式是世界上最著名的颁奖典礼之一。

B. 正式仪式，就是颁发奖项的地方，是世界上著名的颁奖典礼之一。

C. 颁发奖项的正式仪式是世界上最突出的颁奖典礼之一。

_____ 4) The Beatles is a fairly legendary band. They created a new musical style and inspired a lot of new ideas in the form of pop music.

A. 披头士乐队是一支相当传奇的乐队。他们创造了一种新的音乐风格，激发了许多新的思想，以流行音乐的形式。

B. 披头士乐队是一支相当传奇的乐队。他们创造了一种新的音乐风格，以流行音乐的形式，激发了许多新的思想。

C. 披头士乐队是一支相当传奇的乐队，开创了一种新的音乐风格，用流行音乐激发了许多新思想。

_____ 5) Elizabeth was determined to make no effort for conversation with a woman who was now more than usually insolent and disagreeable.

A. 伊丽莎白决心不费吹灰之力与一个比平时更傲慢无礼的女人交谈。

B. 伊丽莎白不肯再费力气和这样一个女人交谈，她现在异常无礼，非常令人反感。

C. 伊丽莎白决定不再和这样一个女人说话，这个女人现在异常无礼，非常令人反感。

Section B. Sentence translation (5 items*6 points=30 points)

1) As one of the most prominent and glittering award ceremonies in the world, the Academy Awards ceremony, more popularly known as the Oscars, is televised live to more than one billion viewers in about 200 countries each spring.

2) Every year since 1929, the big names and shining stars have gathered annually in Hollywood for a lavish evening of celebration and recognition of excellence in cinematic achievements.

3) When the recording executives chosen for the Walk of Fame committee were compiling a list of important recording industry people who might qualify for a Walk of Fame star, they realized there were many more people who were leaders in their business who would never earn a star on Hollywood Boulevard.

4) The Beatles— with their buoyant spirits, their bottomless charm, their irrepressible wit and talent — could probably have boosted the mirth quotient at a clown convention.

5) They have changed the aesthetics of rock and pop music in the world. And they also changed almost all other music styles as well.

Section C. Paragraph translation (50 points)

The Academy Awards ceremony is a glittering popular annual affair which is broadcasted to more than one billion viewers in about 100 countries each spring. Originally hosted by academy presidents, the ceremony soon came to be led by entertainers. The winners' names are announced by celebrities. They are kept in sealed envelopes until the event.

Unit 6

BRITISH AND AMERICAN LITERATURE

I Ernest Hemingway

When it comes to the heroic style in American literature, we cannot but come up with the works by Ernest Hemingway, one of the most influential American writers in the 20th century, whose life of adventures and public image influenced later generations. In this section, we are going to appreciate an excerpt from *The Old Man and the Sea* and learn the techniques of adjusting the linguistic ranks (调整语言层级) in E-C translation.

↳ 1. Cultural Background

Ernest Hemingway ranks as the most famous of twentieth-century American writers, like Mark Twain. Hemingway is one of those rare authors most people know about whether they have read him or not. The difference is that Twain, with his white suit, **ubiquitous**[1] cigar, and easy wit, survives in the public imagination as a basically, lovable figure, while the deeply imprinted image of Hemingway as **rugged**[2] and **macho**[3] has been much less **universally**[4] admired, for all his lame. Hemingway has been regarded less as a writer dedicated to his craft than as a man of action who happened to be afflicted with genius. When he won the Nobel Prize in 1954. *Time* magazine reported the news under Heroes rather than Books and went on to describe the author as "a globe-trotting expert on bullfights, booze, women, wars, big game hunting, deep sea fishing, and courage." Hemingway did in fact address all those subjects in his books, and he acquired his **expertise**[5] through well-reported acts of participation as well as of observation; by going to all the wars of his time, hunting and fishing for great beasts, marrying four times, **occasionally**[6] getting into fistfights, drinking too much, and becoming, in the end, a worldwide celebrity recognizable for his signature beard and challenging physical pursuits.

Words and Expressions:

1 ubiquitous /juːˈbɪkwɪtəs/ *adj.* 普遍存在的，无所不在的

2 rugged /ˈrʌɡɪd/ *adj.* 粗犷的；坚毅的

3 macho /ˈmɑtʃoʊ/ *adj.* 男子汉的

4 universally /ˌjuːnɪˈvɜːrsəli/ *adv.* 普遍地；一致地

5 expertise /ˌekspɜːrˈtiːz/ *n.* 专门知识 (或技能等)，专长

6 occasionally /əˈkeɪʒnəli/ *adv.* 偶然；偶尔；有时候

2. Translation Examples Explained

Please read this passage and focus on the bold parts.

> He was an old man who fished alone in a skiff in the Gulf Stream ①*and he had gone eighty-four days now without taking a fish*. In the first forty days a boy had been with him. ②*But after forty days without a fish the boy's parents had told him that the old man was now definitely and finally salao, which is the worst form of unlucky*, and the boy had gone at their orders in another boat which caught three good fish the first week. ③*It made the boy sad to see the old man come in each day with his skiff empty* and he always went down to help him carry either the coiled line or the gaff and harpoon and the sail that was furled around the mast. The sail was patched with flour sacks and, furled, it looked like the flag of permanent defeat.
>
> ④*The old man was thin and gaunt with deep wrinkles in the back of his neck.* ⑤*The brown blotches of the benevolent skin cancer the sun brings from its reflection on the tropic sea were on his cheeks.* The blotches ran well down the sides of his face and ⑥*his hands had the deep-creased scars from handling heavy fish on the cords*. But none of these scars were fresh. They were as old as erosions in a fishless desert.

---

① "... and he had gone eighty-four days now **without taking a fish**."

Since the prepositional phrases (介词短语) in English often serve to express the condensed meaning in the form of the clause while the Chinese language has verbs bound and tends to be more dynamic, we'd better adjust and expand the prepositional phrase to a clause. The prepositional phrase "without taking a fish" is upshifted (调高层级) to a clause in the Chinese translation. There we have "出海八十四天了，连一条鱼都没有捕到。"

---

② But after forty days without a fish the boy's parents had told him that the old man was now definitely and finally salao, **which is the worst form of unlucky**.

To achieve a more fluent and emphatic sentence to the Chinese readers, the attributive clause is downshifted (调低层级) to the four straight characters and forms a compact verbal phrase to function as the predicate. There we have "可是一连四十天都没捕到鱼后，孩子的父母就说，这老头倒了血霉，晦气透顶。"

③ It made the boy sad **to see the old man come in each day with his skiff empty**...

To clarify the cause of the feeling followed by the focus of information to come, the "to-infinitive" is separated and upshifted to a clause. The translation becomes "看着老人天天空船而归，孩子心里很难受。"

④ The old man was thin and gaunt **with deep wrinkles in the back of his neck**.

As we mentioned before, the prepositional phrase should be upshifted to a clause. In this way, we get a Chinese translation with two loosely connected short clauses – a style preferred by Chinese speakers. The translation becomes "老人瘦骨嶙峋，颈背上刻着深深的皱纹。"

⑤ The brown blotches of the benevolent skin cancer **the sun brings from its reflection on the tropic sea** were on his cheeks.

The attributive clause is separated from the modified noun "cancer". We should upshift the attributive clause to an independent clause in Chinese. Then, we get a translated sentence: "脸上留着良性皮肤肿瘤引起的褐色斑块，那是阳光在热带海面上的反射造成的。" The version has two loosely connected clauses, with a simpler sentence structure and a clearer expression of ideas to Chinese speakers.

⑥ ... and his hands had the deep-creased scars **from handling heavy fish on the cords**.

In this sentence, the word "scars" has two modifiers: one pre-modifier and one post-modifier. If we translate the two modifiers and places both of them before the noun "scars" according to the linguistic rules in Chinese (拉拽网上大鱼形成的深深的疤痕), the use of two long-modifiers in sequence makes Chinese speakers breathless and tongue-twisted.

Therefore, we should upshift one of the modifiers from a phrase to a clause. In this way, the complex meanings in the two modifiers are expressed clearly in two simple clauses. "双手因为拉拽钓线上的大鱼，镌刻下了很深的伤疤。" This version is clearer to Chinese speakers.

3. Parallel Texts

The following are the original text and its Chinese translation. Read them in comparison to see how the method of adjusting linguistic levels was strategically used in E-C translation.

An Excerpt from The Old Man and the Sea

He was an old man who fished alone in a skiff in the Gulf Stream and he had gone eighty-four days now **without taking a fish**. In the first forty days a boy had been with him. But after forty days without a fish the boy's parents had told him that the old man was now definitely and finally salao, **which is the worst form of unlucky**, and the boy had gone at their orders in another boat which caught three good fish the first week. It made the boy sad **to see the old man come in each day with his skiff empty** and he always went down to help him carry either the coiled line or the gaff and harpoon and the sail that was furled around the mast. The sail was patched with flour sacks and, furled, it looked like the flag of permanent defeat.

The old man was thin and gaunt **with deep wrinkles in the back of his neck**. The brown blotches of the benevolent skin cancer **the sun brings from its reflection on the tropic sea** were on his cheeks. The blotches ran well down the sides of his face and his hands had the deep-creased scars **from handling heavy fish on the cords**. But none of these scars were fresh. They were as old as erosions in a fishless desert.

《老人与海》选段

他是个老人，独自驾着一条小船，在墨西哥湾流捕鱼。出海八十四天了，**连一条鱼都没有捕到**。前四十天，还有个男孩跟着。可是一连四十天都没捕到鱼后，孩子的父母就说，**这老头倒了血霉，晦气透顶**。孩子听从吩咐，上了另一条船，第一个星期就捕到了三条好鱼。**看着老人天天空船而归**，孩子心里很难受。他常下岸去帮老人的忙，把成卷的钓线、或是手钩、鱼叉和缠在桅杆上的帆卸下船来。船帆用面粉袋打过补丁，卷起来时，活像是常败将军的旗帜。

老人瘦骨嶙峋，**颈背上刻着深深的皱纹**，脸上留着良性皮肤肿瘤引起的褐色斑块，那是**阳光在热带海面上的反射造成的**。褐斑布满了他的双颊，双手因为**拉拽钓线上的大鱼**，镌刻下了很深的伤疤。不过，没有一处伤疤是新的，每个伤疤都像无鱼可打的沙漠中被侵蚀的沙土一样古老。

4. Translation Skills Summarized

Let us summarize the translation skills in this section: the adjustment of linguistic levels. All the language units at different levels can be upshifted or downshifted in E-C translation if necessary.

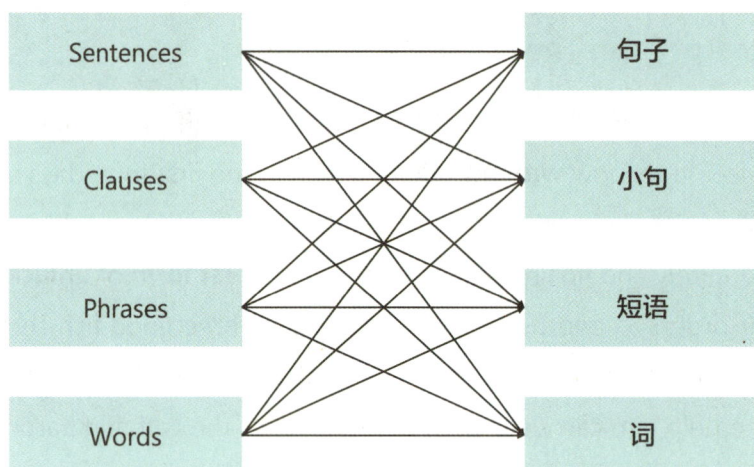

Sentences	句子
Clauses	小句
Phrases	短语
Words	词

The Cause of the Adjustment

Upshifting 上推	Downshifting 下移
To clarify the contextual meaning 赋予语境意义	To contract the structure 简约结构
To change the expressions rhetorically 修辞转换	To condense the meaning 锤炼语言

5. Cultural Expressions

1) Hemingway's Novels:

- *The Sun Also Rises*《太阳照常升起》(1926)
- *A Farewell to Arms*《永别了，武器》(1929)
- *For Whom the Bell Tolls*《丧钟为谁而鸣》(1940)
- *The Old Man and the Sea*《老人与海》(1953) (won a Pulitzer Prize (普利策奖) and the Nobel Prize in Literature)

The Sun Also Rises 《太阳照常升起》	*A Farewell to Arms* 《永别了，武器》	*For Whom the Bell Tolls* 《丧钟为谁而鸣》	*The Old Man and the Sea* 《老人与海》
1926	**1929**	**1940**	**1953**

 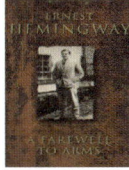 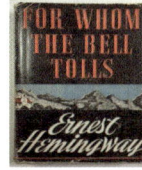 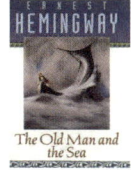

2) Hemingway Code Hero （硬汉形象）

- Enduring and overcoming some sort of physical or psychological wound before he can prove or re-prove his manhood;
- Facing death with dignity;
- Maintaining free-will and individualism.

3) Iceberg Style （冰山风格）

- Making readers feel the emotion of the characters directly;
- Avoiding any authorial comments;
- Avoiding conventionally emotive language;
- Employing a bare minimum of adjectives and adverbs.

↳ 6. Questions for Discussion

1) Can you give your examples of adjusting linguistic levels in E-C translation?

2) Why is Hemingway important to American literature?

II

Jane Austen

Have you noticed the lady featured on the British £10 note? Who is she? Yes, she is Jane Austen (简·奥斯汀), a very influential and brilliant English novelist (小说家). In this section, we're going to talk about Jane Austen, her life and works, and the translation method: adjusting the order of language elements (调整语序).

1. Cultural Background

It is a truth universally acknowledged that a single man in possession of a good fortune, must be in want of a wife.

However, little known the feelings or views of such a man may be on his first entering a neighborhood, this truth is so well fixed in the minds of the surrounding families, that he is considered as the rightful property of some one or other of their daughters.

"My dear Mr. Bennet," said his lady to him one day, "have you heard that Netherfield Park is let at last?"

Mr. Bennet replied that he had not.

"But it is," returned she; "for Mrs. Long has just been here, and she told me all about it."

Mr. Bennet made no answer.

"Do not you want to know who has taken it?" cried his wife impatiently.

"You want to tell me, and I have no objection to hearing it."

This was invitation enough.

"Why? my dear, you must know, Mrs. Long says that Netherfield is taken by a young man of large fortune from the north of England; that he came down on Monday in a chaise and four to see the place, and was so much delighted with it that he agreed with Mr. Morris immediately; that he is to take possession before Michaelmas, and some of his servants are to be in the house by the end of next week."

"What is his name?"

"Bingley."

"Is he married or single?"

"Oh! single, my dear, to be sure! A single man of large fortune; four or five thousand a year. What a fine thing for our girls!"

"How so? how can it affect them?"

"My dear Mr. Bennet," replied his wife, "how can you be so tiresome! You must know that I am thinking of his marrying one of them."

"Is that his design in settling here?"

"Design! nonsense, how can you talk so! But it is very likely that he may fall in love with one of them, and therefore you must visit him as soon as he comes."

"I see no occasion for that. You and the girls may go, or you may send them by themselves, which perhaps will be still better, for as you are as handsome as any of them, Mr. Bingley might like you the best of the party."

"My dear, you flatter me. I certainly have had my share of beauty, but I do not pretend to be anything extraordinary now. When a woman has five grown-up daughters, she ought to give over thinking of her own beauty."

"In such cases, a woman has not often much beauty to think of."

"But, my dear, you must indeed go and see Mr. Bingley when he comes into the neighborhood."

"It is more than I engage for, I assure you."

"But consider your daughters. Only think what an establishment it would be for one of them. Sir William and Lady Lucas are determined to go, merely on that account, for in general you know they visit no newcomers. Indeed you must go, for it will be impossible for us to visit him, if you do not."

Excerpt from Jane Austen, *Pride and Prejudice*, Oxford University Press, 2008

↳ 2. Translation Examples Explained

Please read this passage and think about how to rearrange (重新排列) the language elements in the numbered sentences in E-C translation.

①*Jane Austen (1775—1817) was born in Hampshire, a small town in southwest England.* *She was mostly tutored at home, but received a broader education than many women of her time.* ②*She developed powers of shrewd perceptiveness by her persistent reading and writing as well as her observation of social behaviors. Her reputation as one of the best English novelists depends upon six novels:* Sense and Sensibility, Pride and Prejudice, Mansfield Park, Emma, Persuasion, *and* Northanger Abbey. *Austen restricted the subject to a narrow range of society and events: a quiet, prosperous, middle-class circle in provincial surroundings, and her main literary concern was about human beings in their social relationships, especially in love and marriage.*

③*Everything of the novel was handled with extreme care, as if she was working on a fine engraving made upon a little piece of ivory.* ④*She was always able to find the precise expression that accurately fitted the character and the occasion.* Her wonderful skill in the treatment of humorous and a little satirical conversation helped a lot to reveal characters through their own words.

① Jane Austen (1775 — 1817) was born in **Hampshire, a small town in southwest England.**

The phrase, "a small town in southwest England", is in apposition (同位语) to "Hampshire". The appositive phrase provides extra information of the location without wrecking the sentence structure.

When translating the appositive into Chinese, there are two typical ways to place it. The first way is to keep the order and translate it as a Chinese appositive. Then we have "简·奥斯汀生于汉普郡，英国西南部小镇".

The second way is to swap (交换) the order of the noun and its appositive. In other words, the appositive phrase is put ahead of the noun, serving as a modifier to "Hampshire". Then we have a second version of translation: "简·奥斯汀生于英国西南部小镇汉普郡".

Then please look at the phrase, "a small town in southwest England". The word "town" is the head noun. There is one adjective word "small" before the word "town", and one prepositional phrase "in southwest England" after it. In English, attributive words or phrases can be placed before or after the noun, while in Chinese those are usually put in front of the noun. Meanwhile, when speaking of places, English prefers the order from the smaller one to the bigger one, such as "southwest England" here. In contrast, Chinese prefers to speak the bigger one before the smaller one. Thus, "southwest" and "England" are swapped and translated to "英国西南部" in Chinese.

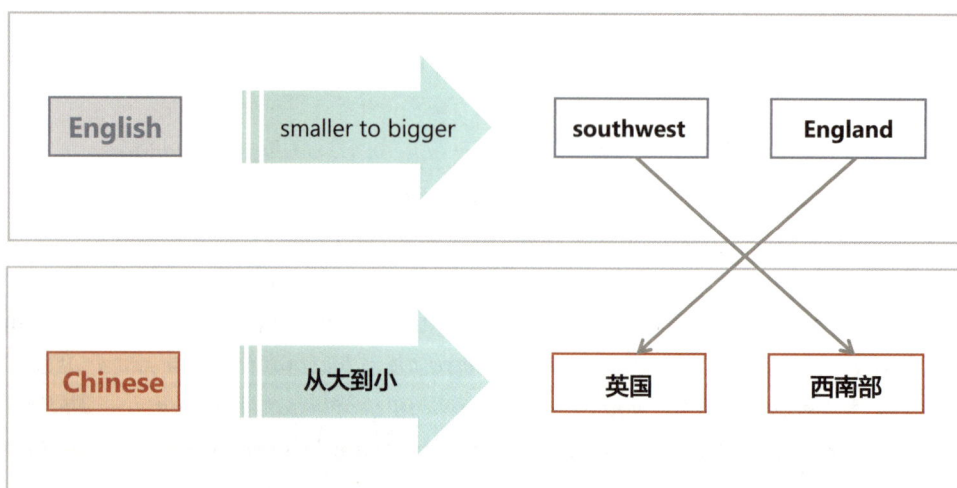

② She developed powers of shrewd perceptiveness **by her persistent reading and writing as well as her observation of social behaviors.**

There is a long adverbial, a prepositional phrase (介词词组), placed after the sentence core. If we keep the same order in Chinese, we get "她形成了敏锐的洞察力，通过长期的阅读和写作，以及对社会的观察", which reads awkward. It is because in Chinese the adverbial phrases are generally put before the main verb. Thus, we usually need to advance the postpositive adverbial (后置状语) to the front of the main verb in Chinese. So here we have "长期的阅读和写作以及对社会的观察，让她形成了敏锐的洞察力".

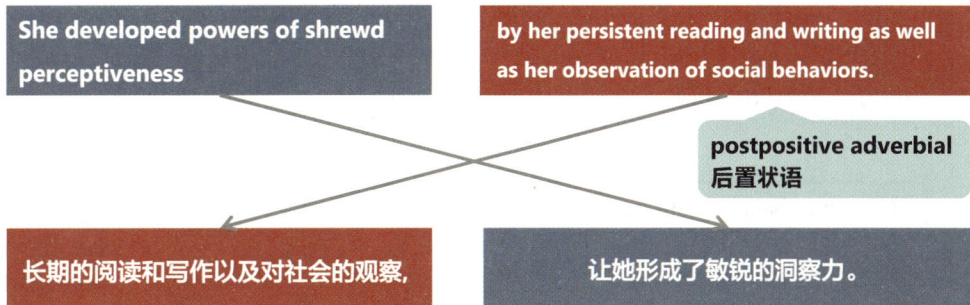

③ Everything of the novel was handled **with extreme care**, as if she was working on a fine engraving made **upon a little piece of ivory**.

There are two prepositional phrases (介词词组). The first one, "with extreme care", modifying the verb "was handled", presents the information of means.

The second one is "upon a little piece of ivory", providing the information of place to the predicate, "was working on".

Both of them play the role of adverbials in the sentence. As explained before, the adverbial phrases are usually put before the verb in Chinese, thus the translated version is " 小说的每一个细节都被精心处理，就好像在一小块象牙上精雕细琢 ".

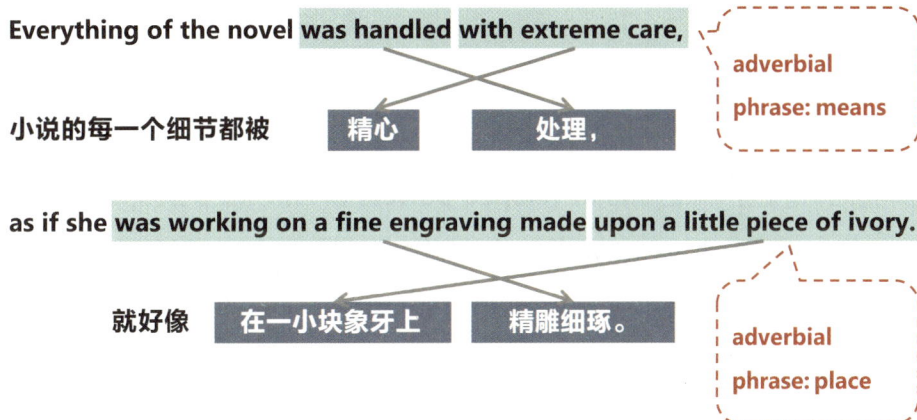

④ She was always able to find the precise expression **that accurately fitted the character and the occasion**.

The clause, "that accurately fitted the character and the occasion", is an attributive clause led by "that", to provide more detailed information for "precise expression". How can we translate the attributive clause from English into Chinese appropriately? If we keep the same order of the antecedent (先行词) and the attributive clause, the Chinese translation might be " 她总能找到精准表达最契合人物与事态 ". It reads confusing and unnatural.

In Chinese, the attributive clause is usually placed before the noun. Thus, we adjust the order by moving the attributive clause prior to the antecedent. Here comes a better Chinese version: " 她能找到最契合人物与事态的精准表达 ".

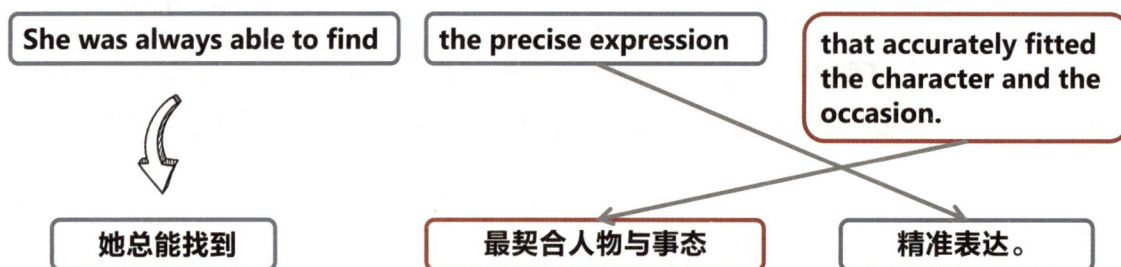

3. Parallel Texts

Please read the source and target texts in comparison and see how the order of language elements was rearranged in E-C translation.

Jane Austen

Jane Austen (1775 — 1817) was born in Hampshire, a small town in southwest England. She was mostly tutored at home but received a broader education than many women of her time. **She developed powers of shrewd perceptiveness by her persistent reading and writing as well as her observation of social behaviors.** Her reputation as one of the best English novelists depends upon six novels: *Sense and Sensibility*, *Pride and Prejudice*, *Mansfield Park*, *Emma*, *Persuasion* and *Northanger Abbey*. Austen restricted the subject to a narrow range of society and events: a quiet, prosperous, middle-class circle in provincial surroundings, and her main literary concern was about human beings in their social relationships, especially in love and marriage. **Everything of the novel was handled with extreme care, as if she was working on a fine engraving made upon a little piece of ivory. She was always able to find the precise expression that accurately fitted the character and the occasion.** Her wonderful skill in the treatment of humorous and a little satirical conversation helped a lot to reveal characters through their own words.

简·奥斯汀

　　她主要接受的是家庭式教育，但她的知识面比许多同时代女性更广阔。**长期的阅读和写作，以及对社会的观察，让她形成了敏锐的洞察力**。作为英国最优秀的小说家之一，她的代表作有六部：《理智与情感》《傲慢与偏见》《曼斯菲尔德庄园》《爱玛》《劝导》及《诺桑觉寺》。奥斯汀的作品关注特定的社会群体和事件，即乡土环境下宁静而欣欣向荣的中产阶层以及他们的生活，重点描述社会关系中的人物，特别是处于爱情和婚姻中的人物。**小说的每一个细节都被精心处理，就好像在一小块象牙上精雕细琢。她总能找到最契合人物与事态的精准表达。**她十分擅长使用幽默手法和捎带讽刺意味的对话来揭示人物自身的性格特点。

↳ 4. Translation Skills Summarized

Let us summarize the translation skills in this section: adjusting the order of language elements. English and Chinese have the same basic sentence structure. It is "subject plus verb plus object", shorten as SVO. Such a structure implies the same logic, which is "actors (施事者) + do (行为) + sth./recipients (受事者)."

However, the difference of word arrangement does exist between the two languages. There are two noticeable types of adjustment when we do translation from English to Chinese. We are supposed to reposition the placement of adverbials and attributives in E-C translation.

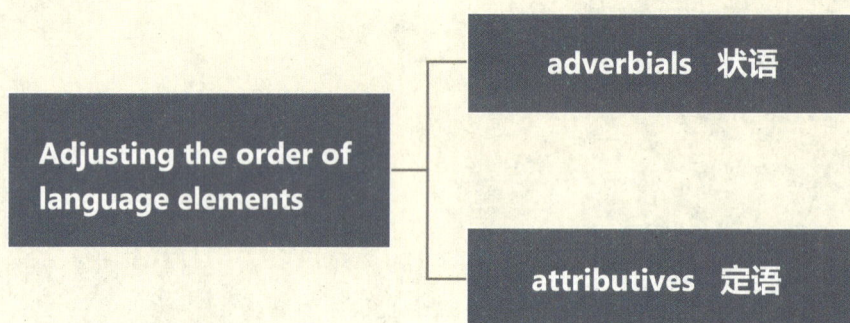

```
                                        ┌─── adverbials  状语
Adjusting the order of ─────────────────┤
language elements                       └─── attributives  定语
```

Adverbials present additional information for the verb. They can be a single word, a phrase or a clause.

In English, the position of adverbial words or phrases is more flexible. It can be placed in the beginning, the middle and the end of an English sentence. Comparatively, adverbial words or phrases in Chinese sentences are usually positioned in front of the subject or the verb.

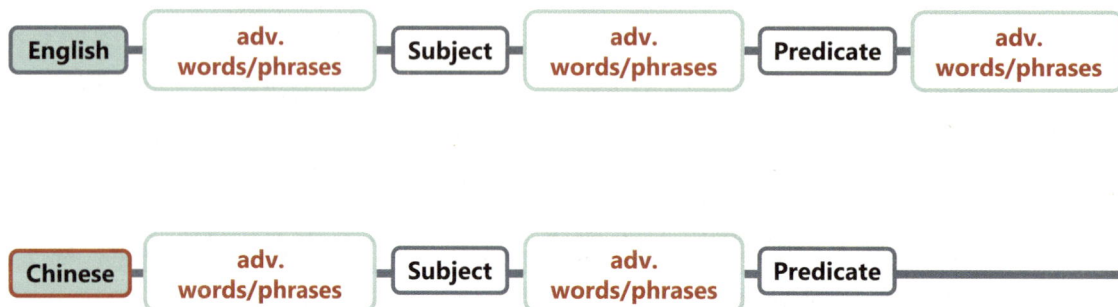

```
English — adv. words/phrases — Subject — adv. words/phrases — Predicate — adv. words/phrases

Chinese — adv. words/phrases — Subject — adv. words/phrases — Predicate
```

English adverbial clauses are also much more flexible in arrangement. They can be placed in the beginning, the middle and the end of an English sentence through appropriate connectives (连接词).

The position of adverbial clauses in Chinese follows the temporal (时间的) sequence but is quite less decided by connectives. It means that the order of the main clause and the subordinate clause is decided by natural time sequence — first thing first and last thing last. For example, the clause of cause is usually arranged prior to the clause of effect.

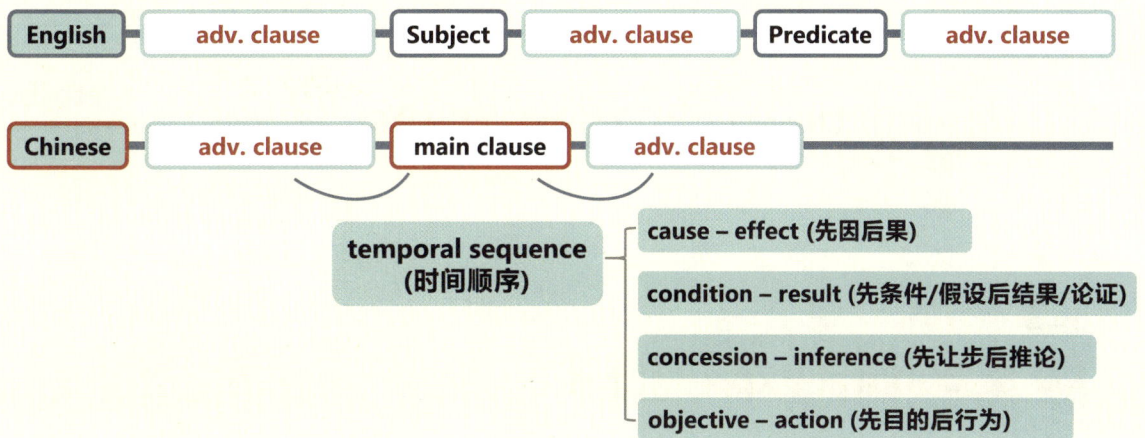

| English | adv. clause | Subject | adv. clause | Predicate | adv. clause |

| Chinese | adv. clause | main clause | adv. clause |

temporal sequence (时间顺序)
- cause – effect (先因后果)
- condition – result (先条件/假设后结果/论证)
- concession – inference (先让步后推论)
- objective – action (先目的后行为)

Attributives describe the qualities or states of nouns. They can be a single word, a phrase or a clause. In English, attributive words or phrases may be positioned before or after the noun, but they are generally placed before nouns in Chinese. The attributive clause, in English, is usually placed after the noun. However, it is often placed before the noun in Chinese.

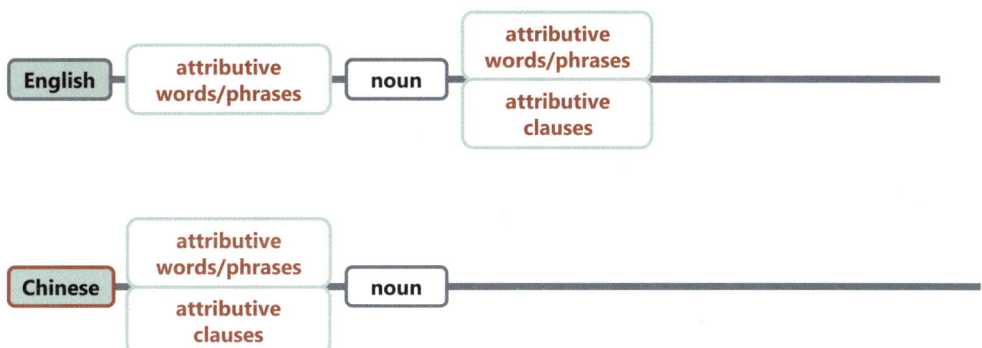

| English | attributive words/phrases | noun | attributive words/phrases / attributive clauses |

| Chinese | attributive words/phrases / attributive clauses | noun |

To sum up, in terms of the order of sentence elements, English is more flexible while Chinese is more inflexible.

Apart from that, when translating English into Chinese, whether to adjust the word order depends on various factors, such as the fluency and accuracy of the target language, coherence between sentences, and the translator's purpose.

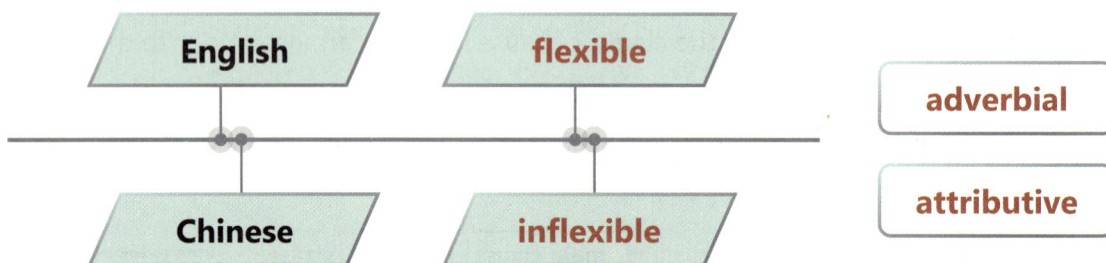

5. Cultural Expressions

1) Jane Austen's Six Novels:

- *Sense and Sensibility*《理智与情感》(1811)
- *Pride and Prejudice*《傲慢与偏见》(1813)
- *Mansfield Park*《曼斯菲尔德花园》(1814)
- *Emma*《爱玛》(1815)
- *Persuasion*《劝导》(1818)
- *Northanger Abbey*《诺桑觉寺》(1818)

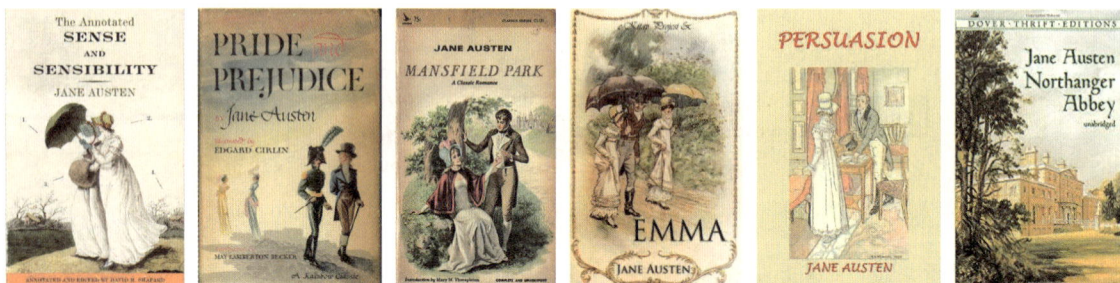

2) Great Themes of Her Literature

- Marriage
- Class structure
- Social roles of men and women
- Financial opportunities for lower class and upper class

PRIDE AND PREJUDICE: THEMES

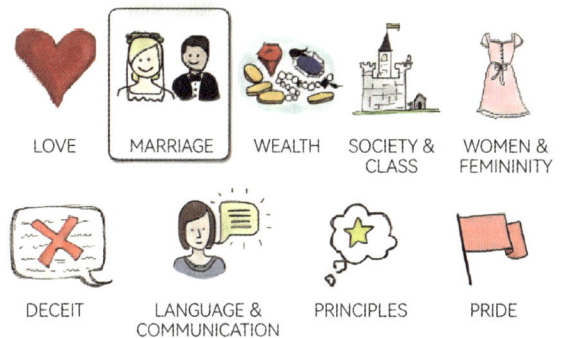

LOVE   MARRIAGE   WEALTH   SOCIETY & CLASS   WOMEN & FEMININITY

DECEIT   LANGUAGE & COMMUNICATION   PRINCIPLES   PRIDE

3) Jane Austen's Trademark Features

- insightful observation（敏锐的洞察力）
- astute characterization（巧妙的人物塑造）
- brilliant wit（机敏睿智）

4) Jane Austen's Life

- Jane Austen grew up in a family neither wealthy enough nor poor enough, kind of an awkward middle status in rural England.
- Austen was writing something reflective of the time in 18th and 19th century, when women did not have a lot of options on marriage which was absolutely expected, but almost expected as a business proposition. Marriage, to some degree, was for money and family status.

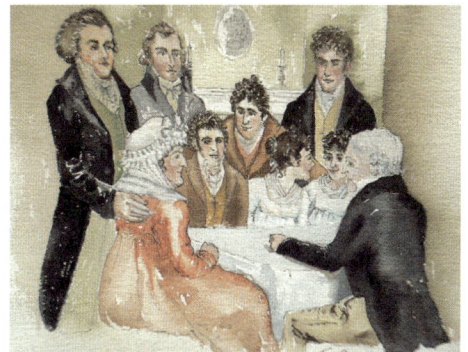

Marriage in the 18th, 19th century
- **absolutely expected**
- **a business proposition**
- **wealth and status**

- However, the resonating plots easily found in her novels were people trying to balance the tension between the quest for love and the economic benefits of marriage. Austen viewed marriage as something beneficial in a lot of ways, but not something happy. Like what Charlotte Lucas said to Elizabeth in *Pride and Prejudice*, "Happiness in marriage is entirely a matter of chance". That might explain a little bit why Austen didn't end up marrying.

Happiness in marriage is entirely a matter of chance.
Jane Austen

- Jane Austen's love for reading and writing were encouraged and nurtured well by her parents. She developed a sharp wit through cultured education. Her real gift was skewering social establishments.

- All these experiences helped her to build up the complexity of heroines, who generally were well-cultured ladies with intelligence, pragmatic personalities and rich inner lives.

Complexity of heroines:
- **well-cultured ladies**

↳ 6. Questions for Discussion

1) How many completed novels did Jane Austen write? Could you list the names?

2) Can you provide some examples of adjusting sentence order in E-C translation?

III Exercises

Section A. True or false (5 items)

_____ 1) In 1954, Ernest Hemingway was awarded the Nobel Prize for Literature for his novel *A Farewell to Arms*.

_____ 2) Jane Austen is the only woman featured on an English bank note.

_____ 3) Language units at different levels usually can be upshifted or downshifted in E-C translation if necessary.

_____ 4) Although Chinese and English share the same basic sentence structure, modifiers sometimes are put in different places in the sentence.

_____ 5) The novel *Jane Eyre* was written by Jane Austen.

Section B. Multiple choice (5 items)

_____ 1) Shakespeare has an unmatched genius for stagecraft, poetry, and insight into human character.

　　A. 在编剧技巧、吟诗作唱及洞察人性方面，莎士比亚的天赋无人能及。

　　B. 莎士比亚拥有无人能及的天赋，在编剧、诗歌和观察人物方面。

　　C. 莎士比亚拥有对编剧、诗歌和观察人物方面的无人能及的天赋。

_____ 2) Ernest Hemingway was above all famous for his literary style: spare, understated and direct.

　　A. 海明威尤其是以简约、朴素、直截了当的文学风格而著称。

　　B. 海明威尤其著名，因为他的文学风格：简约、朴素、直截了当。

　　C. 海明威因为他的文学风格尤其著名：简约、朴素、直截了当。

_____ 3) One never fully accepts the juxtaposition of the Hemingway – person in his writing with the simple man.

　　A. 一个人从来不完全接受海明威的并列——在他的写作与简单的人中。

　　B. 一个人永远无法完全接受海明威式的人物在他的作品中和简单的人物并列在一起。

　　C. 海明威在作品中经常把自己写进去，混迹于普通人之中，这一点我们很难苟同。

_____ 4) Hemingway's first novel, *The Sun Also Rises*, painted the image of a whole generation, the Lost Generation.

    A. 海明威的第一本小说——《太阳照常升起》，塑造了一代人的形象 ——"迷惘的一代 "。

    B. 海明威的第一本小说《太阳照常升起》，塑造了 "迷惘一代 " 的形象。

    C. 海明威的第一本小说，《太阳照常升起》，塑造了一代人的形象，"迷惘的一代 "。

_____ 5) Many laws of nature exist in nature though they have not yet been discovered.

    A. 虽然许多自然的法律确实存在于自然界中，但是它们尚未被发现。

    B. 虽然许多自然规律尚未被发现，但是它们确实在自然界中存在。

    许多自然法律实际上存在于自然界中，尽管它们尚未被发现。

IV Test

Section A. Multiple choice (5 items*4 points=20 points)

_____ 1) The structure of an atom can be accurately described though we cannot see it.

    A. 原子的结构可以被准确地描述，尽管我们看不见它。

    B. 虽然我们看不见原子结构，但能准确地描述它。

    C. 虽然原子结构可以被准确地描述，但我们看不见它。

_____ 2) The man who has begun to live more seriously within begins to live more simply without.

    A. 开始在内心生活得更严肃的人开始更简单地生活在没有。

    B. 内心生活得越严谨的人，外在生活越简单。

    C. 心灵愈加严谨，外表愈加简单。

_____ 3) Santiago is a typical Hemingway hero, a man of action and one of few words.

    A. 桑地亚哥就是一个有代表性的海明威英雄，喜欢行动，少言语。

    B. 桑地亚哥就是一个有代表性的海明威英雄，少言语，喜欢行动。

    C. 桑地亚哥就是一个典型的海明威式主人公，少言寡语，以行动见真章。

_____ 4) These novels are essentially of the same type with simple plots and marvelous characterization.

        A. 这些小说从根本上看类型相同，情节简单，人物塑造惟妙惟肖。

        B. 这些小说从根本上看是情节简单、人物非凡的相同类型。

        C. 这些小说从根本上看类型相同，伴有相同情节与非凡人物。

_____ 5) Time goes fast for one who has a sense of beauty, when there are pretty children in a pool and a young Diana on the edge, to receive with wonder anything you catch!

        A. 当你跟可爱的孩子们站在池子里，又有个如戴安娜似的年轻女子在池边好奇地接受你捉上来的任何东西的时候，如果你懂得什么叫美的话，时间是过得很快的！

        B. 时间总是过的很快，对于一个拥有美感并充满惊喜的捕捉任何事物的人来说，当有小孩在池塘里，年轻的女子在旁边时。

        C. 要是你和一群可爱的孩子在池塘中捉鱼摸虾，池边站着一个天仙般的姑娘，在快活地捡起你们的"战利品"，你若知美，定会觉得时间如白驹过隙，一晃即逝。

Section B. Sentence translation (5 items*6 points=30 points)

1) The old man was thin and gaunt with deep wrinkles in the back of his neck.

2) Mr. Bingley was good looking and gentlemanlike; he had a pleasant countenance, and easy, unaffected manners.

3) She developed powers of shrewd perceptiveness by her persistent reading and writing as well as her observation of social behaviors.

4) Dreadful to me was the coming home in the raw twilight, with nipped fingers and toes.

5) Before me was the breakfast-room door, I stopped, intimidated and trembling.

⤷ Section C. Paragraph translation (50 points)

It is a truth universally acknowledged that a single man in possession of a good fortune must be in want of a wife. However, little known the feelings or views of such a man may be on his first entering a neighborhood, this truth is so well fixed in the minds of the surrounding families that he is considered the rightful property of some one or other of their daughters.

Unit 7
SPORTS

Football

1. Cultural Background

Football (England) or Soccer (America) is a sport in which two teams play **defense**[1] and **attack**[2] against each other on the same **rectangular**[3] field according to certain rules. The ball is controlled and advanced by the feet. Soccer is called "the world's best sport" because of its strong **antagonism**[4], changeable **tactics**[5] and large number of participants.

The **predecessor**[6] of modern football, it is alleged, originated from the ball game "Cuju" in Zizhou (now Zibo City), Shandong Province in ancient China. After that, it was spread to Europe by the Arabs and gradually evolved into modern football. Modern football began in England. In 1848, The Cambridge Rules, the first written rules in football history, were created. On October 26, 1863, England established the world's first football association and unified the rules of the game. In 1872, the first official inter-association match in football history was held between England and Scotland. In 1900, football was added as an official sport at the second Summer Olympics. Football is widely translated as "Football" around the world, and only in a few countries such as the United States is translated as "Soccer". "Football" in the United States and Canada is called "American Football" (美式足球).

The **supreme**[7] organization of football is the International Football Federation (**FIFA**)[8], which was founded in 1904 and is headquartered in Zurich, Switzerland. The highest organization in China is the Chinese Football Association (CFA), which was established in Beijing on January 3, 1955.

Words and Expressions:

1 defense /dɪˈfens/ *v&n.* 防守

2 attack /əˈtæk/ *v&n.* 进攻

3 rectangular /rekˈtæŋgjələr/ *adj.* 长方形的，矩形的

4 antagonism /ænˈtægənɪzəm/ *n.* 对抗；对立，敌对

5 tactic /ˈtæktɪk/ *n.* 策略；手段；招数

6 predecessor /ˈpredəsesər/ *n.* 前任；前辈

7 supreme /suˈpriːm/ *adj.* （级别或地位）最高的，至高无上的

8 FIFA 全称 Fédération Internationale de Football Association 国际足球联合会，简称 " 国际足联 "

2. Translation Examples Explained

Please read this passage and pay attention to the use of cohesive devices (衔接手段) and their translaiton.

①*Football is a game played by two teams on a rectangular field, with the object (目标) of driving the ball into the opponent's goal.* ②*Each team has 11 players, plus several substitutes (替 补) who can take the place of injured players. The ball is controlled and advanced primarily by using the feet; only goalkeepers are allowed to handle the ball.*

Evidence from many ancient societies such as Chinese, Greek, Mayan, and Egyptian reveals that kicking games were played in those cultures. The modern game of football began in the 19th century in England, where a variety of football games developed, all of which involved both handling and kicking. Now, football is the world's most popular sport, played by men and women of all ages, with millions of fans throughout the world. A chief reason for football's vast popularity is that it has proved to be among the most accessible and adaptable of the world's sports. All that is needed to play is an area of open space and a ball. Much of the world's football is played informally on patches of ground, without field marking or real goals (球门).

① Football is a game played by two teams on a rectangular field, with the object (目 标) of driving the ball into the opponent's goal.

As we know, in English, the definite article "the" is often used to help the reader understand an element in a text by referring backwards to something that has already been mentioned. It builds connection between different elements and thus achieves cohesion.

the object => the object of the two teams

the ball => the ball played by the two teams

the opponent => each of the two teams

Take this sentence as an example. The three definite articles respectively link the words "object", "ball", and "opponent" back to "two teams" mentioned in the previous clause and help to clarify what those words exactly mean.

However, as a common device, the definite article does not exist in Chinese. Therefore, it is usually omitted in E-C translation. And there is no need to use overt means to create grammatical relations between different elements, since those relations in a Chinese text depend more on the context instead of grammatical devices.

Football is a game played by two teams on a rectangular field, with the object of driving the ball into the opponent's goal.

A. 足球是两支队伍在一块矩形场地上竞技的体育运动，双方队员的目标是把他们踢的球射入他们对手的球门。

B. 足球是两支队伍在一块矩形场地上竞技的体育运动，Ø目标是把Ø球射入Ø对方球门。

For example, even without specifying the meaning of "the object", "the ball", and "the opponent", the clause "目标是把球射入对方球门" in this translation is not difficult for Chinese readers to understand. And compared with the translation " 双方队员的目标是把他们踢的球射入他们对手的球门 ", this clause is clearer and more concise, given that conciseness is a typical feature of Chinese sentences. Thus, we get the translation as: 足球是两支队伍在一块矩形场地上竞技的体育运动，目标是把球射入对方球门。

② Each team has 11 players, plus several substitutes (替补) who can take the place of injured players. The ball is controlled and advanced primarily by using the feet; only goalkeepers are allowed to handle the ball.

In addition to the definite article, another device used to achieve cohesion in the first paragraph is repetition.

Repetition, which involves reusing a lexical item (词项), a word, a part of a word, or a sequence of words, is the simplest way to create semantic links within a sentence or among sentences.

For example, in this paragraph, the lexical items such as "team" and "the ball" are repeated successively to connect the second and the third sentences to the first one. In this way, new information about the team and the ball can naturally build onto the old one, thus making the whole paragraph consistent.

Despite a common cohesive device in English, repetition is even comparatively more frequently used in Chinese.

> Football is a game played by two **teams** on a rectangular field, with the object of driving the **ball** into the opponent's goal. Each **team** has 11 **players**, plus several **substitutes** who can take the place of injured **players**. The **ball** is controlled and advanced primarily by using the feet; only **goalkeepers** are allowed to handle the **ball**.

A. 足球是两支队伍在一块矩形场地上竞技的体育运动，双方球员的目标是把踢的球射入他们对手的球门。每支队伍由11名球员和数名候补队员组成，候补队员可以代替受伤的球员上场。球的控制和传送主要由脚来完成，只有守门员允许以手持球。

B. 足球是由两支队伍在一块矩形场地上竞技的体育运动，目标是把球射入对方球门。每支队伍由11名球员和数名替补队员组成，替补队员可以代替受伤的球员上场。球员主要用脚控球和运球，只有守门员允许以手持球。

This translation establishes a strong semantic links. It is because when translated, the passive sentence "The ball is controlled and advanced primarily by using the feet" was deliberately changed into an active one, with the omitted agent (施动者) "players" added onto the subject position.

Repeating the lexical item "球员", the clause "球员主要用脚控制和运球" establishes a strong semantic link to the previous sentence. Along with other repeated words "队伍" "球" and "候补队员", it also helps to form a smooth semantic chain that efficiently ties the whole paragraph together.

In contrast, with "球" as the subject, "球的控制和传送主要由脚来完成" only creates a weak connection to the sentence on by repeating the word "球". What is lost in translation is the referential tie made by the definite article "the" back to "the ball" in the first sentence, given the fact that the definite article does not exist in Chinese and is often omitted in E-C translation.

In this sense, changing the passive-voice sentence into an active one can in a way compensate for the loss brought about by the omission of the definite article. So, the sentence can be translated to be: 每支队伍由 11 名球员和数名替补队员组成，替补队员可以代替受伤的球员上场。球员主要用脚控球和运球，只有守门员允许以手持球。

Below are the original text and its Chinese translation. Read them in comparison to see how cohesive devices were used in E-C translation to re-create connections.

Football

Football is a game played by two teams on a rectangular field, with the object (目标) **of driving the ball into the opponent's goal. Each team has 11 players, plus several substitutes** (替补) **who can take the place of injured players. The ball is controlled and advanced primarily by using the feet; only goalkeepers are allowed to handle the ball.**

Evidence from many ancient societies such as Chinese, Greek, Mayan, and Egyptian reveals that kicking games were played in those cultures. The modern game of football began in the 19th century in England, where a variety of football games developed, all of which involved both handling and kicking. Now, football is the world's most popular sport, played by men and women of all ages, with millions of fans throughout the world. A chief reason for football's vast popularity is that it has proved to be among the most accessible and adaptable of the world's sports. All that is needed to play is an area of open space and a ball. Much of the world's football is played informally on patches of ground, without field marking or real goals (球门).

足球

足球是两支队伍在一块矩形场地上竞技的体育运动，目标是把球射入对方球门。每支队伍都由 11 名球员和数名候补队员组成，候补队员可以替换受伤的球员上场。球员主要用脚控球和运球，只有守门员允许以手持球。

许多古国比如中国、希腊、玛雅和埃及都有证据表明踢球游戏是它们文化的一部分。现代足球发源于 19 世纪的英格兰。在这里，各式各样的足球运动都得以发展，但所有的种类都包含手持和脚踢。现在，足球是世界上最流行的体育运动，男女老少皆可参与，在全世界拥有数以百万计的球迷。而其中主要原因是，实践证明足球是一项最容易开展、最不受场地限制的运动之一。一块空地、一个球足矣。世界各地多数足球比赛都是随意在一块空地上进行的，不必标画场地，也不需要设真正的球门。

4. Translation Skills Summarized

Cohesion is the way we use vocabulary and grammar to create connections between the ideas in a text. It is an important device to build discourse coherence (连贯).

There are two categories of cohesion: grammatical and lexical cohesions. Grammatical cohesion is the meaningful connections in a text that is achieved by grammatical structures, while lexical cohesion is based on words and background knowledge.

Cohesion 衔接

cohesion

grammatical
语法衔接手段

lexical
词汇衔接手段

In the grammatical cohesion, there are four types: reference, substitution, ellipsis, and conjunction.

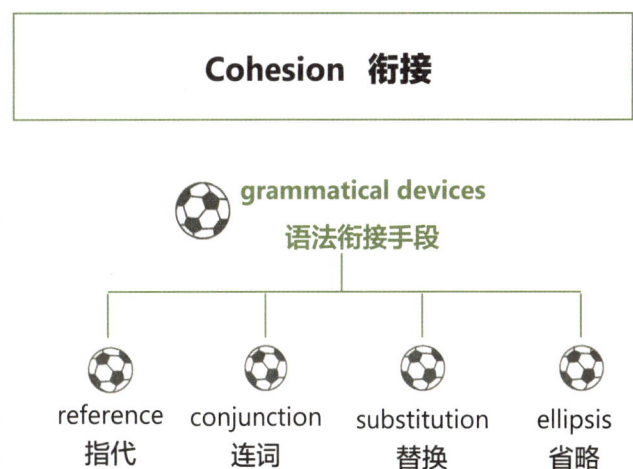

Cohesion 衔接

grammatical devices
语法衔接手段

reference
指代

conjunction
连词

substitution
替换

ellipsis
省略

Reference refers to the situation in which one element is understood by referring to another in the text. A good example of referring devices is the definite article "the" we have discussed earlier. Articles, pronouns, and demonstratives all belong to referring devices of this type. Here is another example from the passage.

> ① Evidence from many ancient societies such as Chinese, Greek, Mayan, and Egyptian reveals that kicking games were played in those cultures.
>
> 许多古国比如中国、希腊、玛雅和埃及都有证据表明踢球游戏是它们文化的一部分。

In this example, the demonstrative "those" refers back to "many ancient societies" and the cohesion is re-established by "许多古国" and "它们" in the Chinese translation.

Conjunction refers to the linking device used to establish logic relations among different ideas. Connective words may include conjunctions, adverbs, prepositions or prepositional phrases, and even clauses with connective meaning functions. In the following example, the conjunction "if" is used to express a condition for the main clause.

> ② If teams are still level after extra time, then a penalty shootout must take place.
>
> 如果加时赛后两队仍是平局,则会通过点球大战决出胜负。

Substitution refers to placing one item with another in the text to avoid repetition, including "one", "do", and "so", which are common words of this type. In the following example, "one" substitutes "game".

> ③ At the time, football was the most widely played game of its kind, but it wasn't the only one.
>
> 当时,足球虽是同类运动中受众最广的,却并不是唯一的。

Ellipsis refers to the omission of the unnecessary elements that have already been mentioned earlier in the context or that have been known by the writer and the reader. In the following sentence, the nominal "British people" is omitted.

> ④ British people like sports. In fact, many love football.
>
> 英国人喜欢运动。事实上,许多人都喜欢足球。

In terms of lexical cohesion, there are four types: repetition, synonym/antonym, hyponym/meronym, and collocation.

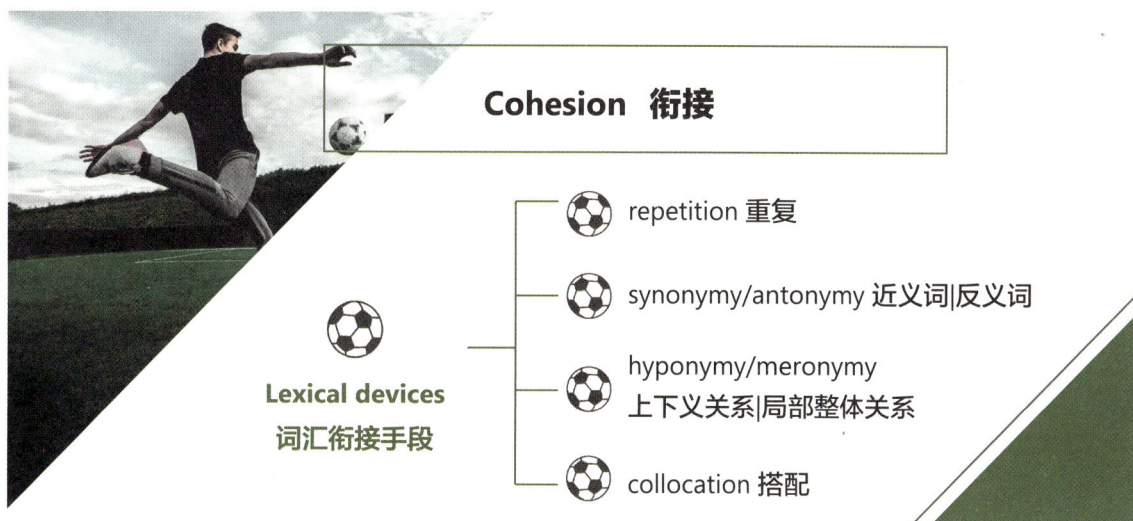

Cohesion 衔接

Lexical devices 词汇衔接手段

- repetition 重复
- synonymy/antonymy 近义词|反义词
- hyponymy/meronymy 上下义关系|局部整体关系
- collocation 搭配

Repetition is the restatement of the same lexical item. The cohesive device has been explained earlier. Another example would be the repetition of "football" throughout the whole text, which helps to link different ideas into a meaning one.

Synonym is a device that creates cohesion among lexical items of similar meaning. It is commonly used in both English and Chinese. Examples of synonyms are "kicking game" and "football" in the English original, which are translated as "踢球游戏" and "足球" in Chinese.

Antonym is a device that establishes a contrastive relation between two items of the opposite meaning. This can be exemplified by the sentence:

It will be good for them, but it will be bad for the game.

对他们来说是好事，对比赛来说是坏事。

In this example, "good" and "bad", as well as "好事" and "坏事" help to form a contrastive cohesion in semantic meaning.

Hyponymy is a device that establishes a cohesive relationship between a general concept and specific concepts. For example, in the first paragraph, "team", "players", "substitutes" and "goalkeepers" form a cohesive relationship in which the "team" is the superordinate (上义词), and "players", "substitutes" and "goalkeepers" are subordinates (下义词) or hyponyms (下义词) of "team." And this device helps to strengthen the connection among the three sentences in the first paragraph. Accordingly, this hyponymic relation is rebuilt in the Chinese translation among the words "队伍", "球员", "候补队员" and "守门员".

Meronymy is a "whole-part" relationship between items. For example, a "whole-part" relationship can be established among the words "football" "ground" "penalty area" "goal area" and "corner area". They can establish a cohesive relationship in a text.

Collocation is a device that creates some semantic relation among items that are likely to co-occur in a text. For example, in the passage above, the topic-related words such as football, play, ball, team, players, goalkeepers, handle the ball, kicking and handling, just to name a few, are likely to appear with each other.

Although the two types of cohesion exist both in English and Chinese, grammatical cohesion is more commonly used in English while lexical cohesion is more frequently used in Chinese.

The reason, however, as we have repeatedly mentioned, is due to the differences in the sentence structure between English and Chinese.

English	**Chinese**
grammatical cohesion	lexical cohesion
hypotaxis 形合	parataxis 意合

English is a hypotactic (形合的) language. It means the logical relations between different sentences and paragraphs are often expressed by overt grammatical means, such as conjunctions and connectives (连接词).

In contrast, Chinese is a paratactic (意合的) language. Its logic relations between sentences depend more on notional words (实义词) and the context instead of grammatical items.

The differences between English and Chinese cohesion may cause difficulty in E-C translation, especially when there is no grammatical or lexical equivalent to re-create cohesion. In that case, we need to look for alternative ways, that is, to skillfully use the translation methods we have learned so far to solve those problems.

5. Cultural Expressions

Although football is the most popular sport in the world, there is no agreement in terms of how to call it. While the majority of the worlds call it "football", a handful of countries, most notably the US, prefer to call it "soccer". Well, the answer lies in how the sport developed in each country.

Football-type games have been around for centuries. The earliest evidence of football comes from ancient China in the 3rd century B.C., a sport that people called *Cuju*. Over the ages, various kinds of football spread throughout the world.

But the modern football we know today is often said to have begun on October, 26th, 1863 when the England's newly formed Football Association wrote down a set of rules. At the time, it was the most widely played game of its kind in the country. However, there were still other versions of the game around.

Cuju 蹴鞠

China, in the 3rd century BC

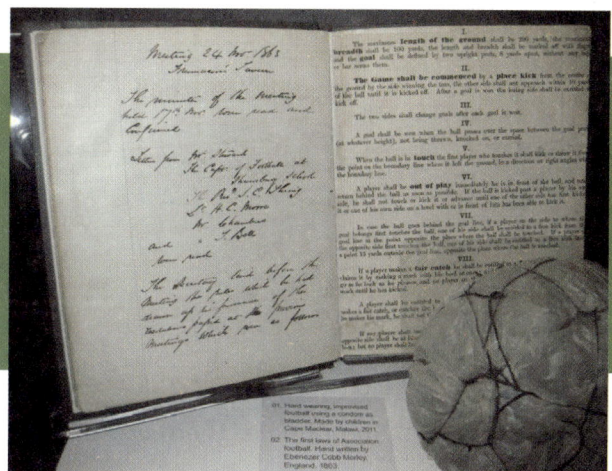

The original hand-written "Laws of the Game" drafted for The Football Association in 1863 on display at the National Football Museum, Manchester, England.

Rugby football, named after an English boarding school, was a variation that allowed players to carry and run with the ball to advance it toward the goal. The game is played under the Football Association's rules; thus, it became known as association football.

rugby football
英式橄榄球

association football
英式足球

Inevitably, the names would be shortened. Linguistically creative students at the University of Oxford in the 1880s distinguished between the sports of "rugger" (rugby football) and "assoccer" (association football). The latter term was further shortened to "soccer" (sometimes spelled "socker"), and the name quickly spread beyond the campus. However, "soccer" never became much more than a nickname in Great Britain. By the 20th century, rugby football was more commonly called rugby, while association football had earned the right to be known as just plain football.

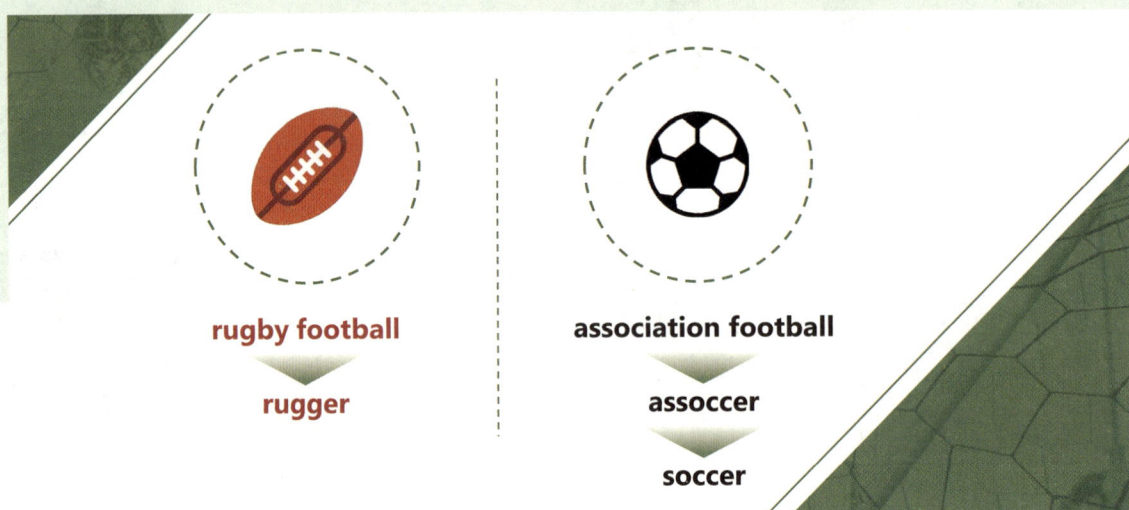

rugby football

rugger

association football

assoccer

soccer

Meanwhile, in the United States, a sport emerged in the late 19th century that borrowed elements of both rugby and association football. Before long, it had proved more popular than either of them. In full, it was known as gridiron football, but most people never bothered with the first word. As a result, American association-football players increasingly adopted soccer to refer to their sport. The United States Football Association, which had formed in the 1910s as the official organizing body of American soccer, changed its name to the United States Soccer Football Association in 1945, and it later dispensed with the "Football" altogether. No longer just a nickname, soccer had stuck.

By the time "football" found its way to the U.S.

Gridiron football
烤盘足球｜橄榄球

Gridiron football
烤盘足球｜橄榄球

Other countries where the word "soccer" is common include those that, like the United States, have competing forms of football. For instance, Canada has its own version of gridiron football; Ireland is home to Gaelic football; and Australia is mad about Australian rules football (which is derived from rugby). In places where football can be ambiguous, soccer is usefully precise.

soccer   football

the U.S.   Canada   Australia

Japan   South Africa   Southern Philippines

New Zealand   Ireland   Papua New Guinea

Rest Of The World

↳ 6. Questions for Discussion

1) How much do you know about football? Can you introduce it briefly?

2) What are two categories of cohesion?

II Baseball

↳ 1. Cultural Background

"Baseball" is one of the ball games. It is a competitive event of attack and defense with metal stick hitting.

Baseball originated in the 15th century as a popular game of paddle and ball in England. It later spread to the United States. In 1839, the first baseball game was played in Cooperstown, N.Y. In 1978, the International League of Baseball was recognized by the **International Olympic Committee** *, and in 1994, the International Baseball Federation established its headquarters in Lausanne, Switzerland. Baseball was introduced as an Olympic sport in 1992.

Baseball's highest organization is the International Baseball Federation, founded in 1938. The highest organization in China is the Chinese Baseball Association, which was founded in Beijing in 1979.

↳ 2. Translation Examples Explained

Please read the following passage and see how coherence（连贯）is created in the English text and recreated in the Chinese translation.

①*Long known as America's "national pastime", baseball actually evolved from the English game of "rounders".* ②*Baseball is a team sport, in which a fist-sized ball is thrown by a defensive player called a pitcher and hit by an offensive player called a batter with a round, smooth wood or aluminum stick. The ball itself is also called a baseball. Scoring is accomplished by the batter running counter-clockwise around the diamond after hitting the ball and trying to touch four bases on the ground in sequence before the opposing players can put him out. After the team at bat has three outs the two teams switch their roles. They switch back and forth between batting and fielding. The team that scores the most runs after nine innings wins the*

◇◇◇◇◇◇◇

* International Olympic Committee 国际奥林匹克委员会，简称"国际奥委会"，是一个非政府、非营利的国际体育组织，负责组织举办夏季奥林匹克运动会、冬季奥林匹克运动会、青年奥林匹克运动会等。

game. ③*Virtues of talented players shine in baseball games—accuracy and speed, the practices eye and hefty arm, the mind to take in and readjustment to the unexpected, the possession of more than one talent and the willingness to work in harness without special orders.*

① Long known as America's "national pastime", baseball actually evolved from the English game of "rounders".

Please look at the first example. Its main structure appears in the end, which is a "Subject + Verb" sentence pattern. The beginning part of the sentence is a pre-modifier, describing the word "baseball". We can translate this sentence by following its original order: "久被人们视为美国'全民运动'的棒球实际上是由一种叫'圆场棒球'的英格兰游戏演变而来". In this version, the pre-modifier (前置修饰语) was kept as background information. Alternatively, we can translate it as in the second version: "棒球一直被视为美国的'全民运动'，实际上它是由一种叫'圆场棒球'的英格兰游戏演变而来".
In this version, the pre-modifier (前置修饰语) in the English sentence is divided (分译) and upshifted (升级) in Chinese to a clause (小句), parallel to the second clause. These changes can help to highlight (强调) and foreground (凸显) the beginning part, making it as the topic statement of the whole passage. This part better summarizes what is mainly talked about in the whole passage. In this way, a more coherent (连贯) passage was rebuilt in the second Chinese translation.

棒球一直被视为美国的"全民运动"(国球)，实际上它是由一种叫"圆场棒球"的英格兰游戏演变而来。

② Baseball is a team sport, in which a fist-sized ball is thrown by a defensive player called a pitcher and hit by an offensive player called a batter with a round, smooth wood or aluminum stick. The ball itself is also called a baseball. Scoring is accomplished by the batter running counter-clockwise around the diamond after hitting the ball and trying to touch four bases on the ground in sequence before the opposing players can put him out.

Here comes the second example. To better understand and achieve coherence (连贯) among sentences, we will regard these sentences as a whole unit of translation.

As we read along, we can get the main idea of this unit by reading the leading parts in two sentences. This unit introduces baseball by describing how to play it and how to score points.

Here comes our first Chinese version, which follows the original order.

V₁: 棒球是一项团队运动，在比赛之中，一名叫投手的防守的球员扔出一枚拳头大小的球，一名叫击球手的进攻的球员用一支木制或铝制的光滑圆棒来击打。这个球也叫做棒球。得分方式是这样：击球手在将球击出之后，围绕着钻石逆时针方向奔跑，并在被对方球员赶出去之前依次跑完地面的四个基地。

This version is not good because we cannot get a good translation by simply summing up all the equivalent (对应的) words in another language.

Also, you will find some expressions wordy, like "一名叫投手的防守的球员" and "一名叫击球手的进攻的球员".

In addition, there are also some incorrectly translated terms (术语), for example, "钻石", "赶出去" and "基地". These Chinese translations sound unprofessional and difficult to understand, because they do not align well with the context (语境) — a professional sports that we are talking about.

Most importantly, some translated parts seem to jump out of nowhere. They cut off the semantic (语义的) connection between information chunks (信息块) coming before and after.

V₂: 棒球是一项团队运动，防守方一名投手先扔出一枚拳头大小的球，即棒球，而后进攻方一名击球手用一支木制或铝制的光滑圆棒击球。击球手在将球击出之后，围绕着钻石型内场逆时针方向跑垒，并在被守方球员打出局之前依次跑完地面的四个垒位，最后即可得分。

You will get a better idea by comparing it with Version 2, where accurate Chinese baseball terms (棒球术语) are used. They are: "防守方一名投手" (the pitcher playing defense), "进攻方一名击球手" (a batter playing offense), "钻石型内场" (a diamond-like infield), "跑垒" (running bases), "打出局" (being out) and "地面的四个垒位" (four bases on the ground). These accurate terms help readers to understand what is being talked about, building a better coherence between the text and the context (语境).

Please pay special attention to the highlighted parts. In the first version, the short sentence "这个球也叫做棒球" is not closely related to the context that precedes and follows it. But in Version 2, it was brought ahead as an appositive (同位语). This change obviously builds a better logical connection (连通) in the text.

The same is true for the clause "得分方式是这样". In the first version, it is misplaced (放错位置) because it is not so relevant to its neighboring clauses. When moving it to the end as in the second version, we have a sequence of clauses talking about the same person "击球手": "……击球手用……圆棒击球……击球手在将球击出之后……". In short, we usually put together information chunks with closer meanings. This helps to create a better coherence as in the second translation.

Additionally, the second translation adds time signal words (表时间的信号词) as cohesive devices (衔接手段) like "先", "而后", "在将球击出之后", "在……之前" and "最后".

The above-mentioned methods, the use of accurate terms in Chinese, the rearrangement of information chunks and the adding of time signal words work together to create a clear time flow and a better coherence (语义连贯).

③ Virtues of talented players shine in baseball games — accuracy and speed, the practices eye and hefty arm, the mind to take in and readjustment to the unexpected, the possession of more than one talent and the willingness to work in harness without special orders.

For the third example, we also offer two translations.

The first version follows a general-to-specific pattern, while the second version uses a specific-to-general pattern.

总 → 分：先表态后叙事

V₁: **棒球比赛能体现出优秀球员的众多品质**：准确和速度，丰富的经验和粗壮的胳膊，计谋多端的头脑和灵活的应变能力，每名队员都才华横溢，不需过多指点就能很好地合作。

分 → 总：先叙事后表态

V₂: 准确和速度，丰富的经验和粗壮的胳膊，计谋多端的头脑和灵活的应变能力，每名队员都才华横溢，不需过多指点就能很好地合作，**这些都是棒球比赛中所体现出的优秀球员品质**。

The two versions are both optional, but the second pattern is more frequently used in Chinese expressions.

In this way, we also repeat the specific-to-general pattern used in the previous example, building up consistency (一致性) for the whole unit.

3. Parallel Texts

Let us compare the source text and its translation and review what methods were used to achieve coherence in the Chinese translation.

Baseball

Long known as America's "national pastime", baseball actually evolved from the English game of "rounders". Baseball is a team sport, in which a fist-sized ball is thrown by a defensive player called a pitcher and hit by an offensive player called a batter with a round, smooth wood or aluminum stick. The ball itself is also called a baseball. Scoring is accomplished by the batter running counter-clockwise around the diamond after hitting the ball and trying to touch four bases on the ground in sequence before the opposing players can put him out. After the team at bat has three outs the two teams switch their roles. They switch back and forth between batting and fielding. The team that scores the most runs after nine innings wins the game. Virtues of talented players shine in baseball games – accuracy and speed, the practices eye and hefty arm, the mind to take in and readjustment to the unexpected, the possession of more than one talent and the willingness to work in harness without special orders.

棒球

棒球一直被视为美国的"全民运动"(国球)，实际上它是由一种叫"圆场棒球"的英格兰游戏演变而来。棒球是一项团队运动，防守方一名投手先扔出一枚拳头大小的球，即棒球，而后进攻方一名击球手用一支木制或铝制的光滑圆棒击球。击球手在将球击出之后，围绕着钻石型内场逆时针方向跑垒，并在被守方球员打出局之前依次跑完地面的四个垒位，最后即可得分。进攻方三次出局以后，两支队伍交换角色。他们来回换位、轮流攻防。九局比赛之后，得分多的一队获胜。准确和速度，丰富的经验和粗壮的胳膊，计谋多端的头脑和灵活的应变能力，每名队员都才华横溢，不需过多指点就能很好地合作，这些都是棒球比赛中优秀球员所体现出来的品质。

208 | 译言英美文化教程

4. Translation Skills Summarized

How to achieve coherence in translation? Generally speaking, there are several aspects that deserve special attention.

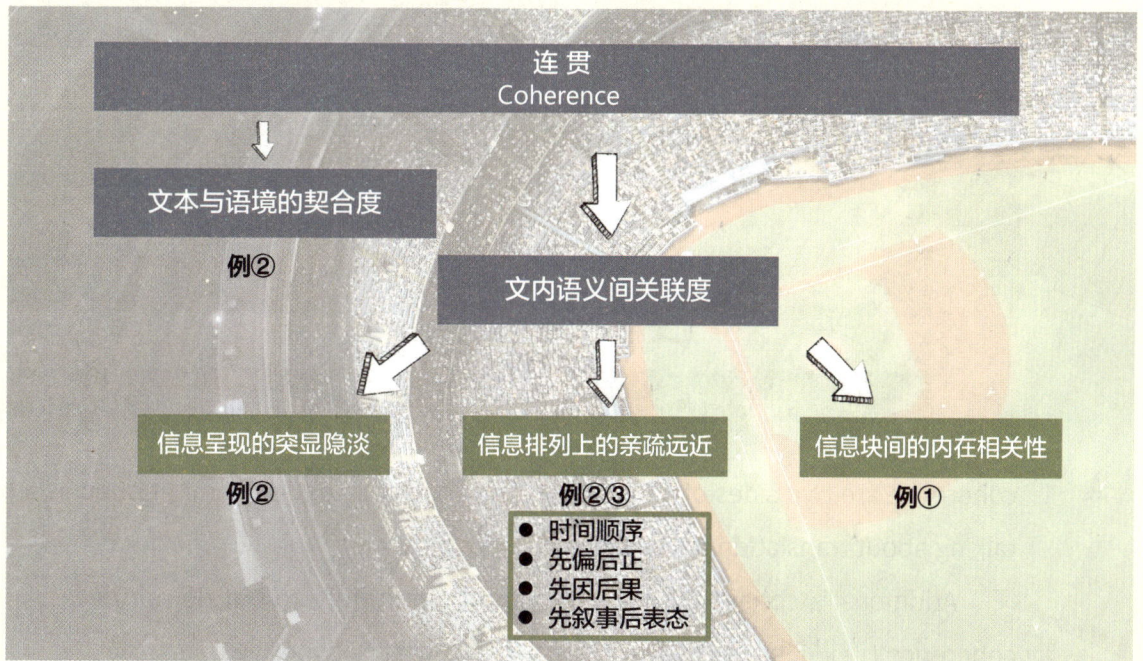

Firstly, what we say in the text, especially the use of terms (术语), should well match the context.

Secondly, the ideas we express in the text should be relevant to each other in content, either with or without using connective words.

Thirdly, when we arrange information chunks in text, the chunks with meanings closer to each other should be put closer to each other in the sentence order. There are some preferred orders for arranging information in the Chinese language.

Finally, when we present information chunks in the text, we would better foreground the most important information chunks, like the topical words or ideas, while moving to the background the less important ones.

By using these methods, we can rebuild a natural flow and coherence between ideas in the target text and between the text and the context.

In general, coherence is the covert, implicit and underlying logical connectedness (连通) in the text.

In contrast, cohesion, what we have learned in the previous section, is the overt, explicit and surficial formal linkage between the elements of a text. Cohesion and

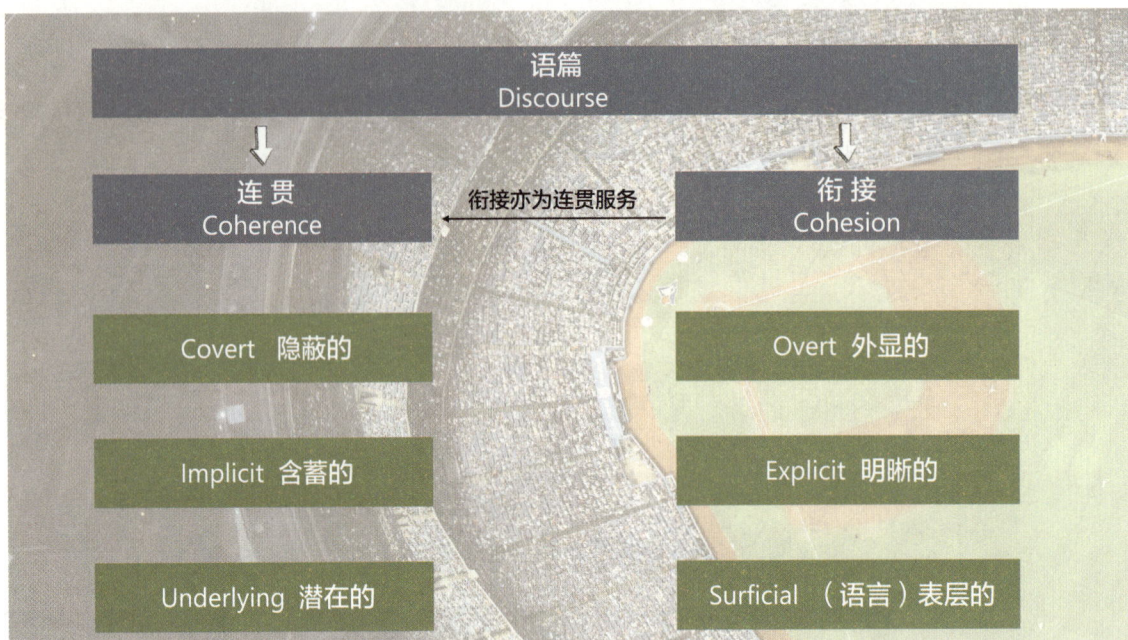

語篇
Discourse

連貫　　　　　衝接亦為連貫服務　　　　　衝接
Coherence　　　　　　　　　　　　　　　　Cohesion

Covert 隐蔽的　　　　　　　　　　　Overt 外显的

Implicit 含蓄的　　　　　　　　　　　Explicit 明晰的

Underlying 潜在的　　　　　　　　　Surficial （语言）表层的

coherence are two sides of a discourse, and they are frequently mentioned as a pair when talking about translation at the discourse (语篇) level.

Additionally, cohesive (衔接的) methods contribute to but do not necessarily ensure coherence (连贯), but a coherent discourse is surely a cohesive one.

5. Cultural Expressions

Baseball plays a crucial role in American life. It is not only played by professionals, college and high school teams, but also by children.

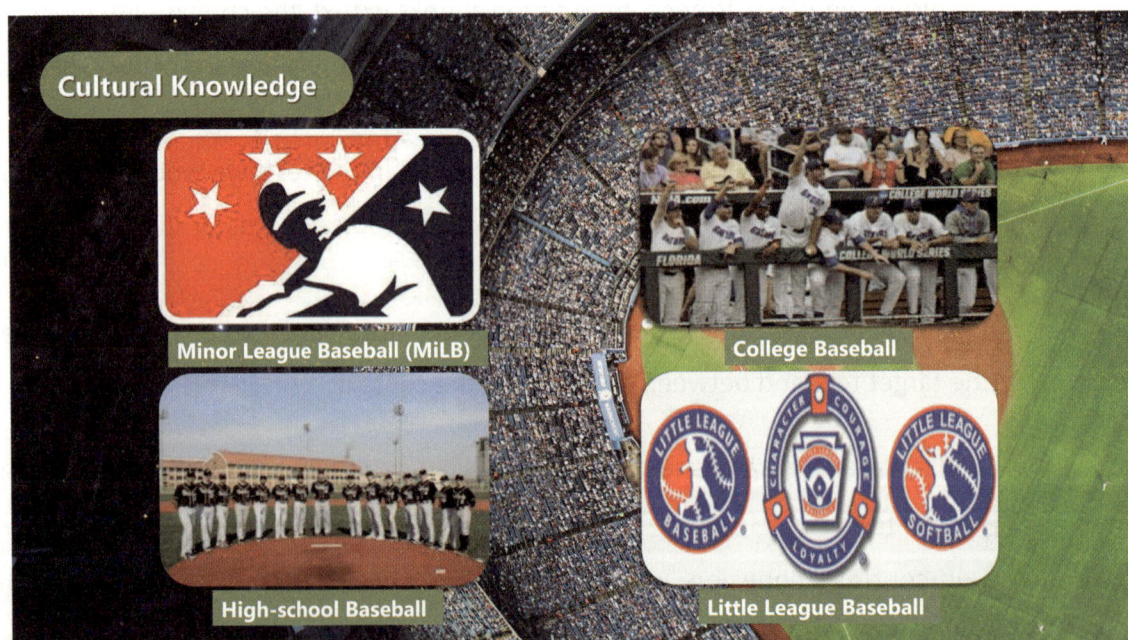

Cultural Knowledge

Minor League Baseball (MiLB)

College Baseball

High-school Baseball

Little League Baseball

Many American boys begin to play baseball when they are only five or six years old, and they continue to play until they become adults. Official data shows that in 2018 more than 25 million American kids played baseball or softball, a variant (变体) of baseball. From kids to professionals, players get organized into teams, and teams into leagues (联盟) to play the games.

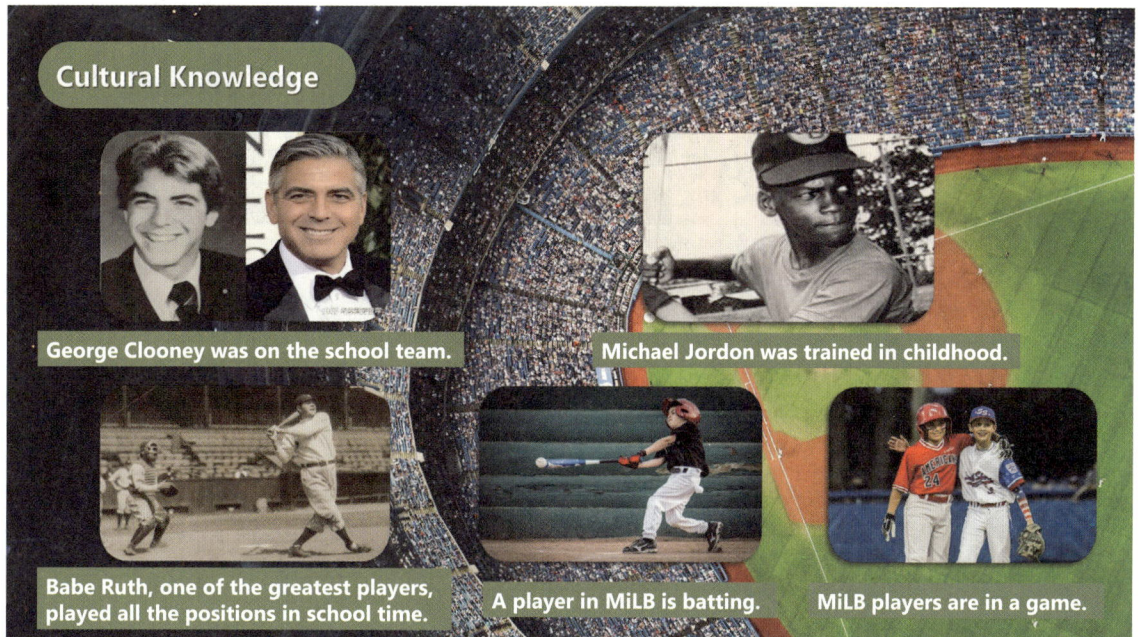

Cultural Knowledge

George Clooney was on the school team.

Michael Jordon was trained in childhood.

Babe Ruth, one of the greatest players, played all the positions in school time.

A player in MiLB is batting.

MiLB players are in a game.

Among different leagues, the oldest and highest ranked professional league is Major League Baseball, MLB for short. Today, a total of 30 teams play in two separated leagues: the American League (AL) and the National League (NL), with 15 teams in each league.

American League (AL)
美国联盟

Major League Baseball (MLB)
美国职业棒球大联盟

National League (NL)
国家联盟

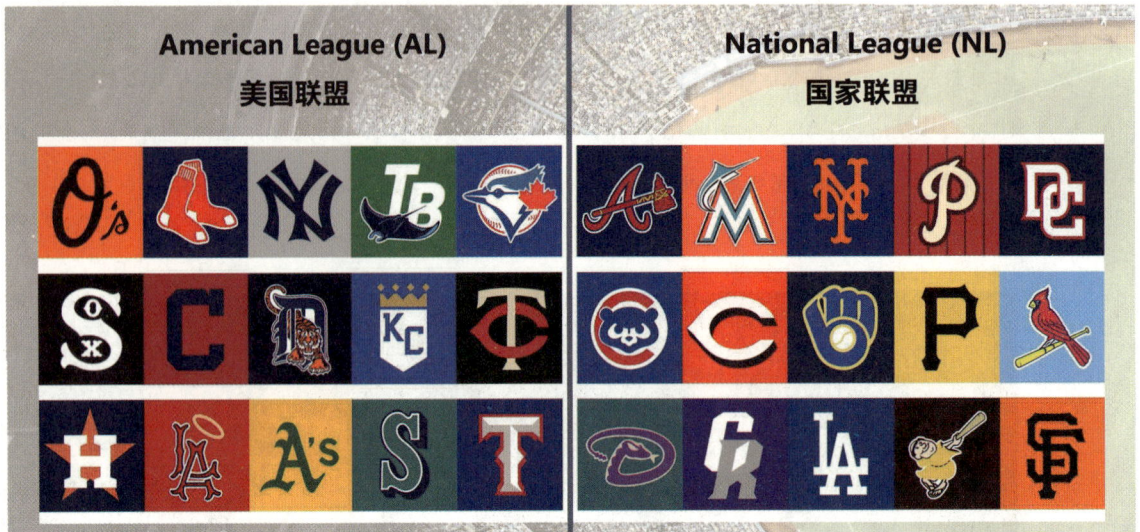

| American League (AL) 美国联盟 | National League (NL) 国家联盟 |

The MLB annual season is a game of episodes (节段). It is enjoyed by fans from spring throughout autumn.

Before the start of a new season, there is a six-week spring training which is a series of practices and exhibition games (表演赛).

Then begins the regular season. Each team in MLB plays 162 games for six months, usually from the beginning of April to the end of October.

Just after the midway point of the regular season, the MLB All-Star Game is held during a break from the season schedule.

In October, five winning teams in each league advance to the post-season games.

Eventually, the world series is played between the winner of each of the two leagues, and the big winner is determined through a best-of-seven (七场四胜制) championship series.

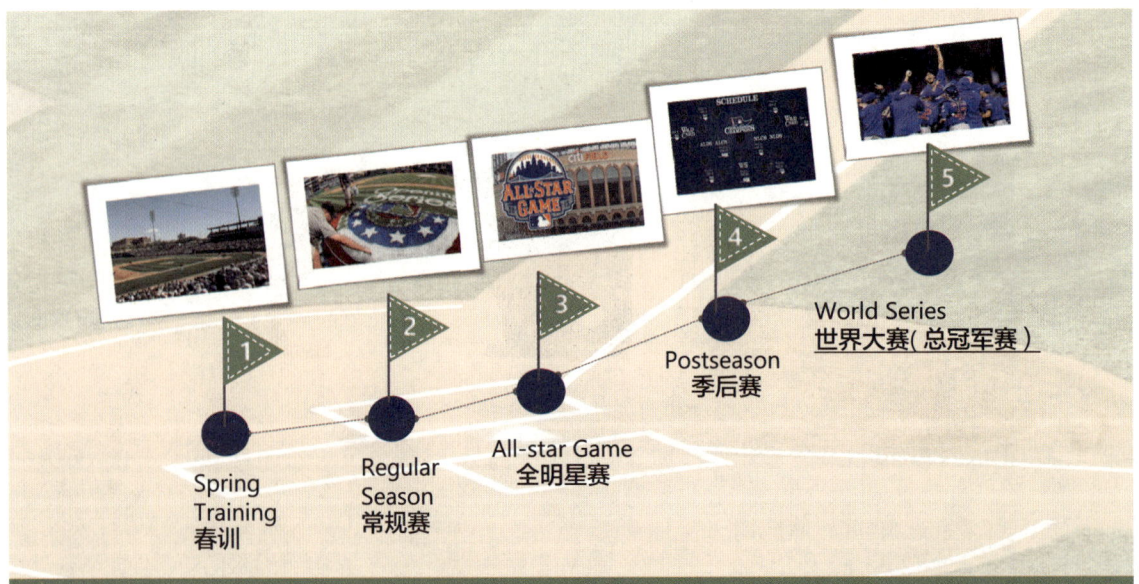

Spring Training 春训

Regular Season 常规赛

All-star Game 全明星赛

Postseason 季后赛

World Series 世界大赛(总冠军赛)

Baseball is so popular in America that many technical terms in baseball games become everyday American English.

Here lists some typical ones.

1) Step up to the plate

As you see in the diamond, there are four bases there. One base where the batter stands being prepared and hits the coming ball is named home plate (本垒) or plate. So, someone who steps up to the plate is ready to do his job.

Here is an example: It's time for Tom to step up to the plate and take on his share of work.

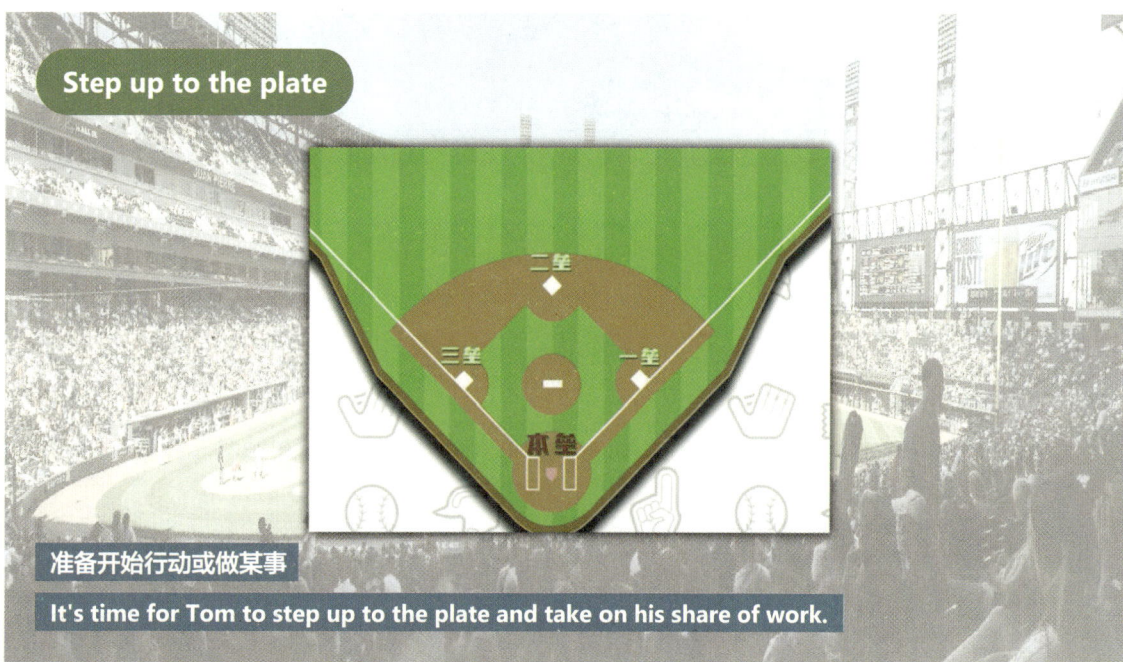

Step up to the plate

二垒

三垒   一垒

一

本垒

准备开始行动或做某事

It's time for Tom to step up to the plate and take on his share of work.

2) Throw a curve ball

We have been told in the passage that "the baseball is thrown by a defensive player called a pitcher". If the pitcher throws a curve (曲线的) ball, it will be difficult for the batter to hit due to its curving path. So, the phrase "throw a curve ball" indicates "to meet or do something unexpected".

Please look at this sentence: The weather threw a curve ball at their picnic and they had to eat indoors.

Throw a curve ball

做出意料之外的事，抛出意外的难题

The weather threw a curve ball at their picnic and they had to eat indoors.

3) Strike out

If the batter misses a ball, it is called a strike. If he gets three strikes, he loses his turn at bat and he is out of the game. So, a person who strikes out or stuck out attempted something but failed.

For example: I hear you struck out on that proposal. Better luck next time.

Strike out

棒球运动中 三击不中你便出局
In baseball, three strikes and you're out

三振出局，淘汰出局

4) Get to first base

As we learned, the batter runs counter-clockwise around the diamond after hitting the ball and tries to touch four bases one by one. When he gets to the first base, he starts the first step toward scoring a run（得一分）for his team. Thus, if we get to the first base, we begin to make progress with our plans.

We might say, "they were delighted that they'd got to first base in the negotiations."

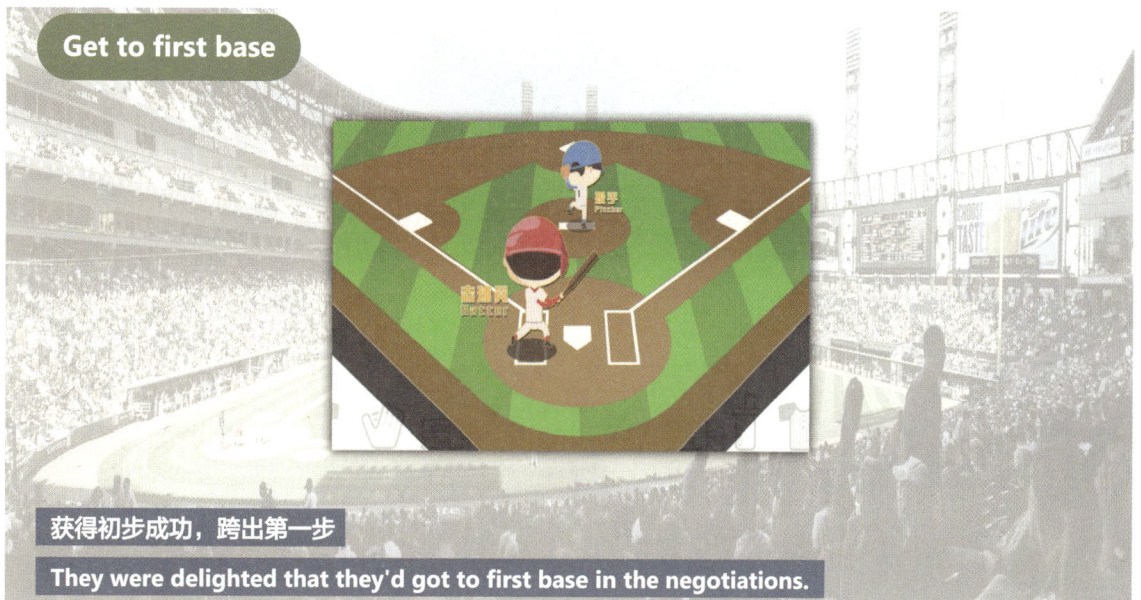

Get to first base

获得初步成功，跨出第一步

They were delighted that they'd got to first base in the negotiations.

5) Hit a home run

In the baseball game, the runner rounds all three bases and finally touches the home plate. This process of scoring a run is called "hit a home run". Someone who hit a home run did something extremely well, or he performed a very successful action.

Here is a sample sentence: It was an unexpected interview question, but I really feel like I hit a home run with my answer.

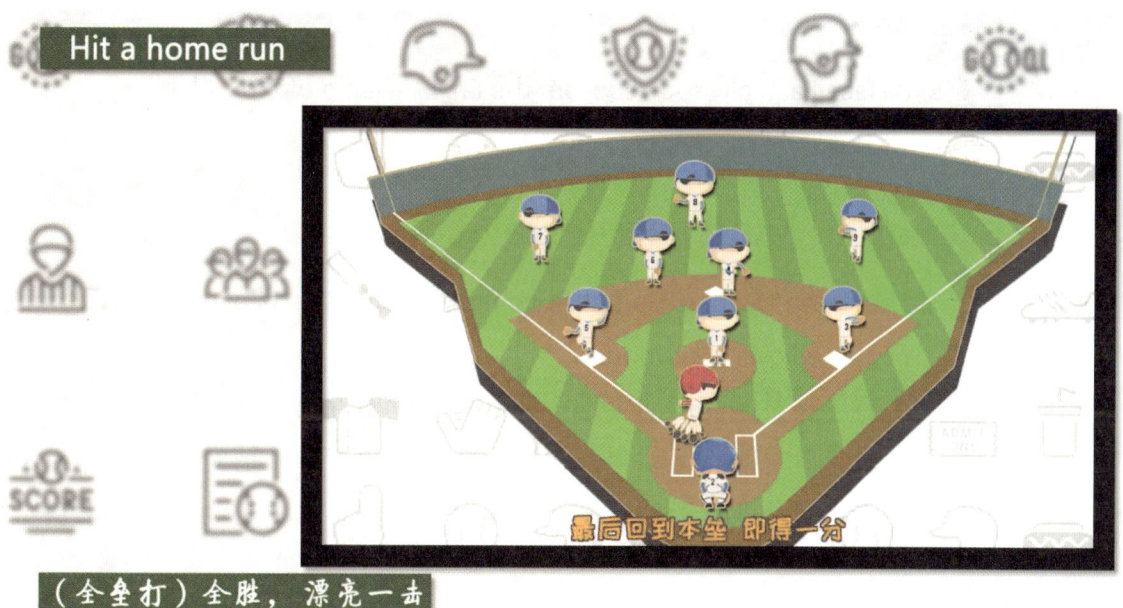

Hit a home run

最后回到本垒 即得一分

（全垒打）全胜，漂亮一击

6. Questions for Discussion

1) Have you ever played baseball? Do you know the rules of playing baseball?
2) What are the differences and connections between the coherence and cohesive methods?

III Exercises

Section A. True or false

_____ 1) The modern game of football began in the 19th century in England.

_____ 2) The oldest and highest ranked professional league is Major League Baseball (美国职业棒球大联盟).

_____ 3) Grammatical cohesion can be realized by different devices, for instance, references, conjunctions, repetitions and ellipses.

_____ 4) A good translation cannot be achieved by simply summing up all the equivalent words.

_____ 5) Baseball actually evolved from the English game of "rounders".

Section B. Multiple choice

_____ 1) The Youth Olympic Games, a comprehensive sports event, is designed for young people all over the world.

    A. 青年奥林匹克运动会是一项专为全世界青年人设立的综合体育赛事。

    B. 青年奥林匹克运动会，一项综合的运动赛事，是为全世界青年人设立的。

    C. 青年奥林匹克运动会，一项综合的运动赛事，是为青年人来自全世界的而设立。

_____ 2) Own goals (乌龙球) have so far scored for Iran and France. They've also popped up with one for the host, Russia.

    A. 目前，" 乌龙球 " 已经帮助伊朗队、法国队取得胜利，同时也为东道主俄罗斯队锦上添花。

    B. 目前，" 乌龙球 " 已经帮助伊朗队、法国队取得胜利。" 乌龙球 " 也为东道主俄罗斯队锦上添花。

    C. 目前，" 乌龙球 " 已经帮助伊朗队、法国队取得胜利。伊朗队和法国队同时也为东道主俄罗斯队锦上添花。

_____ 3) One photo showed him at an award ceremony, where he had been honored for his financial contribution to a local baseball team.

    A. 一张照片显示他在一个颁奖仪式上，在那里他因对当地棒球队的财政贡献而受到了荣誉。

    B. 照片中，他因对当地棒球队的财务支持在颁奖典礼上得到了嘉奖。

    C. 有一张照片显示他在一个颁奖典礼上，在那里他受到的荣誉是因为他对当地棒球队的财政贡献。

_____ 4) The football is controlled and advanced primarily by using the feet; only goalkeepers are allowed to handle the ball.

    A. 足球的控制和传送主要由脚来完成，只有守门员允许处理球。

    B. 足球主要通过使用脚来控制和推进，只允许守门员处理球。

    C. 球员主要用脚来控球和运球，只有守门员允许以手持球。

_____ 5) Scoring is accomplished by the batter running counter-clockwise around the diamond after hitting the ball and trying to touch four bases on the ground in sequence before the opposing players can put him out.

    A. 击球手在将球击出之后，围绕着钻石型内场逆时针方向跑垒，并在被守方球员打出局之前依次跑完地面的四个垒位，最后即可得分。

    B. 得分方式是这样：击球手在将球击出之后，围绕着钻石逆时针方向奔跑，并在被对方球员赶出去之前依次跑完地面的四个基地。

    C. 得分是由击球手在击球后逆时针方向绕着钻石跑，并试图按顺序在地面上触摸四个基地，然后对方球员才能把他放出来。

Section A. Multiple choice (5 items*4 points=20 points)

_____ 1) Badminton is a racket sport played by two opposing players, who take positions on opposite halves of a rectangular court.

    A. 羽毛球是一种球拍类运动，双方选手分别站在长方形场地两侧。

    B. 羽毛球是一种由双方选手展开的球拍类运动，双方选手分别站在长方形场地两侧。

    C. 羽毛球是一种球拍类运动，有双方选手参与的，他们分别站在长方形场地两侧。

_____ 2) A fist-sized ball is thrown by a defensive player called a pitcher in a game.

    A. 在比赛中，一个叫投手的防守的球员扔出一枚拳头大小的球。

    B. 一枚拳头大小的球被一名叫投手的防守员扔出。

    C. 在比赛中，防守方一名投手扔出一枚拳头大小的球。

_____ 3) The style of the Chinese Women's Volleyball Team in a competition is indomitable, bold and vigorous.

    A. 中国女排在比赛中的风格是不屈不挠、大胆和蓬勃的。

    B. 中国女排比赛时，作风顽强、朝气蓬勃。

    C. 中国女排在比赛中的风格是作风顽强、大胆有力的。

_____ 4) Football originated from a ball game called Cuju in ancient China, and then after the Arabs to Europe, developed into a modern football.

    A. 足球起源于中国古代的一种球类游戏"蹴鞠"，后来经由阿拉伯人传到欧洲，发展成为现代足球。

    B. 足球起源于中国古代的球类运动，称为"蹴鞠"，然后在阿拉伯人到欧洲后，发展成为现代足球。

    C. 足球起源于中国古代的一种称为"蹴鞠"的球类游戏，然后在阿拉伯人到欧洲后，发展成为现代足球。

_____ 5) Repetition is a cohesive device that involves repeatedly using a single word, a part of word, or a sequence of words, to create links between different ideas within a sentence or among sentences.

A. 重复是一种衔接手段，它涉及到反复使用一个单个单词、单词的一部分或单词序列，在句子内或句子之间建立不同思想之间的联系。

B. 重复是一种衔接手段，它包括反复使用一个单词、一部分单词或一串单词，在句内或句子之间建立不同思想之间的联系。

C. 重复是一种衔接手段，目的是在句内或句子之间建立不同思想之间的联系，它包括反复使用一个单词、单词的一部分或一串单词。

Section B. Sentence translation (5 items*6 points=30 points)

1) Long known as America's "national pastime", baseball actually evolved from the English game of "rounders".

2) Virtues of talented players shine in baseball games — accuracy and speed, the practices eye and hefty arm, the mind to take in and readjustment to the unexpected, the possession of more than one talent and the willingness to work in harness without special orders.

3) Football is a game played by two teams on a rectangular field, with the object (目标) of driving the ball into the opponent's goal.

4) Each team has 11 players, plus several substitutes (替补) who can take the place of injured players. The ball is controlled and advanced primarily by using the feet; only goalkeepers are allowed to handle the ball.

5) Baseball is a team sport, in which a fist-sized ball is thrown by a defensive player called a pitcher and hit by an offensive player called a batter with a round, smooth wood or aluminum stick. The ball itself is also called a baseball.

Section C. Paragraph translation (50 points)

The FIFA World Cup (often called the World Cup) is one of the most exciting competitions in the world, and the most important festival of the world's football fans. It is held every four years, but the qualifying rounds of the competition take place over a three-year period, using regional qualifying tournaments. The final tournament phase includes 32 national teams competing over a four-week period.

FINAL EXAMINATION

↳ Section A. True or false (10 items*3 points = 30 points)

_____ 1) A number of major rivers like Missouri River, Arkansas River, and Ohio River all flow into the Mississippi River.

_____ 2) The Emmy Awards are awards presented to honor distinction in the field of music in the United States.

_____ 3) A pub is an establishment licensed to sell alcoholic drinks. It functions as a social center for folks, offering them opportunities to meet and relax.

_____ 4) Hemingway defined the Code Hero as one who offers up and exemplifies certain principles of honor, courage and endurance which in a life of tension and pain make a man a man.

_____ 5) The non-core elements of a sentence make the meaning of the sentence rich and complete but at the same time make the sentence longer and more complex. Therefore, we need to sort out various, layered, and embedded non-core elements before we come to a good understanding and translation.

_____ 6) The method of combination is to cut a long stretch of language into small pieces whereas division is to integrate words, phrases or clauses into one.

_____ 7) There is always a best translation to every text.

_____ 8) In translation, the expression stage is more important than the understanding stage.

_____ 9) The translation of a text may involve the use of different methods and techniques at the same time.

_____ 10) To be a good translator, one needs not only to be bilingual but also bicultural.

Section B. Multiple choice (8 items*5 points = 40 points)

_____ 1) In the early days, the Mississippi was the most important means of transportation for people and commercial goods, and now it is still one of the major in-land carriers of freight.

A. 在以往的日子里，密西西比河是最重要的人员和商业货物的运输手段，现在，密西西比河依然是陆上货运的主要运输方式之一。

B. 在以往的日子里，密西西比河是最重要的客运和商业货运的运输手段，现在，密西西比河依然是陆上货运的主要运输方式之一。

C. 早期，密西西比河曾是最重要的客运和商业货运手段，如今，其仍是内陆货运的主要方式之一。

_____ 2) Yellowstone Park has numerous recreational activities, including hiking, camping, boating, fishing and sightseeing.

A. 黄石公园有许多娱乐活动，包括远足、露营、划船、钓鱼和观光。

B. 黄石公园的娱乐活动种类繁多，包括徒步旅行、山间露营、湖面泛舟、岸边钓鱼以及观光浏览。

C. 黄石公园有无数的娱乐活动，包括远足、露营、划船、钓鱼和观光。

_____ 3) Frequently, a relative or close friend will be asked to give a eulogy (悼词), which details happy memories and accomplishments.

A. 通常，逝者的一个亲朋好友会念悼词，追述逝者的美好点滴和种种成就。

B. 通常情况下，逝者的一个亲戚或亲密朋友会被叫去念悼词，其中详细描述了对逝者美好的回忆和其成就。

C. 通常情况下，逝者的一个亲戚或亲密朋友会念悼词，其中详细描述了对逝者美好的回忆和其成就。

_____ 4) Although nominally a Christian holiday, Christmas is also widely celebrated by many non-Christians, much like the Chinese Spring Festival which is very lively and ceremonious.

A. 尽管是有名无实基督教节日，圣诞节也被广大非基督徒所庆祝，这颇似中国的春节，热闹而隆重。

B. 尽管通常是基督教节日，但广大非基督徒也庆祝圣诞节，这颇似中国的热闹而隆重的春节。

C. 尽管名义上是基督教节日，但广大非基督徒也庆祝圣诞节，这颇似中国的春节，热闹而隆重。

_____ 5) Other decorations such as lights and wreaths of evergreen and signs wishing a "Merry Christmas" can be found inside and outside of many homes.

 A. 其他装饰品，如灯光、常青花环以及写着"圣诞快乐"的标签，可以在众多家庭的里里外外找到。

 B. 像灯光和常绿花环这类的装饰和祝愿"圣诞快乐"的许愿标签可以在许多家庭的里里外外被找到。

 C. 像灯光和常绿花环这类的装饰和祝愿"圣诞快乐"的许愿标签在许多家庭的里面和外面都可以找到。

_____ 6) The British have many traditions but there is nothing more quintessential (典型的) than taking afternoon tea.

 A. 英国人有许多传统，但没有什么比喝下午茶更具有典型性了。

 B. 英国有许多传统，但喝下午茶是其中最典型的。

 C. 喝下午茶是最典型的传统，尽管英国有许多传统。

_____ 7) It is a truth universally acknowledged that a single man in possession of a good fortune must be in want of a wife.

 A. 有钱的单身汉总要娶位太太，这是举世公认的真理。

 B. 这是一条真理，举世公认的，有钱的单身男人总需要一位太太。

 C. 这是一条举世公认的真理，那就是占有大量钱财的单身男人总要娶位太太。

_____ 8) Between 1589 and 1613, Shakespeare produced most of his known plays. Some of them are quite famous and highly appreciated by readers and scholars of later centuries.

 A. 在 1589 年到 1613 年间，莎士比亚生产了他的大部分知名剧作。它们中的一些非常出名，受到后来几个世纪的读者和学者赞赏。

 B. 在 1589 年到 1613 年间，莎士比亚生产了他的大部分知名剧作，它们中的一些非常出名，受到后来几个世纪的读者和学者赞赏。

 C. 莎士比亚的大多数知名剧作创作于 1589 年到 1613 年，其中不乏举世闻名、备受后世读者和学者欣赏的经典剧作。

↳ Section C. Paragraph translation (1 items*30 points = 30 points)

In 1926, he published his first novel, *The Sun Also Rises*. It paints the image of a whole generation, the Lost Generation. This includes the young English and American expatriates as well as men and women caught in the war and cut off from the old values and yet unable to come to terms with the new era when civilization had gone mad.

BIBLIOGRAPHY

Baker, Mona. Routledge Encyclopedia of Translation Studies [M]. Shanghai: Shanghai Foreign Language Education Press, 2004.

Shuttleworth, Mark, and Cowie Moira. Dictionary of Translation Studies [M]. Shanghai: Shanghai Foreign Language Education Press, 2004.

博伊尔. 英国原来是这样2: 英国传统与习俗50主题 [M]. 北京: 外文出版社, 2010.

曹颖哲, 等. 英语畅谈畅听美国文化 [M]. 大连: 大连理工大学出版社, 2014.

陈宏薇. 汉英翻译基础 [M]. 上海: 上海外语教育出版社, 2011.

陈毅平, 秦学信. 大学英语文化翻译教程 [M]. 北京: 外语教学与研究出版社, 2014.

范仲英. 实用翻译教程 [M]. 北京: 外语教学与研究出版社, 1994.

方梦之. 译学辞典 [M]. 上海: 上海外语教育出版社, 2004.

古今明. 英汉翻译基础 [M]. 上海: 上海外语教育出版社, 2000.

海明威. 海明威短篇小说全集[M]. 天津: 天津人民出版社, 2017.

何礼, 刘璐. 英美国家概况 [M]. 重庆: 重庆大学出版社, 2018.

金利, 等. 每天聊点美国文化 —— 一本书读懂美国 [M], 北京: 化学工业出版社, 2017.

刘云波, 虎松菊. 漫游美国(Roam Around America)[M]. 郑州: 大象出版社, 1999.

马钟元. 每天读点英文 —— 英美文化常识全集 [M]. 北京: 中国宇航出版社, 2013.

美国大使馆文化处. 美国地理简介(英汉对照) [M]. 北京: 美国大使馆文化处, 1981.

王淑花. 英美文化博览 [M]. 北京: 科学出版社, 2013

吴(M. Woo), 杨小兰. 一本书读透美国: 社会·文化[M]. 北京：中国致公出版社, 2014.

许鲁之. 新编英美概况 [M]. 北京: 中国海洋大学出版社, 2017.

姚宗立. 大洋彼岸的移民国家: 美国 [M]. 武汉: 武汉大学出版社, 2003.

《英语学习》编辑部. 性情人生 [M]. 北京: 外语教学与研究出版社, 2002.

张培基, 等. 英汉翻译教程 [M]. 上海: 上海外语教育出版社, 2001.

郑杰. 了解英美一本就够 [M]. 北京: 中国纺织出版社, 2017.